SECRET HISTORY
OF THE
WIZARDING PHENOMENON

SECRET HISTORY OF THE WIZARDING PHENOMENON

HOW THE HARRY POTTER BOOKS, MOVIES, FANDOM AND MORE CAME TO LIFE

PATRICIO TARANTINO

TRL Books

TRL Books
www.trlbooks.com

Cover illustration by Débora Olivaes.

First edition: September 2021
Second edition: June 2022

ISBN 979-8-88992-166-0

To my mom,
who gave me my first "Harry"
and built my first bookcase.

Table of Contents

Foreword

When Patricio asked me to write the foreword to this book, it was just the latest surprise in a long list of exciting Harry Potter-related incidents that have been occurring to me in regular intervals since 1997.

Back in the mid-90s, working in publishing was something I found my way into accidentally, and I was still developing my secretarial/office management skills alongside learning all I could about working for a literary agency; I was inexperienced and had no idea of how my life or career would go. What I did know very well already though, was how to use the power of children's books to entertain, educate and delight. As a child, I had no TV until I was ten; my parents introduced me to books at a very young age and read to me daily. I was soon escaping into fiction on my own, reading under the covers after lights out, and absorbing the power of a good tale without it being any effort whatsoever. It was a natural part of my life. It has not been the same for many other children since; TV and, more recently, computer games and the internet have taken up large parts of the time which I would have used for reading, and teachers (especially with the UK's new stringent curriculums) don't seem to have as much time to introduce the pleasure of reading great stories to their classes.

So, I was delighted to find a book I recognized spoke to me as the tales of my childhood had. A book that I couldn't put down, where the world was fully realized and the story had many satisfying elements, was all mine. When I was selling the manuscript, I had no way of knowing at the time that it would give the world the same great entertainment than it had given me; I just wanted it out there to see what it could do. The fact that a book could expand its audience and start to become a phenomenon by word of mouth through children was incredible. I left the agency before it was published, but I kept going into bookshops to make sure they had copies on display, and listening out for mentions of it in the papers.

I started to hear more about Harry in the press during the first year of publication, including spotting an article in *the London Evening Standard* in August 1998 about a lawyer who had gone by mistake to a court in Dudley for a case, instead of to Dursley, two hours away. I wrote a letter to the paper pointing out the Harry Potter connection and it was published a couple of days later. The first of my special Harry treats came a couple of months later when my aunt invited me to hear J.K. Rowling speak at the Cheltenham Literary Festival, and I was able to give her a copy of that letter at the signing afterwards.

Other treats over the next few years included being interviewed and photographed for *the Times*, *The Scotsman* and *People magazine*, amongst others; being invited to appear on *The Oprah Winfrey Show* in 2005 (which included filming with the excellent Barry Cunningham ahead of the show); being invited to speak at Chicago Ideas Week in 2013 on the same bill as Buzz Aldrin (who said my dress looked like galaxies!); being taken to see the Cursed Child as a birthday present; and being filmed for a Japanese documentary to commemorate the 20th anniversary of publication. It was also great to be on a BBC radio panel with Christopher Little in 2017, talking about the books 20 years on—I think it was evident how proud we both were of the creation we'd helped to bring to the world.

Some of my more thrilling pleasures have been much simpler, but in many ways more profound: noticing people reading the books on the tube or bus in the early days; finding a pile of Chamber of Secrets all labelled up in a classroom as part of as school reading scheme; ubiquitous references to Harry Potter in films, books and across popular culture; and seeing my 6-year-old niece's letter to Santa this Christmas ("some Gryffindor Quidditch robes, a Nimbus 2000 and a real wizard's wand"). Meeting fans who've grown up with the books and are totally immersed in Harry's world is amazing. I mentioned to two young American women at *The Casual Vacancy* launch event that the first time I'd met Jo at a book signing, she was a redhead, and they were excited: "You were there at the beginning!" They were such devoted fans they'd even studied the author's sartorial details over the years. I'm a huge fan of the band Duran Duran, so I recognize that sort of obsessive behavior. It's totally normal, of course! It was also a privilege to meet Geoff and Vicki of "All the Stations" in summer 2017. They were engaged in a project to visit every railway station in the UK and had built up a worldwide following on YouTube; Vicki, being a dedicated Harry Potter fan, was looking for related adventures as part of her epic journey, and I went to join them for a chat when they came along my local railway line, which was very exciting as I also love train journeys.

I've been approached for interviews by writers from fan websites over the years, which is how I was first in touch with

Patricio, and it's always an honor to help them out with their research. I feel that if they've taken the time to track me down, I want to give them a good experience in return. My story is only a small part of Harry's journey, but it's one which I've had great pride and pleasure in over the years, and respecting that achievement is something I do for myself. I've talked to fans for various online Potter communities and their breadth of knowledge and dedication always impresses me greatly.

I've been lucky enough to meet Jo Rowling on a few occasions and she always remembers me; she remembered Patricio too, when he fixed it for me to meet her at *The Casual Vacancy* signing in his absence. My tremendous aunt arranged again for me to see her speaking at the Harrogate Crime Writing Festival around the time of the third Robert Galbraith book and the organizers were kind enough to let me ask 'Robert' a question in the session; I was able to thank her for her secret references to me in *The Cuckoo's Calling*, only two of which I'd spotted. The third she had to point out to me. I consider this a mark of thanks from the author to me for my small part in her story and am still in awe that she did it!

There are many Harry Potter-related experiences which I have not yet had, for example visiting the studio tour in England, or the theme park in America, or the Pottermore online community, and I still haven't read some of the spin-off books e.g., *Fantastic Beasts* or *Beedle the Bard.* Some readers may be surprised to hear this, but I have my own special experience of the Harry Potter phenomenon to sustain me, just as the novels have done for millions of young people across the world. Patricio's research for this book has been extensive and wide-ranging and he's been dedicated in searching out all the details about the novels and what they mean to everyone whose lives they touch. I hope you recognize some of your own special experience with the Wizarding World captured in these pages.

Bryony Evens,
"the enormously important
Harry-Potter-champion"
according to J.K. Rowling.

CHAPTER ONE

Before Harry

"I have no nostalgia, whatsoever... Childhood...
I mean, I wouldn't go back if you paid me. Ever."
J.K. Rowling (Stahl, 2002)

It's impossible to talk about the Harry Potter story without knowing the story of its author. Different events and circumstances occurred that have made her life an obvious comparison to a fairy tale. In fact, this comparison is as old as the publication of her first book, the one that introduced the Harry Potter series —which has revolutionized the literary world more than any other series has done in history. It turned its author into the first female multi-millionaire writer, broke both sales and printing records across the different launches; and has not only changed the book industry, but also the film industry, influencing the market and the treatment of other series. The phenomenon has generated countless merchandise, theme parks on different continents, museums, tours, and auctions of valuable items associated with the brand. The Harry

Potter series also took the world of theater by storm with a new story taking place after the Harry Potter book series.

The main character begins his journey to Hogwarts School of Witchcraft and Wizardry by way of the Hogwarts Express, a scarlet train which takes him from London into the Wizarding World. This train, stationed at King's Cross station in London, England, is where the adventure begins, and it takes Harry to the place where he finally feels comfortable with those who appreciate and love him. Just like the adventures of Harry, the story of Peter Rowling and Anne Volant also starts at King's Cross station.

It was 1963 when eighteen-year-old Peter Rowling and Anne Volant served their country. Peter was part of the British Royal Navy and Anne served with the Women's Royal Naval Service, a group of women who provided administrative support to the British Royal Navy. They saw each other for the first time at the station in London, on one trip that was headed 800 km to the north towards Arbroath, Scotland. The nine-hour journey was enough time for them to get to know each other.

The meetings between Peter and Anne continued throughout the following months. The couple continued to grow together, and Anne became pregnant. Expecting a child made them realize that they didn't want to return to the city, but to a rural area where their future children could grow close to nature. Peter got a job as an apprentice at the Bristol Siddeley factory near Bristol, the largest city in the English West Country. However, before moving and starting a new family life, the couple had to follow the social norms of the time and get married since they were expecting a child.

The wedding took place on March 14, 1965 at All Saints Parish Church, a temple in North London near the home of Anne's family. The Victorian building is no longer available as a religious temple, but it has been converted into eight luxurious apartments (one of them with 4 rooms went on sale for £1,750,000). Anne, who was only twenty years old at the time, was five months pregnant and her current state didn't go unnoticed.

Opportunities for a young couple with a baby on the way were not as favorable in the 1960s as they are now. However, the Rowlings worked hard. They moved, when the pregnancy reached its ninth month, into a one-story house located at 109 Sundridge Park, Yate, England, a city 15 km from Bristol. The area wasn't fully developed yet. The closest place to shop was Yate Town Shopping Centre which had opened the previous year and was 300 meters away. Today, Yate is a city that hasn't stopped growing and has hundreds of shops in the center of the city.

The Cottage Hospital, where J.K. Rowling was born, operated at 240 Station Road, less than 500 meters from their new home. Originally a private house called Melrose House in 1920, it had been transformed into a health center in honor of those killed in the First World War. In 1951, it ceased to function as a hospital and its medical units were transferred to the city of Bristol, after which The Cottage Hospital became exclusively a maternity ward. Anne Rowling was admitted to The Cottage Hospital at the end of July and took her place in one of the twelve beds there. She was cared for by Irene Norton, the head of nursing. On July 31, 1965, Anne gave birth to a 'fat and blonde' baby, as J.K. would describe herself years later. The baby was registered under number B006725 in the Sodbury district, and her parents, Peter and Anne, decided to give her only one name: Joanne.

Despite being born in Yate, and having lived her early years there, whenever Joanne Rowling was asked about where she was born years later, she would say Chipping Sodbury. The town is less than a kilometer away, is known as Yate's "wealthy neighbor", and noted for its picturesque architecture and antique shops.

The Rowlings' only daughter did not remain as such for very long. Before Joanne was two years old, the Rowlings had their second daughter, Dianne. The birth this time was at home. The reasons are unknown, although it was probably because The Cottage Hospital did not allow visits by minors, not even the siblings of newborns. Dianne was born on June 28, 1967, and that was the day of little Jo's first memory. Joanne remembers that her father gave her modelling clay in order to entertain her, and she admits that she was so entertained that she didn't see her sister that day.

The two sisters were known by the abbreviation of their names, Jo and Di. They did not live long in Yate, as Peter was promoted at the Bristol factory that would soon be merged with the Rolls-Royce factory in 1971. Despite bearing the name of the automaker, Rolls-Royce also worked on aircraft engines. Peter Rowling was in-charge of them at the company.

Six kilometers from Yate was Winterbourne, a community larger than a town, but not as big as a city. The population in Yate was growing, becoming the city the Rowling family didn't want, and Winterbourne became the community that they were looking for in their new life. They bought a three-bedroom house at 35 Nicholls Lane from the Evans family for just over £3,000. They settled there the same year Dianne was born. It was at the Nicholls Lane house that Joanne began connecting with books. A reading of *The Wind in the Willows*, performed by her father, is one of the first readings that Joanne and her sister remember.

When she was just five years old, Joanne went to school for the first time. The Saint Michael's Church of England School in Winterbourne was just a few blocks from her home, and she enjoyed her very first day. However, when her mother went to pick her up at the end of the day, Joanne thought school was over forever and that she would never have to return.

Over the years, it has been rumored that the school's principal, Alfred Dunn, and various teachers, were the inspiration for the Hogwarts teachers, but J.K. Rowling never confirmed this and there is no obvious connection to the theory.

Joanne Rowling's first writing came a year later, at age six, and was titled "Rabbit". As she recalls: "Certainly the first story I ever wrote down (when I was five or six) was about a rabbit called Rabbit. He got the measles and was visited by his friends, including a giant bee called Miss Bee. And ever since Rabbit and Miss Bee, I have wanted to be a writer, though I rarely told anyone so. I was afraid they'd tell me I didn't have a hope" (The Not Especially Fascinating Life So Far of J.K. Rowling). In other stories, the protagonist was simply her sister. Other characters were animals capable of communicating with humans. With the passing of time, Di would stop being the protagonist and would leave the stories to become Joanne's number one reader. This would be noted in the dedication of the first book published by Joanne years later.

But rabbits were not only part of a fantasy world; neighbors with a familiar name had two (one white and one black) that the Rowling sisters fed while hiding their jealousy (they also wanted one). Just six houses away, at 29 Nicholls Lane, lived Ian and Vikki Potter, brothers almost the same age as Jo and Di. Ruby Potter was the boys' mother and had also befriended Anne, with whom she exchanged books. Ruby remembers Anne spending her time reading to her daughters because she believed it was important for their education.

The four of them, and sometimes Christopher White, another neighbor, spent the afternoons playing on the pavement. "The children were forever pinching the brooms from the garage to use as broomsticks," recalls Ruby Potter (Smith, 2003). They sat under a tree and made up spells and magic potions. The one who actually did it was Jo while the others listened. Although the little girl was still too shy to show or read her own stories, it didn't mean that she deprived her friends of her imagination when it came to playing. When *Harry Potter and the Philosopher's Stone* was published many years later, Ruby contacted Joanne Rowling to congratulate her. In Joanne's response to Ruby's letter, Joanne clarified that Harry Potter was not based on Ruby's son Ian, although she had borrowed the last name. In 2014, however, Rowling said that although she had decided to use the name Harry for the character, she wasn't very sure about the last name, so she considered several alternatives. Among them was the last name Batt, so Harry Potter could have been Harry Batt.

Life in Winterbourne was quiet, but it would not last much longer. The Potters and Rowlings ceased to be neighbors in 1974 when Peter and Anne were enchanted by a small town on the other side of the Severn Bridge. The bridge, opened almost ten years earlier by the Queen, connected Bristol with the Welsh town of Chepstow. Tutshill, a neighboring town to Chepstow, separated only by the River Wye (which in turn functions as a boundary between Wales and England), was the place where the Rowlings eventually moved.

Tutshill was a paradise for little Jo and Di. There was nature everywhere. The town, which stood between the River Wye and the River Severn and the Forest of Dean behind them, was a region of more than 100 square kilometers that apparently remained in J.K. Rowling's memory. The Forest of Dean is where Harry, Hermione, and Ron appear in the early chapters of the seventh book when they flee from the Death Eaters. At the age of seven and nine, the move was the most important change in the lives of the Rowling sisters. The stone house where they moved to was called The Church's Little House as it was adjacent to the St. Luke Church. It is also where Jo and Di worked a few times, cleaning to earn extra money. (They were also baptized there at age eleven).

On the other side of the church was Tutshill Church of England School where Joanne continued her education for two years. It wasn't a school that Rowling cared for, mainly because of her experience with Miss Morgan. In the autumn of 1974, on the first day of school, Miss Morgan gave a math test to her new group of 40 students. The math test included topics such as fractions, which Joanne had never seen before. This caused Joanne to receive a low score—and Morgan, who divided and seated her students according to their abilities—placed Joanne in the 'least brilliant' section.

As the year went by, Joanne improved her grades with a lot of effort and was moved to the left section of the classroom for the 'brilliant' students. Rowling remembers that this change came at a cost, because when she was moved, she stopped sitting with her friends at school. Never confirmed, it's suspected that this initial policy to discriminate students based on their aptitudes may have been inspiration for the Hogwarts Sorting Hat. What was confirmed by J.K. Rowling herself is that Miss Morgan inspired Severus Snape, the Hogwarts potions teacher who mistreated Harry Potter and his classmates in the early years: "There are a number of people who influenced the character of Snape in my books, and that teacher was definitely one of them. I found it extremely scary" (Fraser and Rowling, 2001).

On the school's 150th anniversary, which coincided with the publication of the third book in the Harry Potter series, Rowling was invited to the school to lead a presentation and launch of *Harry Potter and Prisoner of Azkaban.* She ultimately declined. In 2001, she decided to honor the school in her book, *Quidditch Through the Ages*, and named one of the teams, the Tutshill Tornados. It is no coincidence that she has also given them a blue and light blue uniform, the same colors of the uniform she wore for two years.

Another one of the teams named in the book is the Wimbourne Wasps. Less than two kilometers away was West Moors, where J.K. Rowling's paternal grandparents, Kathleen, and Ernie, had a grocery store where the Rowling sisters loved to play. The grandparents, who lived in a house above the store, let their granddaughters play with the real merchandise. Little Joanne helped by weighing each product carefully and Di played as the customer. It was at age nine (the same year she moved to Tutshill) that her grandmother, Kathleen, passed away from a heart attack. "I adored her, and my saddest memory of that time is of her death" (Fraser and Rowling, 2001). Years later, when the publisher suggested adding an initial for her fictitious middle name, Joanne thought of her grandmother and choose the letter "K".

Rowling was inspired by her other grandparents in *Harry Potter and the Prisoner of Azkaban.* Stanley and Frieda Volant, Anne's parents, lived in the same house in Tufnell Park for more than 30 years until Stanley's death in 1977. Joanne remembers them as an unhappy couple, but she remembers her grandfathers, Stanley and Ernie, with affection and their names are identified by Harry Potter fans: they are the drivers of the

Knight Bus that rescue the protagonist at the beginning of the book. However, Joanne and her sister were not too fond of their grandmother Frieda, who preferred the company of her many dogs over them. Although it was not confirmed by the author, it isn't difficult for fans to suspect that Aunt Marge may have been inspired by Frieda. Despite having moved houses, the Rowlings ensured that literature was as present as ever in the household. After her first attempt at writing "Rabbit", Joanne wrote "The Seven Cursed Diamonds", a short story. No known copies of these stories exist, and unless the author herself keeps them, we may never read them. Note, however, that the idea of seven cursed objects was already present in her mind. It is the main plot in the series of the boy wizard.

Literature was also present through classics (and not so classic books, since Anne's sister sent boxes with romance novels every month). Enid Blyton and C. S. Lewis were the children's authors that young J.K. Rowling read, though the one that definitely had an impact on her was Elizabeth Goudge's *The Little White Horse*, which became her favorite book. "And perhaps more than any other book, it has a direct influence on the Harry Potter books" (Fraser, 2002). Beginning in 2000, *The Little White Horse* editions have a recommendation from Rowling on their cover: "I absolutely adored *The Little White Horse*" (The Bookseller, November 9, 1999) which prompted many to read the book. The similarities seen with the boy wizard series are clear: a thirteen-year-old orphan protagonist, characters with unusual names, animals who speak and hide things, and even a magical creature who prepares food (think of house-elves in the Hogwarts kitchens).

When little Joanne, who was a fan of books, entered adolescence, she wanted to leave that image for her private life, because being an ardent reader wasn't considered popular among teenagers. "Hermione was very easy to create because she is based almost entirely on myself at the age of 11. She is really a caricature of me" (Weir, 1999).

In 1976, most of the Tutshill School students went to the Wyedean School, a few hundred meters from The Little House of the Church where the Rowling family lived, but still, it was in what would be considered the town of Sedbury. Today, the street that separates the former Rowling house from the high school is a long row of houses, making it difficult to know where Tutshill ends and Sedbury begins. This is where Mr. Nettleship, a chemistry teacher, taught. Although it has never been confirmed, he is believed to have also inspired Professor Snape because of the way he asks questions to the class. Also, it may be true because Chemistry was a subject that Joanne disliked. Nettleship himself finds the possibility of being the inspiration for the character quite humorous.

Once Dianne joined Joanne at Wyedean School, her mother applied for the Department assistant position under Chemistry Department head, Nettleship, and obtained it. From then on, the daily walks of the three Rowling women to and from school became commonplace in Tutshill. Despite this, Lucy Shepherd, the 20-year-old literature teacher, was the most influential person for teenage Jo. It was not only because Jo was able to express herself through writing in Ms. Shepherd's classes, but also because Ms. Shepherd conveyed her passion about women's ability to exploit their potential in the modern society that was taking shape in the 1970s. Rowling still treasures the letter Lucy Shepherd sent her when she published *Harry Potter and the Philosopher's Stone*.

Rowling was fourteen when her great aunt gave her Jessica Mitford's *Hons and Rebels*. She had already read *Emma* several times and Jane Austen was her favorite author, but Mitford's autobiography changed everything. "My most influential writer, without a doubt, is Jessica Mitford. When my great-aunt gave me *Hons and Rebels* when I was 14, she instantly became my heroine" (Fraser, 2002). Years later, when she had her first daughter, Rowling did not hesitate to name her daughter in honor of her favorite writer.

In 1985, Anne Rowling was 40 years old, twenty years older than her oldest daughter, when doctors gave her troubling news. It had been confirmed that she suffered from multiple sclerosis, a chronic disease that manifests with coordination problems and muscle weakness. Two years before the diagnosis, Anne's first symptom appeared as having difficulty lifting a tea kettle. Today, multiple sclerosis, or MS, remains uncurable, which is why Joanne Rowling founded The Anne Rowling Regenerative Neurology Clinic in 2013. It assists the University of Edinburgh in investigating neurological conditions, especially neurodegenerative diseases.

While Peter Rowling continued to move up in rank at Rolls-Royce, Anne Rowling had to leave her position as a chemical assistant at the Wyedean School. Due to her illness, she couldn't manipulate the test tubes and other instruments. She settled back in her house and read as much as she could about her affliction. All the while, she faced good days and bad days, having difficulty walking at times. As an excuse to leave the house, when her health allowed it, Anne Rowling visited the church next to her house to clean. Sometimes her daughters would accompany her. Joanne and Di signed the church's guestbook on at least five occasions. That guest book remained open to the public until a few years ago, and visitors could see the author's signature. Due to the fear that it would be stolen, the book was saved and is no longer available for viewing.

In her last years at Wyedean School, Joanne instantly became friends with a Welshman named Sean Harris who had enrolled at the school. Harris owned a turquoise-colored Ford Anglia, which led the pair of friends on adventures in pubs in nearby cities, both to the English side (such as Bath or Bristol), and to Cardiff, the capital of Wales.

Those trips were moments of distraction when Joanne could free her mind and think about the future. It wasn't just the distance that helped Rowling, but also the support of Sean himself. "[Sean] was the first person with whom I really discussed my serious ambition to be a writer and he was the only person who thought I was bound to be a success at it, which meant much more to me than I ever told him at the time" (WalesOnline, 2004).

In *Harry Potter and the Chamber of Secrets*, Joanne had the opportunity to thank Sean, not only by dedicating the book to him, but also by showcasing the turquoise Ford Anglia. It would no longer belong to Sean Harris, but its new owners would be the Weasleys, and just as the car rescued her from the grey Tutshill, this time it would rescue Harry not once, but twice. First from his uncle's house where he had been locked up and then from the forbidden forest.

In her final year at Wyedean School, Joanne was elected by the teaching staff and her fellow students as the "Course Representative". This was a sign of the popularity she had achieved at school, something very different from those early years where she had suffered verbal and even physical abuse for being the responsible girl who kept reading.

Jo applied to the University of Oxford to study Modern Languages. Her parents, who had not been university students, were amazed at the idea. Joanne Rowling took the exam and, after a time on the waiting list, was notified that she had not been accepted. The rejection didn't stop Joanne's ambitions.

At the age of eighteen, she started school at the University of Exeter. A two-hour drive from Tutshill (and a little less by train), Exeter was the only university to the southwest of Bristol, and that may have been why Rowling chose it. With her books and acoustic guitar, she left her parents' house and went to live in the student housing.

The freedom to be away from home, and the fact that she was no longer the brightest in her class, were possibly the reasons that caused her more Hermione-like personality to fade and brought out one more interested in a social life than in academics. Her teachers don't remember her as a brilliant student, but as an average one who hardly had any gift for writing. Her parents also didn't have much confidence in her. They even argued that a degree in English Philology would not be useful and influenced her to study a foreign language, claiming that such a degree could help her get a job as a bilingual secretary. At their advice, Joanne then decided to study French and Classic Philosophy, the latter clearly due to her interest in the historical and mythological side of things, something latent in the Harry Potter books.

While listening to albums by The Smiths, her favorite band at the time, Rowling continued to give free rein to the imagination. Her friend, Yvette, remembers that Joanne wrote stories about the men of that time, who were the villains captured by a group of female spies consisting of her and her friends. It was during this time in the English West Country that she met someone who would inspire her character Rubeus Hagrid years later. He was a member of the very big and scary Hells Angels motorcycle gang. Every time this person entered the pub, he made people feel insecure, but then this person would sit down and start talking about his garden and how his plants had been withering lately, and people would relax.

With ups and downs, and difficulties with tests, Rowling managed to get through the first two years of college. However, the third year required that she moved to France. Joanne taught English for a year in Paris at a French school. She shared an apartment in the capital with an Italian named Fernando, a Spanish girl, and a Russian woman. Rowling used her experiences in France as inspiration for the Beauxbatons Academy in *Harry Potter and the Goblet of Fire.* In fact, the name *Voldemort,* the name of Harry Potter's nemesis, means "Escape from Death" in French.

In Rowling's fourth and final year at the University of Exeter, her most important concerns were about the final exams and her approximately 3,000-word French thesis. Joanne spent a tremendous amount of her senior year in the campus library, oftentimes forgetting to return books and racking up a fine of £50.

However, despite spending hours in the library, she did not read for her thesis or for her final exams. English literature was what fascinated her, and it was at the library that she became an admirer of J.R.R. Tolkien after reading *The Lord of the Rings* saga. While the similarities are vast, Rowling denies having been inspired by the epic story. "Tolkien created a whole mythology. I don't think anyone could claim that I have done that. On the other hand, he didn't have Dudley" (J.K. Rowling chat, 2000b). Rowling did eventually spend a lot of time studying between her readings for pleasure and passed her exams. The graduation ceremony came in the summer of 1987, and Peter and Anne, who was now confined to a wheelchair, attended. Peter and Anne were happy to see their daughter finish college after working so hard. It was a very proud day for the family.

After graduation, Joanne Rowling moved to the Clapham neighborhood in London with other colleagues from the university. Her first job after school was with a temp agency that led her to an editorial office where Rowling was in charge of typing rejection letters for the manuscripts that had been sent. For a time, she worked for Amnesty International, where she started, enthusiastically, but little by little the difficulty of achieving real change lowered her expectations. Despite the variety of work she found, her spare time and energy was spent writing an adult novel. Whenever her colleagues went to a pub during lunch, Joanne decided to go on her own to continue writing. Her co-workers suspected that Rowling was having an affair. Loneliness allowed Joanne to move forward with her novel (which, to date, has not been published).

In June 1990, Joanne moved to Manchester with a boy she had started dating at the University of Exeter. She had made up her mind to move in with him, but after a weekend of trying and failing to find an apartment in Manchester, it was time for her to head back to London.

When twenty-four-year-old Joanne arrived back at Piccadilly Station, she did not know what was about to happen. She got on the full train and found a seat by the window. Unfortunately, the engines were damaged, and the train was stopped for four hours.[1] If the mechanics hadn't taken so long to fix it, today the world's libraries and bookstores would be

---

[1]I have tried, by all means, to get the exact date of this event. All UK train companies I have contacted assured me that they do not keep a record of damage from almost 30 years ago. I got the same response from government organizations, as well as non-profit organizations. There's nothing I would have liked more than to know the exact date that Harry Potter came into the world. For now, it will remain a mystery.

very different from how we know them. As Joanne watched the cows graze along the English countryside through the train window, the idea of an orphan boy attending a school of witchcraft and wizardry entered her head. Joanne Rowling hadn't been looking for any inspiration, but the most important idea of her life came to her that day.

"The idea came out of nowhere and I could see Harry very clearly; this scrawny little boy and it was the most physical rush of excitement. I've never felt that excited about anything to do with writing. I've never had an idea that gave me such a physical response. So, I'm rummaging through this bag to try and find a pen or a pencil or anything. I didn't even have an eyeliner on me. So, I just had to sit and think. And for four hours, because the train was delayed, I had all these ideas bubbling up through my head" (Harry Potter and Me, 2002).

When the long journey ended at Euston Station, in the city of London, Rowling had already thought of certain characters, not necessarily by name: Ron Weasley, Hagrid, and the ghosts Peeves and Nearly Headless Nick. She even thought of Hogwarts Castle. When she got to her room in the Clapham neighborhood, she started writing down everything she remembered in her notebook. It would still take seven years until her first book was published, and several more years for the arrival of the worldwide phenomenon that we know today.

The recession attacked England even though Prime Minister Margaret Thatcher didn't want to accept it. In just a few months, the Iron Lady would leave office. That night none of that mattered. For the first time, a feather left its ink trail on a sheet of Harry Potter. The Wizarding World had just been conceived.

CHAPTER TWO

First Pages

"When the American deal came through, that meant security. It means that I can buy a flat. It means not worrying."
J.K. Rowling (Treneman, 1997)

Rowling's idea for Harry Potter in 1990 changed her life. She moved with her boyfriend to Manchester where she got a secretary job at the Chamber of Commerce and continued working on the story of the boy wizard. Meanwhile, she decided that the series would consist of seven books, one for each year at Hogwarts school, and she filled a shoe box with her written notes, ideas, and illustrations. This was the third time overall that she began to write a new novel.

Anne Rowling died on December 30, 1990. Rowling had spent Christmas with her family that year and received the news in Manchester through a call from her father. This death had a profound effect on Joanne and on the book she was working on. One of Rowling's favorite chapters from the entire series, "The Mirror of Erised", reflects on Rowling's desire to be able to reunite with her mother again. Rowling confessed that, when rereading the chapter years later, she realized that Harry's feelings mirrored her own when it came to losing a parent. She had written her feelings into the book through Harry.

The following year did not start much better for Joanne and her boyfriend. The relationship was in decline. One night, after a fight, Rowling left the apartment and spent the night at the Bourneville Hotel in Didsbury, a suburb near Manchester. She took her notebooks and spent the entire night doing what she liked best—writing. It was then that she invented Quidditch and its main rules. She wanted a mix of basketball and soccer. The fury she felt during their recent fight served as inspiration for the bludgers. Regarding the name, Rowling admits: "The truth is that I invented the word [Quidditch] for a totally whimsical reason. I just wanted a word that began with Q. Don't ask me why. [...] I just really liked the sound of it" (Feldman, 1999). She also wrote about Platform 9 3/4 while in Manchester. Being away from London, she confused King's Cross with Euston, so the description of the station in the novel doesn't coincide with reality. The choice of King's Cross station is in honor of where her parents first met.

The relationship with her boyfriend ended, and in September Joanne flew to Porto, Portugal, where she found a job as an English teacher. The two-and-a-half-hour flight could have gone unnoticed if it hadn't been for Rowling inventing the names of the four Hogwarts houses: Gryffindor, Slytherin, Hufflepuff, and Ravenclaw (although the original names were a bit different, like Slytherite instead of Slytherin). For lack of a place to write, she wrote the names down on disposable motion sickness bags given to passengers during the flight. Despite associating her writing routine in cafées to Edinburgh, she began this tradition in Porto, Portugal.

Upon arrival in Porto, she moved in with two young English women who also worked as teachers: Aine Kiely and Jill Prewett[2]. If those names sound familiar to Harry Potter fans, there is a reason. She dedicated *Harry Potter and the Prisoner of Azkaban* to the two of them, nicknaming them as "the godmothers of Swing". This nickname is not because they had swing dancing prowess, but because the Swing Club is a night bar that the three friends used to frequent. Rowling often went to the Swing Club at night and wrote in cafés during the day. Although never confirmed, her stay in Portugal may also have inspired the title of the first book. While there, she could have read "Pedra Filosofal", a famous poem by António Gedeão which Manuel Freire set to music in 1969. The author also confirmed that Salazar Slytherin's name was taken from the Portuguese dictator António de Oliveira Salazar.

Within a few months, Joanne met Jorge Arantes, a Portuguese journalist who she married in 1992. She had her first daughter, Jessica, on July 27th, 1993. The relationship, which was mostly focused on jealousy, ended in November that year when Arantes' violent attacks on Joanne began. The bitter pill to swallow was that the union became a joke in *Harry Potter and the Prisoner of Azkaban*, where Divination professor Sybill Trelawney predicts to Lavender Brown that what she fears will happen on October 16th. On that date Lavender Brown discovers that her rabbit was killed by a fox. October 16th was Rowling and Arantes' wedding day. It was not the first time that Rowling used dates from her personal life in her books. December 31st was the date that she received the news of his mother's death, the same date as the birth of Tom Riddle, the series' villain.

---

[2] The last name Prewett appears in the Harry Potter series. It's Molly Weasley's maiden name.

With the help of her friends and lawyers, Joanne managed to leave Portugal with her four-month-old daughter and return to her country. She could have gone to her father's house, but the relationship with Peter Rowling had not been the best since he had married his secretary, who was eight years younger than Peter, shortly after Anne's death. So, Joanne decided to live with her sister, Dianne. She arrived in Edinburgh for Christmas 1993 with her young daughter, Jessica, and three completed Harry Potter chapters along with a box full of notes.

The chapter that opens the series, "The Boy Who Lived", was difficult for her to write: "The trouble with that chapter was (as so often in a Harry Potter book) I had to give a lot of information yet conceal even more" (Rowling, 2006h). Among the different versions of that chapter that Rowling came to write, there is one where readers see Voldemort committing the murder of Harry's parents in Godric's Hollow, while in another version, a muggle betrays the Potters and gives up the location Potter home. Another draft included a character named Pyrites[3], a henchman for Voldemort, who was meeting Sirius Black in front of the Potter house. Rowling comments that Pyrites was a dandy with white gloves which would end up artistically stained with blood. Another version of the first chapter showed Hagrid visiting the Muggle Prime Minister named Fudge and asking him to notify the Muggle community of a red-eyed creature (Voldemort). It is very similar to the first chapter of *Harry Potter and the Half-Blood Prince* when the Muggle Prime Minister receives a visit from the Minister of Magic to alert him about Voldemort (Rowling also tried to use this chapter in the third and fifth book, but without success).

---

[3] Pyrites is a mineral that, due to its great resemblance to gold, was called "fool's gold". Even in the earliest versions of his writings, Rowling paid great attention to the origin of his character's names.

This first chapter also told how a certain "Vernone" Dursley works with Fudge who took his baby nephew, with a cut on his forehead, to Fudge's office wondering what to do. Another interesting preliminary version shows the Potters living on an island in the middle of the sea near Hermione's family on the coast. Hermione's father notices the explosion caused by the murder and leaves in the middle of the storm on a boat to the island where he finds the bodies of James and Lily, and little Harry. All these sketches were discarded in favor of the chapter that we know in which we follow Vernon at work, and we also see Dumbledore, along with McGonagall and Hagrid, leave Harry on Privet Drive.

Rowling toyed with many ideas concerning the first book, including the Sorting Hat. Among the original ideas, there was a court made up of ghosts who decided which house the student belonged to. Also considered was an election committee made up of the prefects and heads of each house, and even the possibility of four statues, one for each founder of Hogwarts, that came to life and chose their own students (this idea was eventually used for Ilvermorny, the American wizard school). Finally, the author thought of something simpler: taking names out of a hat, and then taking names out of a talking hat which eventually evolved into the idea for the Sorting Hat as we know it today.

As soon as she settled in Edinburgh, in the first week of January, Joanne gave the first chapters of the book to her sister. She was the first person to read them. Dianne was enthralled. "It's possible that if she hadn't laughed, I would have set the whole thing on one side" (Dunn, 1997). But Di laughed, says Rowling, who only needed that approval to continue. But while the writing was on track, other aspects of her life were not. She applied for welfare benefits and began receiving £69 (equivalent to $103.50 at the time). With that money, she had to cover food, clothes and a home for her and her daughter. Because this was practically impossible, she received 600 pounds ($900) from her friend, Sean Harris, and tried to find a place to rent, but most landlords refused to rent to someone without a job and who received social assistance. However, this changed when a woman allowed her to rent a one-bedroom apartment located at 7 South Lorne Place in the Leith neighborhood. Years later she would finish writing her first book on the kitchen counter in that apartment. These were the hardest moments for Joanne and her daughter, Jessica. The criminal activity in the neighborhood (a broken window one night and an attempted robbery) was a problem, and added to that problem was the little weekly money she had had during that time: "I don't want to dramatize, but there were nights when, though Jessica ate, I didn't" (Dunn, 1997).

Luckily for Rowling, her brother-in-law, Roger Moore (married to her sister Di months before Joanne's arrival in Edinburgh, Scotland), opened Nicolson's, a café located on the first floor at the corner of Nicolson and Drummond St.[4]. Perhaps so as not to feel so alone, Rowling preferred to write in a café and not in the solitude of her new apartment (The rumors that she did it because she couldn't pay for the heating in her home have been denied by the author). In order to get there, she would leave her apartment in Leith and push Jessica in a stroller. If her daughter was asleep when they arrived, Rowling would climb the stairs and sit at the corner table. She would order a coffee and spend two or three hours writing. Employees recognized her and remember her writing several pages by

[4] For fans visiting today, the café has been sold and is now a restaurant called Spoon. A plaque on its exterior wall commemorates the fact that Rowling has written part of her early books there.

hand while Jessica slept at her side. Rowling says that the reason why she wrote in a café was simply because, if she stayed at home, she had to prepare the coffee herself, and that distracted her.

Another place Rowling frequented was The Elephant House at 21 George IV Bridge, which is still open today. In addition to posters in the window and photos on the interior walls where Rowling is seen at some of the tables, the café even has a book signed by the author in an interior display case. If you ever pass by, do not skip the bathroom. The walls are covered with messages written by fans from all over the world. For £1, you can also buy a postcard with a painting showing the now celebrity writing on the premises.

Rowling recalls one of her visits to those cafés. When asked if she rewrote a lot, she says, "Yes, a lot. Once ever in the four books that I'm published, I've sat down written something beginning to end and let it stand and that was in the chapter in *The Philosopher's Stone* where Harry learns to fly. I remember vividly the afternoon, my daughter fell asleep I ran into the café on a beautifully sunny day, I sat down, and I wrote that chapter from beginning to end, and I think I changed two words and that's very unusual for me" (Mzimba, 2001).

Due to Edinburgh's geography, The Elephant House is on a slanted street, causing the back block to be at a lower level. The back windows, where Rowling used to sit, have an elevated view of the rest of the city. From there you can see George Heriot's School, a school that many say was the inspiration for Hogwarts. However, even better is the view over Greyfriars Kirkyard Cemetery, which is freely accessible, just a few meters from the café. Joanne has confessed several times that she used names from tombstones of the deceased, and many of the fans go there to find Rowling's inspirations. From the poet

McGonagall to the grave that has received the most photos: Thomas Riddle. If you search well enough, you can find other names that Rowling might have written down for future use, such as "Scrymgeour" with only one letter different from the Minister of Magic (Scrimgeour) who assumes the role in *The Half-Blood Prince*.

In the summer of 1995, things continued to improve. Rowling was able to stop receiving Social Security thanks to financial help from a friend. Also, she received a grant from the Scottish Officer of Education and Industry in order to attend a university program. There, she pursued a postgraduate certificate to become a foreign-language teacher in Scotland. Lastly, Rowling's divorce process with Jorge Arantes came to an end along with the approval of a restraining order against him (he had flown to Edinburgh several times unexpectedly). But perhaps most notable of all was that in August, Rowling completed the first manuscript of *Harry Potter and the Philosopher's Stone* in its entirety. She took six months to reread it and make final changes, and in February of 1996, she decided it was time to publish it.

Joanne went to the Edinburgh Central Library and picked up the 1995 edition of *The Writers' and Artists' Yearbook*, a red book that lists contacts in the publishing industry for authors, designers, and illustrators. She looked for possible agents there and wrote down names and addresses. Due to her economic situation, she could only make two copies of the first three chapters (which is what was normally requested by agents) and her cover letter. She then bought two black folders and sent them to two agents.

The first of them replied and said that their client list was full and returned the manuscript without the folder, because it did not fit in the envelope. Rowling recalled that moment saying, "I was furious, I wanted to write and say, 'You owe me five pounds"' (O'Donnell, 1999). She had better luck with the second agency. She had noted the agency previously because the name caught her attention, and also because their listing stated that there was "no reading cost."

Christopher Little founded a new literary agency alongside his partner, Patrick Walsh, and Bryony Evens as their secretary in the new agency. The agency did not publish children's books, so Rowling's manuscript went directly to the reject basket as soon as it arrived. But on one February morning, Bryony was struck by the black folder in which the manuscript had been shipped. She was also surprised, and still remembers, the four illustrations attached with the manuscript: Harry standing in the Dursleys' living room, another with the Quidditch players, a third featuring the scar most prominently, and a fourth with Fluffy[5]. Bryony enjoyed reading the first chapters she had received, which were funny, and decided to share them with people in the agency. With the passage of time, Bryony earned, with good reason, the recognition of having discovered Harry Potter, because if it were not for her, the manuscript would have continued to be passed between agent offices. J.K. Rowling met Bryony at a signing event years later and signed one of the designated copies to her: "For Bryony, who did discover Harry Potter," and "For the huge and important champion of Harry Potter, Bryony Evens." The last time they crossed paths was at a publicity event for *The Casual Vacancy*, and Rowling recognized Bryony right away. Rowling thanked her again.

The agency sent Rowling a letter asking for the rest of the book to read. Rowling remembers that letter as being the best

[5] The first two mentioned illustrations were published: one in the Collectors' Edition of Harry Potter and the Sorcerer's Stone in the United States, and the second on the Pottermore.com website.

she had received in her life and acknowledges that she read it several times. To avoid any delay, she took less than a week to send the rest of the requested book.

This time it was Fleur Howle's turn to look over the manuscript. She had worked as a producer on several television series and movies, but now she was a freelance reader at the agency and oversaw determining whether the complete manuscript was worthwhile and, in that case, contact the author and share editorial notes. She took the book, knowing that Bryony had already given her go-ahead, and liked it. “It stood out from other books. I was homesick for all the wonderful books I had grown up with.” Little had also added Fleur to the team because of her experience in the world of television and her desire to search for novels with the potential of being adapted to TV and film. "When he asked me if I felt it had the potential to be adapted, I said yes," recalls Howle. However, she also admits that she didn't see much of a commercial future for the book.

Once Little read the material, they discussed the changes between the three of them. Howle felt that: "Reading the Quidditch match felt like listening to it on the radio, and if you don't know the rules, you don't understand," so she suggested that the rules of the sport be added in a very descriptive way. Bryony suggested that Neville's character be more prominent. Howle also suggested that the illustrations be discarded because they added nothing to the story. Only three letters between the agency and Rowling were enough to make the necessary changes and the manuscript was very similar to the version that was finally published. The agency proposed a contract containing the usual terms: 15% of gross profits in the UK, and 20% for film rights and translation rights. Joanne was surprised that an agent was interested in her book, and she immediately accepted.

It was time for *Harry Potter and the Philosopher's Stone* to be shipped to publishers. Christopher had given Bryony the order not to spend too much and only three copies of the manuscript could be made, each one naming the author as "Joanne Rowling". When a publisher did not accept it, Bryony requested that the copy be returned so that it could be forwarded. Around twelve publishers rejected the book (among them were Transworld, Penguin, and Orion) for various reasons. The most common excuse was its length, which came in at around 200 pages. It was considered too long for a book without illustrations that was aimed at children between the ages of eight and ten.

Fortunately, the manuscript arrived at the Bloomsbury offices in Soho Square. This publisher had been founded in 1986 and was still under the command of Nigel Newton. Following his most famous publication, Michael Ondaatje's *The English Patient*, he formed a children's book department under the command of Barry Cunningham alongside Elinor Bagenal, Janet Hogarth, and Rosamund de la Hey. Christopher Little called Barry Cunningham, pitched the book, and sent the manuscript to him immediately. All four of them on the team were fascinated by the novel. "I loved the beginning—it reminded me a little of Roald Dahl (who I had also worked with). Then I most liked the friendship between the three of them which I have always thought was the real magic! Of course, all the details are great too, but that's why I wanted to buy it," says Cunningham. De la Hey added: "From the very beginning, while we may not have predicted the full global phenomenon, we knew that Harry was special. In fact, Barry's words to me when he passed me the manuscript, were 'Read this, I think it's a bit special."' But the team had to convince the rest of the publishing house to acquire the rights. To do this, Rosamund de la Hey had the idea to distribute the manuscript among her colleagues, rolled up like a tube, and with Smarties chocolates inside, symbolizing the prizes for children's books in the United Kingdom that bear the same name as the candy— because they were organized by Nestlé. It was important in this environment because the winners were chosen by children's votes (eventually, the first three books in the series would win this award).

Approval to acquire the rights was swift. The key to this swiftness was Alice Newton, Nigel Newton's eight-year-old daughter, who was the first child to read the book. Nigel gave her the first three chapters and recalls that the night before the meeting to discuss the book, his daughter came down from her room an hour later glowing, saying: "Dad, this is so much better than anything else" (Bloomberg, 2005). When Bloomsbury finally sent its offer to Christopher Little, Harper Collins had also expressed interest. Bryony stood up to the big publisher and expressed that they would have to fight for Harry Potter. When those at Harper Collins heard this, they decided to drop their bid. In this way, Bloomsbury achieved the greatest phenomenon in modern literature for a total of £1,500 ($2,550), of which Joanne Rowling obtained £1,275 ($1,910). The book would be published in June of the following year, and the publisher secured not only the first book, but the second book as well.

Bloomsbury wanted to meet the author, so they organized a lunch in London where they could meet. Rowling traveled from Edinburgh that day. She didn't want to leave her daughter alone for long. The lunch, where she met Christopher Little and Barry Cunningham, would go on to become one of Rowling's favorite anecdotes. Towards the end of the lunch, as Rowling started talking about Harry growing up, as she was already planning sequels, the Bloomsbury publisher advised her not to quit her current job because she would never make too much money writing children's books. "I only meant to be sensible— at that time Children's books were not the road to fame and fortune." Barry now recalls it as his "unfortunate phrase."

In 1997, Rowling began teaching French to students between ages of twelve and eighteen at Leith's Academy in Scotland, a few blocks from her apartment. In her graduation notes from professors in the program, her planning and communication skills with students were highlighted. She got a permanent job there, but life was difficult between work, caring for her daughter, Jessica, and writing *Harry Potter and the Chamber of Secrets.*

Meanwhile, the Scottish Arts Council launched a competition offering financial aid to Scottish residents who were published authors. Although Rowling only met the first requirement, Jenny Brown, the council's director, found *Philosopher's Stone* sympathetic and approved of Rowling's nomination. After a personal interview, the panel selected her as the winner and awarded her the top prize of £8,000 ($12,000). The scholarship not only made life easier for Rowling, who was now able to quit her job and dedicate herself full-time to her second book, but also provided proof of Harry Potter's momentum. With the money, Joanne bought an electric typewriter and a £100 jacket for her television appearances.

The first book was still being prepared for publication, so Christopher Little continued to work against the clock. He suggested that Rowling adopted a pseudonym since the data handled by the sales department concluded that male children did not read books written by female authors. "J. Rowling" was discarded for its simplicity and an attempt was made to add a fictitious middle name. "J.R. Rowling" sounded bad for the replay and "J.R.R. Rowling" was too Tolkienesque. Ultimately, "J.K. Rowling" was the choice, in part, because of the good-sounding consecutive J and K in the alphabet, and because it honored her grandmother, Kathleen. But there was another reason for hiding the name, and it was that Rowling didn't want her ex-husband to know she had published a book. "I actually wanted to publish under a completely different name because I'd come out with this very difficult marriage and I was a little bit paranoid. And it was silly really because my ex-husband knew what I had been writing. He never read it, but we'd talked about it. So if he ever heard about it I suppose he would have known it was me. But I didn't imagine it was going to be a success, I didn't imagine it was going to be in Portugal" (Armitage, 2021). Despite the change of name, the first editions of the book attributed the copyrighted text to Joanne Rowling (this is not the case anymore, and subsequent editions attributed it to J.K. Rowling).

In May, Bloomsbury released *Bloomsbury Autumn Highlights: Extracts From Forthcoming Titles June to December 1997*, its catalogue to promote the new work of twenty-five authors in England. In this catalogue, 14 pages of *Harry Potter and the Philosopher's Stone* appeared. This was the first place where a portion of Harry Potter appeared.

Once the editing was finished, headed by Barry Cunningham and Susan Dickinson, an editor who worked as a freelance editor on the book, there hadn't been many changes in content, but some passages of character introductions were eliminated to speed up the plot. Manuscripts were sent to four influential people, mostly journalists in the field of children's books, and three of them returned with letters showing enthusiasm for the book. "When I then emailed the entire company with quotes from these letters, it had an impact," recalls Rosamund de la Hey. One of the manuscripts had been for Lindsey Fraser, Executive Director of the Scottish Book Council. She was delighted with the book and recommended it to her colleagues. She also formed a good relationship with J.K. Rowling, and, in 2000, she went on to publish *Telling Tales: An interview with J.K. Rowling*, a small book featuring an extensive interview with Rowling. Regarding the original manuscript she received, she confesses: "If I kept it? Well, no ... I loved the book, but I am a very enthusiastic recycler, so I'm afraid it was recycled." Another person who received a copy of *The Philosopher's Stone* was Wendy Cooling, Director of the Children's Book Foundation. Her comment, "A terrific read and a stunning first novel", would be used on the cover of the British First Edition. Because the book was well-received, Bloomsbury decided to make copies for the press to review. This was unusual for children's books, but it showed the confidence that Bloomsbury had in the novel.

Although the subsequent books had a definite publication date for fans who were looking forward to it, for the first book of the series this was not the case. *Harry Potter and the Philosopher's Stone* began selling when it reached bookstores in late June of 1997. June 26, 1997 was later chosen as its official publication date with a circulation of 500 hardcover copies (only 200 of which were for sale while the rest went to libraries) and 5,150 in paperback (as reported by the publisher). Rowling recalls that she spent the day walking around Edinburgh with the book under her arm, looking for it in different store displays. In her interview with Lindsey Fraser, she confessed that her daughter's first words were "Harry" and "Potter," and that little Jessica yelled them at the bookstore door. It seemed like a good publicity stunt, but Joanne confessed that the act was her daughter's own, and that she hadn't suggested it.

Seven years after that train journey, Joanne Rowling's dream came true. The book was a reality. The cover, illustrated by Thomas Taylor, featured an astonished Harry in front of the Hogwarts Express. The art had been personally suggested by Barry Cunningham, who wanted it to reflect the humor of the book without being too childish. However, this first edition (which did not feature the Hogwarts crest), contained several errors. One of them is well known by the fans, even by those do not collect the first editions of the books: "A wand" appeared twice on the student supply list.[6].

The publisher had not gotten a large budget to promote the book. They relied on word-of-mouth promotion between booksellers and parents, and barely produced the poster that was displayed in bookstores. *The Scotsman* and *The Sunday Times* published two very favorable reviews, comparing it to Roald Dahl's books. Lindsey Fraser's criticism in *The Scotsman* is considered the first published Harry Potter critique: "I simply included it in a collection of books I wanted to recommend to children for their summer holidays. I just wanted people to know about this first novel by an author living in Edinburgh. We Scots like to celebrate the talent in our midst!"

Rowling's first public event was in Glasgow, at the John Smith and Co. bookstore. Grainne Cooney, the store's manager, remembers that there were about a dozen people there in the basement of the bookstore, and despite that small number, Rowling was so nervous that minutes before starting to read the

---

[6] The mistake of "a wand" appearing twice is necessary for a book to be considered a First Edition but alone is not enough: the mistake was also repeated in future subsequent prints that are worthless.

book she smoked a cigarette. She remembers the day well and recalls reading the chapter when Harry received his wand at Ollivander's Wand Shop. Rowling also read in August for thirty people in the smaller tent at the Edinburgh International Book Festival, and that was followed by a tour of more Scottish bookstores in the fall of 1997. Hundreds of sales made a difference for the book, and that was achieved by Rosamund de la Hey when she convinced the Ottakar's network to highlight Harry Potter as one of the titles of his campaign, *Six For The Summer*. Rowling and her Harry Potter books were slowly beginning to expand throughout the United Kingdom, but the great leap to the United States had not come just yet.

The Bologna Children's Book Fair in Italy is the most important international event dedicated to the children's literature industry. Since 1963, it has been held annually for four days in March. It has gotten more than 1,200 exhibitors from more than 60 countries around the world, and it's where several awards are announced, including the Hans Christian Andersen. The 1997 fair would go down in history for being the seed of Harry Potter's emergence in the United States of America.

Arthur Levine, Editorial Director of Scholastic Books, was on a plane back from Italy when he read a proof of a nearly 200-page children's book to be published in the UK mid-year. Some versions of this accounting claim that he asked for a copy of *Harry Potter and the Philosopher's Stone* because Janet Hogarth, a former Bloomsbury employee who now works for Scholastic, recommended it. He says that Bloomsbury actually suggested it to him when he described what he was looking for: "Well, you know, what I'm really looking for is a book that people will talk about 20 years down the road and say, 'Wow, that was my favorite book!'" (Scholastic a). One way or another, Arthur

Levine left with a copy, and before landing in the United States, he decided to obtain the rights for the book in the U.S. Thus, he organized an auction in New York for the upcoming months.

It was in April[7], a month after the Bologna fair, when the phone rang at Rowling's apartment at nine o'clock at night. Her book was about to be published, and Christopher Little mentioned an auction to her. She didn't believe it was for her book at first, but then realized that the rights to her book were what they were bidding on. In the next hour, the phone rang again and it was Little again. The auction was over and the rights in the United States had been acquired by Arthur Levine for a six-figure deal. Mr. Levine called Rowling directly a few minutes later to discuss the matter. "I called her very late, and we had a very nice conversation," he recalls. "I said don't be scared, and she said, 'Thanks; I am"' (Levine, 1999). Rowling herself later recounted in an article for *The Sunday Times*: "[I] walked around my flat for hours in a kind of nervous frenzy, went to bed at about 2am, and was awoken by the telephone early the next morning. It didn't stop ringing for a week" ("J.K. Rowling's Diary," Sunday Times, July 26, 1998). The news had already reached the press. Newspapers such as *The Daily Mail, The Guardian* and *The Scotsman* published that a recently divorced and penniless mother sold her first book for £100,000. The truth was that Rowling was not *recently* divorced (more than two years had passed since her divorce), she was not without a penny because she had a scholarship from the Scottish Arts Council, and the sale had not been for £100,000, but for $105,000. The media wanted to exaggerate the story, and it

---

[7] Arthur Levine repeatedly said that the bid took place in April. However, some sources place it in the first week of publication in England, which would also make sense because the news appeared in newspapers in July. J.K. Rowling assures that it was in September, which is impossible.

didn't take long for articles about the poor mother who went to write in cafés to keep her daughter in a warm place became popular. But the news, and the way the English media covered it, jumpstarted sales of the book, and Harry Potter's success would hardly have been the same if the amount paid by Arthur Levine had been much less. For the first week after its publication, the English publisher had to launch a second print run. On July 7th, just over 10 days after the book was released, the first media interview with J.K. Rowling was published in the *Daily Telegraph*, a popular English newspaper. The journalist in charge was Nigel Reynolds, an art columnist, who still remembers today having received a copy of the book, a First Edition, and who, without taking it seriously, threw it in the trash. Years later, he publicly regretted it, because today it would be worth tens of thousands of pounds, and even more if he had asked the author to sign his copy.

Rowling also had to fulfil orders to go to the American market. Arthur Levine Books, a Scholastic division made up of less than five people, had claimed the U.S. rights. The size of the division gave Arthur Levine the ability to work on the books in great detail, while also having the distribution channels of a large publisher. Bloomsbury had only paid a small advance for the book, so for them it wasn't a commercial risk, and if their nearly 6,000 copies weren't selling, it would have been just a bad move on their part. However, Levine had to recover the $105,000 he had paid for the rights, and although he intended to do so in the long term, he had to maximize his chances. It had been therefore decided that there would be a hardcover edition with a dust jacket, that each chapter would have its own illustration, and that different fonts would be used in the text, among other things. The U.S. version was designed by David Saylor and illustrated by artist, Mary GrandPré. These editions also included different designs for letters that appeared in the books. One of the additions was a distinctive signature for each one of the characters that wrote or sent a letter. Since this allowed for a bit of fun, different people did the different signatures. Arthur Levine did the signature for Ron Weasley, while Barry Cunningham did the one for Harry. Rossie O'Donnel did the one for Molly Weasley, and Brenda Bowen (who worked at Scholastic at the time) for McGonagall. Arthur Levine is not completely sure, but he thinks Rowling did Hermione's herself, while David Saylor could have done Sirius'.

Arthur Levine wanted Rowling to succeed in America, so he thought the book should be brought closer to children. First, he decided that some very British words should be adapted to American English. Among the many modifications, Joanne refused to change 'mum' for 'mom,' keeping the English term for "mother." What she did accept was to reinclude some cuts from the British version again. This explains why Dean Thomas appears more times in the American edition of the first book than in the British edition (where the editors had cut his introduction and part of his dialogue). Second, Levine believed the title, *The Philosopher's Stone* would make it seem like it was about philosophy for adults, so he suggested changing it. Considering that Hogwarts was the central aspect, he proposed *Harry Potter and the School of Magic*. On a letter that he sent to Rowling on December 19, 1997, he explains the reasons for that title: "What do you think of HARRY POTTER AND THE SCHOOL OF MAGIC. I think it has a nice ring to it; it evokes all the fun to come at Hogwarts without giving too much away, and it's a bit of play on the sense of the world 'school' (i.e. both an institution of learning, and a... philosophy as it were!)".

Rowling, who oversaw each change, declined, and suggested *Harry Potter and the Sorcerer's Stone*, which became the title in the United States. Years later, Rowling would regret this and say that she would have preferred it to be published under the original title, but she knew that at the time she was in no condition to impose it. In France, the book was published as *Harry Potter à l'école des sorciers* (*Harry Potter and the School of Sorcerers*).

Two weeks after the book was published in England, Rowling submitted the manuscript for *Harry Potter and the Chamber of Secrets*. The good reviews that the first book received worried her, since she did not think that the second book was good enough to hold up. The Bloomsbury publisher was no longer Barry Cunningham, who had left to form his own publishing company, so Emma Matthewson took over. Emma went on to oversee editing for the remaining six books in the series. Rowling would establish an almost friendly relationship with her. In 2000, Rowling seemed to remember the change was to her liking by saying that, "In *Philosopher's Stone* I had a game of chess between Harry and Ron which Ron won by using a particularly violent bishop. My editor made me take it out. He didn't want me to have a bad bishop. Well, he's back, I have a different editor now" (Johnstone, 2000)[8]. This phrase could be misinterpreted regarding Rowling and Cunningham's relationship, but the author is still grateful to her first editor. Years later, she would publicly thank him as one of the seven people who had made the phenomenon possible.

Emma told Rowling, in a letter dated August 6th, that *Harry Potter and the Chamber of Secrets* was brilliant, and that Rowling was at no risk of falling short of the first book. Emma suggested, however, that it was too long and that some parts should be cut. They met in person at the end of that month, and Rowling, not

---

[8] Barry Cunningham did not want that the word 'violent' appear next to 'bishop' because of the religious overtones this might have in a children's book.

yet satisfied, asked for the manuscript back. She sent in the final version on October 25th: "I am very happy with it now, which wasn't the case before," said the author in the letter that accompanied the text (Errington, 2015). One of the many cuts included Nick Nearly Headless' song, which Rowling would share with her fans much later, on her website. Also, in 2005, a copy of the song, handwritten by Rowling, would be auctioned to raise funds for a Scottish language research organization. All information about the family and past of Dean Thomas, Harry Potter's classmate, was also removed in the editing process. Rowling ultimately decided that Neville's story was more important to the central plot. The original title of the book was going to be *Harry Potter and the Half-Blood Prince*, and there Rowling planned to introduce the concept of the Horcruxes (although less developed and with a different name), but she decided that it was too early in the series to do so and felt that the correct place to reveal the concept would be in the sixth book. For readers, it's not difficult to note that many things appearing in the sixth book are also present in *The Chamber of Secrets*: Tom Riddle's diary, the wardrobe in Borgin and Burkes, and the budding relationship between Harry and Ginny Weasley. There were other parts of the book that Rowling decided to change. In the first version of the text, Harry and Ron collided the Ford Anglia into Hogwarts Lake, which was full of mermaids, instead of into the Whomping Willow. "Not as pretty as they look in the books, are they, mermaids?" Ron said in the original text, where mermaids also spoke in English above the surface which contradicts what readers later learn in *Harry Potter and the Goblet of Fire*. The suggestion to change this, and the Ford Anglia's crash against the Whomping Willow, came directly from the editor, Emma, who suggested it because including mermaids in that part and never seeing them throughout the book was pointless.

While writing *Chamber of Secrets*, Rowling suffered from writer's block. This was due to the amount of press she had received from the sale of the rights to the United States, and the articles that some newspapers had published with information on her private life. The block lasted, according to the writer herself, five weeks, "and compared to some people, what's five weeks?" (Paxman, 2003).

By the end of 1997, the Potter phenomenon was just beginning. Even though Rowling had already finished the second book, the first one had not yet even been published in the United States. Nonetheless, it was already beginning to win awards. In November, it would go on to win the Gold Medal in the category of books for children between nine and eleven years from Smarties Awards. Rosamund de la Hey in Bloomsbury had anticipated the awards, and in December, *Philosopher's Stone* would become the Book of the Year for Boys from the British Book Awards. To boost sales and take advantage of the award, Bloomsbury organized a television interview on a BBC children's show. De la Hey also comments that the interview made a big difference, not only in sales, but was "partly measurable from her fan mail, as it was from this point that the letters stopped being addressed to 'Dear Sir.'"

As 1998 came into full swing, more awards acknowledged *Philosopher's Stone*, which had already sold more than 35,000 copies by March of that year. Another milestone was that in May—just ten months after publication—*The Scottish Braille Press* published the Braille edition of the book. Despite her successes, Rowling still did not receive much money from Bloomsbury. However, the sale of the rights to the United States had allowed her to move from Leith's apartment and into a house at 18 Hazelbank Terrace, a quieter, more residential neighborhood in Edinburgh with a school nearby for her daughter.

Preparation for publication of the second book in England had already begun, and by April it had already been decided that the book would be released in July. The publisher changed illustrators from Thomas Taylor to Cliff Wright, someone more experienced. Meanwhile, advanced reader copies of *Sorcerer's Stone* had begun to be distributed in the United States to literary experts, critics, and journalists. To make a good impression, this edition featured all the complete illustrations from the final edition and an introduction from Arthur Levine, which cemented the future success of the book and prompted recipients taking care of their copies; in many years they would have significant value.

On July 2nd, *Harry Potter and the Chamber of Secrets*, dedicated to Rowling's friend Sean Harris, would finally be published. In the coming months, Rowling sent Harris a package with at least 10 copies of the title in various languages, all signed by her. The package was lost or stolen, and some of these copies have appeared in online auctions. *Chamber of Secrets* was first published in hardcover with an initial print run of just 706 copies. To encourage sales, Bloomsbury tried to run a press campaign. Out of their efforts, the official fan club, "Potter's Friends", was founded. A membership cost £4.25 a year. Members of the fan received copies of *The Daily Prophet*, a kind of pamphlet that the publisher sent out four times[9]. It consisted of four pages with news articles from the Wizarding World. What made the pages special, were that they were written by J.K. Rowling. The publisher also began sending Rowling to

[9] Published on July 31, 1998; on February 8, 1999; on June 1, 1999; and on October 1, 1999.

different bookstores and schools to read to passages of the book. The first was at a Waterstones branch in Glasgow on the day of the book's launch, and it was followed with one in Edinburgh the next day. She returned to participate in the Edinburgh International Book Festival in late August, and this time, she read and signed books for 400 attendees. There she found a little girl sobbing, who said to her: "I didn't want there to be lots of people here. This is my book." Rowling added: "I know just how she felt. I still haven't got over the novelty of being in a roomful of people who know these characters" (Johnstone, 1999a). The campaign included posters and life-sized cardboard figures that stood in the display window.

The paperback edition would come out in January of the following year. During a launch event at King's Cross, a steam train left the station and children made predictions about what would happen in the seventh book and buried them in a time capsule. Also, for the first time, the English bookstore chain W. H. Smith became involved with the launch and purchased several copies in advance.

For Rowling, however, it was time to go back to the first book, which was published in the United States. It was priced at $16.95. Around 35,000 hardcover copies with a dust jacket were printed. As in the UK, there was no definite publication date. However, the confusion in the United States was worse. The publisher failed to log a specific date, and there are claims that *Harry Potter and the Sorcerer's Stone* was published on September 1, 1998. While the most likely claim places the date exactly one month later, on October 1st, confusion has arisen because the paperback version was released on September 1st, albeit from 1999.

October sounds more likely, because also in that month, J.K. Rowling embarked on an eleven-day tour of the United States.

She visited Denver, New York, San Francisco, Chicago and Seattle (in some cities, she read for hundreds of people, while in others, such as Denver, she only read for just fifteen individuals, including the employees of the bookstore). By the end of the year, *Publishers Weekly* had chosen *Sorcerer's Stone* as the book of the year, and Rowling had been interviewed on National Public Radio (NPR). The team at Scholastic believed that this interview was what invigorated the phenomenon. By the end of December, 190,000 copies had already been printed. Harry Potter began in the United States with a splash.

At the same time in the United Kingdom, *Chamber of Secrets* won the Nestlé Smarties Awards, and this made Rowling the first author to win it two years in a row. American fans, upon finishing the first book, learned that a second book was available in England. Many of them ordered it online on the UK Amazon website. Scholastic noticed this when the numbers became substantial and independent bookstores became concerned. There was a dispute between the publisher and Amazon, as the copies sold on Amazon.co.uk were from Bloomsbury and the publisher did not have the rights to sell in the United States. Jeff Bezos, CEO of Amazon, defended himself by saying that buying it online is “no different than if you go to London on a vacation and pick up a book and take it home in your suitcase” (Carvajal, 1999). Because of this dilemma, Scholastic had to advance the publication date of the second book from September to June 1999, one year after the publication in England. However, those three months would be decisive for the bookstores which received constant inquiries about when the book would arrive in their country. Although it had already reached #1 on the country's bestseller list, the book did not make the bestseller list in the U.S. until some coercion came from the publisher. "We campaigned to have children's books shown on *The Times* bestseller chart," says Rosamund de la Hey.

Bloomsbury was still taking advantage of the Harry Potter success and planned two new editions of *Philosopher's Stone* and *Chamber of Secrets*. The first of these was the adult version. Although the publisher's public excuse was that many adults wanted to read the book but were ashamed to do so in public places, the reality was different. Despite being a bestseller, *Harry Potter* did not leave the children's sections of large bookstores; an adult-centered cover allowed booksellers to put the copies up for sale in front of stores. Therefore, it was decided to launch an edition with a more serious cover. Secondly, the audiobook edition was planned. Rowling spent January 22, 1999 with actor Stephen Fry for the recording of the text. Fry also recorded all the Harry Potter books for the British market.

Harry Potter and the Prisoner of Azkaban was already on the way. Rowling had started writing it in late 1997 and the process took almost half a year. "Finally! I've read this book so much I'm sick of it," she told her editor. In November 1998, after the corrections, she would repeat that "[...] I am so sick of re-reading this one that I'll be hard put to smile when it comes to doing public readings from it." (Errington, 2015). Rowling was referring to how complicated it was to write with time travel, a concept introduced in the third novel with the Time-Turner. The complications this generated required Rowling to pay too much attention to the details of the plot and to create a way to move through the timelines that was consistent, causing constant checks throughout the text so that there was no error. Finally, by December it seemed to be finished, as the publisher kept a copy labeled "Final Final Sketch 12/23" and a print test dated January 7, 1999. Despite what she told her publisher, in

2004, with the release of the film of *Harry Potter and the Prisoner of Azkaban*, Rowling seemed to have another memory: Writing it was "the best writing experience I ever had. Of the five books that are published, writing Azkaban was the easiest, and in some ways, I think it shows. I was in a very comfortable place when I wrote (number) three: Immediate financial worries were over, and press attention wasn't yet by any means excessive" (Puig, 2004).

The Dementors are one of the new beings introduced in this book. Rowling once dreamt of a similar creature: "I had a dream when I was a child that I was hiding from a creature that looked just like a Dementor, the empty black cloak and the withered hand, and it was sort of drifting towards me. It didn't seem to have feet and I was terrified and I woke up" (Armitage, 2021). But then she confessed that she remembered the dream only years after the writing and publication of the book.

But before the publication of the third book, the second was still forthcoming in the United States. *Harry Potter and the Chamber of Secrets* was released on June 1, 1999, with a print run of 250,000 copies (data not confirmed by the publisher). The style remained the same as the first, hardcover with dust jacket illustrated art by Mary GrandPré. At launch, it was estimated that around 20,000 Bloomsbury copies had been purchased online from the United States. On June 20th, *The Chamber of Secrets* topped *The New York Times* bestseller list in both the independent and chain bookstores category (*Harry Potter and the Sorcerer's Stone* ranked second, but only in independent bookstores).

For the third book, Warner Bros. had already acquired the rights to the film adaptations, and the previous two books were already a sales phenomenon, not only in the United Kingdom, but also in the United States. Bloomsbury now had another approach in mind about marketing and the press. For the first time, a specific date and time was chosen for the launch: July 8th, after school, at 3:45 P.M. The idea came from the Bloomsbury marketing team, who wanted to create a "launching moment" for the book, both for fans and for an advertising impact. Rowling had already signed books at events for the releases of *The Chamber of Secrets* (hardcover and paperback), was about to tour the United States soon, and was busy writing *Harry Potter and the Goblet of Fire* already. Therefore, launching the novel at a precise time was an interesting alternative to generate enthusiasm on the part of the public. Just two months later, in her third appearance at the Edinburgh Festival, when asked about her non-appearance at the launch of the third book, Rowling would say, "I wasn't hiding. I just needed to work" (Johnstone, 1999b).

The idea was a success. On the following day, *The Daily Telegraph* published on its cover page a photo of an independent bookstore where children lined up waiting for the launch time[10]. The same thing happened with *Sky News*, which showed a photo on their newscast. Little publicity was as effective as anxious children waiting for a book. Possibly Harry Potter's biggest marketing move was the idea of book releases on specific dates, and it all started with *The Prisoner of Azkaban* in the UK.

Although the plan was to release the book at 3:45 P.M., not all bookstores followed it. Waterstones in Charing Cross Road started selling the book before the agreed time. Its manager at the time, Seraphina Granelli, claimed "We went on a reconnaissance mission and discovered Foyle's and Books Etc were already selling them. The market is very competitive. If

---

[10] The newspaper also had the exclusive to publish an extract of the book days before its launching, on July 3rd.

our opposition have broken the time then we have no choice but to do the same. We were prepared to abide by it but it wasn't possible." (Fisher & Nettleton, 1999).

In May, the publisher had made an initial print of 5,150 copies, but high demand forced it to request reprints before the release date. At launch, an additional 101,800 copies had been ordered, all of which were released on July 8th. On the afternoon of the launch, before 4:00 P.M., a Waterstones from Birmingham had sold more than 30 copies, and Blackwell's had reached almost 100 copies by 4:15 P.M. These numbers may seem too low, but for the time they were phenomenal. Rosamund de la Hey, who was still marketing in Bloomsbury, was confident but not as confident. The circulation of more than 100,000 copies was a record for a children's book (Roald Dahl's *Matilda* had gone on the market with 30,000), but *Hannibal* was at #1 on the bestseller list, and it was very difficult to beat. *Harry Potter and the Prisoner of Azkaban* not only made it to the top of the charts, but also set the book record for fastest sales: 64,000 copies sold in just three days.

The launch in the United States was on September 8, 1999 (just two months after the British release) with a circulation of 500,000 copies. The publisher had to advance the date, because as with the second book, people ordered it online, and not only individuals, but also independent bookstores, which preferred to buy it as final consumers and then resell it in their stores. The situation served to clarify some legal questions about online sales in different countries of products with distribution rights. (One of the main points was that the books did not sell their distribution rights by country, but by language.)

Scholastic copied the idea of launch times, but used what would later become the norm for the following four books: bookstores would start selling at midnight. Amazon.com had received more than 60,000 preorders by the release date, and the country's physical stores reported 50,000 copies sold the first day. Rowling visited the United States again in October, but this time Scholastic did not waste the opportunity. On a three-week tour, she would do signature events at bookstores, radio interviews, and television appearances.

"Two book signings per individual. No questions. No personalization." Those were the rules in a Boston bookstore, one of the many that Rowling went through to promote the third book. At another Massachusetts bookstore, people started camping out at 11:00 A.M., eight hours before the start of the signing. At Book Revue, the largest bookstore in New York, the hysteria was even worse. The event started at 7:30 P.M., but people were already waiting at the door before dawn and some slept in their parked cars. "This is like Beatlemania," said one employee (Farber, 1999). By the end of the signing, the line of people spread across several streets of the New York while Rowling continued to sign more than 2,000 copies for the fans who had attended. This tour, consisting of almost thirty appearances with an attendance of 1,000 people on average per event, would make her understand the magnitude of the phenomenon, and that she was already treated like a pop star. In the case of another Massachusetts bookstore, the event was cancelled. The store had a capacity for 200 people, but more than 2,000 showed up. When Rowling arrived, the mass of people got out of control. Children were separated from their parents and Rowling had to leave as quickly as she arrived.

"Was like [traveling] with a rock star," says Kris Moran, Advertising Director for Scholastic. She oversaw the advertising campaigns for all seven books, and on that tour, accompanied J.K. Rowling to all events. In appreciation, Rowling would use her last name on one of the characters.

Moran is part of the Quidditch team from Ireland. "I was stunned, completely honored," Moran comments, "Then I got the book and [read] that I actually scored!" (EW Staff, 2001).

Harry Potter was also featured on the cover of *Time* magazine on October 4th. The following week, on October 13th, Rowling appeared on NPR, *The Rosie O'Donnell Show*, and *The Today Show*. During those interviews, audiences realized that Rowling already had most of the rest of the story already planned. In addition to admitting that she had already written the ending, she also commented that readers would know more about Severus Snape, and who he loved, in the seventh and final book. In the same radio interview, she commented that one of Harry's friends would become a professor at Hogwarts at the end of the books. She also confessed that in early 1991, when she had already been writing the first book for over six months, she had had the idea to change Harry's character to a female, but "He was too real to me by then to turn him into a girl— he was a boy in my head" (Lydon, 1999). She also said that Harry's eyes and their resemblance to his mother's would be very important in future books, and she gave out clues to the fourth book, *The Goblet of Fire*. Rowling seemed to have everything under control.

In addition to interviews, Rowling also attended schools where she read passages from the books and answered questions. The combination of all this pushed the three Harry Potter books to the bestseller list of both *The New York Times* (the first time in history that the same author conquered the first three places at once) and *The Wall Street Journal*. At this point *Harry Potter and the Philosopher's Stone* had been on the list for 42 consecutive weeks. More than eight million copies had already been sold in the US.

By the end of the year, *The Prisoner of Azkaban* would win the Smarties Awards, and Rowling would receive a special certificate for being honored three consecutive times. The next award would be for *The Goblet of Fire*, and that would come with the new millennium and with various changes, both by J.K. Rowling and by the two publishers that marketed her books in the United Kingdom and the United States.

CHAPTER THREE

Breaking Records

"I was just a little way away from actually thinking, 'How can I break my arm so I can tell my publishers that I can't physically do it?'."
J.K. Rowling (Paxman, 2003)

In the year 2000, the Harry Potter series was no longer simply J.K. Rowling's trilogy of books. The phenomenon had crossed unimaginable barriers. The novels were banned in some religious schools which believed that the books promoted the occult. On the other hand, however, the phenomenon did not stop gaining followers. Harry Potter books had been translated into more than 35 languages and countries around the world, including China, which published a box set of the first three books in a circulation of 600,000 copies, the largest circulation of any book there since Communism had come to power in 1942. Eight million copies had been sold in the United Kingdom and almost 25 million in the United States; but Harry Potter was not just paper and ink. Hollywood coveted it too, and Warner Bros. had already claimed the rights to film adaptations. Despite all that was going on, the highlight of the year 2000 was the publication of *Harry Potter and the Goblet of Fire.*

Rowling had started working on *The Goblet of Fire* in 1993 when she was pregnant with her daughter, Jessica. At that time, she was defining the overall plot. During those years she had thought about the book in a different way—originally, the name of Pettigrew belonged to a different character called Enid Pettigrew. On a handwritten note by Rowling, Enid Pettigrew is in a list along with the names of other *Defense against the Dark Arts* professors, so it would not be too crazy to assume she was going to be the teacher for that subject in the fourth book. In the same notes where Rowling wrote this, we can also see that her plan was for Gilderoy Lockhart to re-appear in the sixth book (he finally did it on the fifth book, although briefly) and Remus Lupin in the seventh (which ended up happening).

The writing process for the fourth book began in early 1999, after Rowling turned in the finished manuscript of *Prisoner of Azkaban.* Writing *Harry Potter and the Goblet of Fire* was not easy. With the first three novels, Rowling's plot planning had worked perfectly, but now it had failed. She was halfway through the book when she realized that there were two holes in the plot, and she had to go back to fix them. The first problem occurred in the chapter "The Dark Mark," where she had to write thirteen different versions. "I hated that chapter so much; at one point, I thought of leaving it out altogether and just putting in a page saying 'Chapter Nine was too difficult' and going straight to Chapter Ten" (J. K. Rowling chat, 2001d). The specific problem in the plot was never clarified, but the solution involved removing a character. Mafalda was a cousin of the Weasleys, in Slytherin house, who gave the golden trio information about the existence of Death Eaters and other exposition about the Wizarding World. One of her most important appearances was in the aforementioned chapter as she went as a guest with her family to the Quidditch World Cup. Rowling found it implausible that an eleven-year-old girl, nosy as she was, knew more about the Wizarding World than Harry and his friends and would tell them things they didn't know yet. Thus, the author decided to use a different character for that purpose: Rita Skeeter, the correspondent for *The Daily Prophet*. She would reveal details about the Death Eaters in the final version. Rowling also used her as a reporter for the trials that Harry views through Dumbledore's pensieve.

The second issue seemed more important to the plot, but Rowling never gave any details about it. She barely mentioned it in an interview: "The problem I'd given Harry was completely solvable and if I solved it then, I couldn't reach the end I needed to get to. I've had some of my blackest moments with this book. At Christmas I sank to the depths: 'Can I do this?' I asked myself. In the end it was just persistence, [...]. It took months. I had to unpick lots of what I'd written and take a different route to the ending" (Johnstone, 2000). By the time Rowling was working on the book full-time, the Harry Potter literary phenomenon was already expanding enough to understand that it could affect her work. "There was no escape. I could hear him, and I could see him, and I was writing about him" (Fry & Rowling, 2005). The author even remembers writing *Goblet of Fire* while her daughter listened to audiobooks read by Stephen Fry in the next room.

The Goblet of Fire continued to be edited until four months before its publication, which was a departure from the previous ones. This book was the first to be released simultaneously in the United Kingdom and the United States. In both countries, the book was released at midnight. Bloomsbury decided to invest £2 million into the book's advertising campaign. The key to the campaign was the secrecy surrounding the novel.

Firstly, no copies were made for the press like what had been done with the previous books. Very few people had access to the original manuscript other than Bloomsbury's editor, Emma Matthewson. Chris Columbus, who was directing the first Harry Potter movie, was able to read *Goblet of Fire*, but couldn't even tell his children about the book. The secrecy came from Rowling herself: "The marketing was literally, 'Don't give out the book.' And it wasn't even a marketing ploy. It came from me. This book was the culmination of 10 years of work, and something very big in terms of my ongoing plot happens at the end, and it rounds off an era; the remaining three books are a different era in Harry's life. Had that got out, there's no way the book would have been as enjoyable to read" (Jensen, 2000).

One of the details that was not released was the title. Originally, the name was planned to be revealed at the same time of the book's publication, when readers saw the cover. The book's advertisements simply said, "Harry is back!" and "Coming Soon: Harry IV". Promotional material distributed by Scholastic to booksellers included *Harry Potter and the Doomspell Tournament* as a tentative title, but the booksellers were unable to make it known because of the contract they had with the publisher. Finally, in late June, *The Sunday Telegraph* leaked the book's final title, *Harry Potter and the Goblet of Fire.* The title was only decided in April, when Rowling was still hesitating between the different options: *Harry Potter and the Death Eaters, Harry Potter and the Three Champions* and *Harry Potter and the Tournament of the Apocalypse*[11]. The latter was the original name of the competition between the three magical

---

[11] Another option was *Harry Potter and the Fire Goblet*, barely different from the final version, *Harry Potter and the Goblet of Fire.*

schools, which was later replaced by 'the Triwizard Tournament.'

There was one exception to the secrecy, and it was Catie Hoch, a nine-year-old girl from New York with neuroblastoma, an aggressive childhood cancer. The relationship between Catie and Rowling began through letters when the girl wrote Rowling, telling her about her situation. The author expressed her solidarity by starting a written relationship with Catie. In the early 2000s, Catie's mother told Rowling that her daughter's health had deteriorated, and she might not live long enough to read the fourth book. Because of this, Rowling offered to call Catie on the phone and read excerpts from the novel she was still writing. "We laid Catie down on the living room couch and Jo read to her over the phone. Catie's face just lit up," recalls her mother (Laurence, 2002). Catie died in May 2000. Rowling donated $100,000 to the memorial fund her family opened.

Natalie McDonald was another fan, from Canada, who had leukemia, a cancer of the blood cells. Natalie's mother wrote to Rowling with a request like Catie's. Rowling read the letter after a vacation in Spain, and despite feeling it was too late, she responded by explaining what was happening to each of the main characters. The email came a day after Natalie's death. In honor of her, a first-year character is named Natalie McDonald in the fourth book. This is the only character in the entire series who shares their full name with a real person. (Other characters have the first name or surname of a real person, but no one else has both). Rowling would later meet the McDonalds on her visit to Canada for the launch promotion.

Being published at the same time in the United States, *Goblet of Fire* went through an extensive editing process. Arthur Levine's editorial team collaborated with Emma Matthewson; it was the first time that both teams worked side by side on the original text. Arthur Levine sent suggestions to Matthewson, who organized them with those from her team and they were sent together to the author (the only suggestions that were sent were those related to American idioms). In this way, Matthewson supervised the process and was the main person responsible for editing the book. This had its risks too: During the six weeks that the process lasted, the manuscript was almost stolen twice from her car.

The fourth book is dedicated to two people. The first one, *Mr. Ridley,* is Ronald Ridley, a friend of Rowling's father. Mr. Ridley is the reason why Ronald Weasley is called Ron, according to a signed book to her father, where the author wrote "Dear Dad, If I had said 'Ronald (Weasley) Ridley' they would have tracked the poor bloke down... but that's why Ron's called Ron, of course!" The second person mentioned in the dedication is Susan Sladden, a close friend of Rowling in Edinburgh who enabled her to finish the first Harry Potter book by babysitting her daughter Jessica. In a book signed and dedicated to Susan, Rowling wrote "though we didn't want it in print, [Susan] helped me out of my cupboard".

Finally, on July 8th, the book arrived: 750,000 hardcover copies for the United Kingdom and 3.8 million copies for the United States. Nigel Newton, director of Bloomsbury, says that the heroes were Clays—the printer that produced the 750,000 copies in record time and in a state of absolute secrecy—, and Macmillan, which was in charge of the distribution and did so perfectly. Arriving early involved a security risk and arriving late would have been a failure for bookstores and readers. In the United States, FedEx used nearly 10,000 trucks and more than one hundred aircraft for deliveries. This was the first time this many resources were needed for a book premiere. In fact, Helena Coryndon, Bloomsbury's Production Coordinator, says that the astronomical amounts of paper required to print so many copies caused problems. First, Clays did not have enough printing capacity, so it was necessary to work with other collaborating printers. Secondly, there was not enough paper, so they had to work with a paper mill from Finland. The day after establishing the purchase order at the paper mill, employees at the plant in Finland went on strike, putting the process at risk. It all worked out, but it still gave Coryndon a major headache.

The pressure from the publication date and a delay from Rowling in delivering the manuscript caused an error that could not be corrected on time. When Harry Potter and Voldemort face off in the graveyard, his victims come out from the villain's wand in the reverse order of their murders. Readers know from *Prisoner of Azkaban* that James died before Lily (who protected her son), so Lily should come out first from Voldemort's wand. However, in the first printing, James comes out first and encourages Harry to wait for his mother. This error was corrected in later editions. The author acknowledged this error on her website and explained the following in response to the correct order: "Lily first, then James. That's how it appears in my original manuscript, but we were under enormous pressure to edit it very quickly and my American editor thought that was the wrong order, and he is so good at catching small errors, that I changed it without thinking then realized it had been right in the first place. We were all very sleep-deprived at the time" (Rowling, 2006g).

The promotion of the book was unprecedented. Rowling arrived in a Ford Anglia at King's Cross Station in London when the Hogwarts Express departed from Platform 1 adorned with a platform $9^{3/4}$ sign. Rowling along with the Bloomsbury staff, journalists and hundreds of copies of the new book that she would sign, were on the departing train. The trip lasted three days, arriving in Perth on July 11th. There were intermediate stops at Didcot, Kidderminster, Crewe, Manchester, Bradford, York, Newcastle and Edinburgh. "The platform's very close to the one in the book, but the train's the wrong color. We won't quibble though," Rowling said of the staging (Mclaughlin, 2000). During the mini tour of the United Kingdom, there were four signing events in London: two on the 17th, one on the 18th and the last on the 19th of July. In August, Rowling also appeared for a signing event at the Edinburgh International Book Festival. In contrast to the release of *Prisoner of Azkaban*, Rowling did appear publicly this time.

In the United States, Amazon.com received 400,000 preorders, and Barnes & Noble received 360,000 and sold 114,000 copies in the first hour of July 8th at their brick-and-mortar stores. The author also participated actively, giving interviews to the press which published positive notes and reviews. *The New York Times* even published an article by Stephen King who spoke wonders about the books, and particularly about *Goblet of Fire*. In total, on the first day, *Harry Potter and the Goblet of Fire* sold 1 million copies. By the end of the week, 3 million copies had already been sold. The advertising campaign continued after the book was published. For example, planes with signs saying "*Harry Potter and the Goblet of Fire* - Read It Now" flew over the beaches of Long Island in New York and Los Angeles, California among other cities.

In October, Rowling embarked on a tour of the United States and Canada to read and sign books. October 20th was a hectic day. In the morning she did a public reading, signed books, and then had breakfast with fans who had won a contest conducted by the publisher. In the afternoon, she participated in a live chat with fans through the Barnes & Noble website, and in the evening, she appeared on *Larry King Live* on CNN. Two days earlier, Rowling had appeared on *The Rosie O'Donnell Show* and in another live chat with fans on AOL. Then, she went to Canada where she hosted four events: two in Toronto and two in Vancouver. Of all these, reading at the Toronto SkyDome, the main event of the International Festival of Authors, stands out. There she read to 20,000 fans. The Canadian publisher, Raincoast, assures fans that this event holds the world record for the largest book reading. However, that data is not confirmed.

The most interesting thing about the entire advertising campaign for the fans—save for those who had had the opportunity to meet the author—was the interview on the *Today Show* on NBC when Rowling first confirmed the title of the fifth book: "I can't really say because there are two titles I'm choosing between." However, after being asked by a child in the audience, she replied, "It's probably going to be called *Harry Potter and the Order of the Phoenix.*"

So far, there had been one Harry Potter book published each summer. However, Rowling claimed that the next book might take a little longer. And so, it did. Before the publication of the fifth book, several things happened. Not only were two films about Harry released, but also Rowling herself published two companion books from the Wizarding World.

Richard Curtis, an English director and writer famous for his films *Four Weddings and a Funeral, Notting Hill* and *Love Actually,* created these books in a way. In 1985, Curtis founded Comic Relief, a charity with the goal of bringing about change in the lives of the poor and disadvantaged through humor. Curtis contacted Rowling to see if she would consider writing a story about Harry to be auctioned off by the fundraising organization: "I'm sure you won't, we'll still love your books, even if you don't but just thought we'd ask" (Raincoast Books, 2001). Despite Curtis' doubts, Rowling supported the initiative, but being aware that short stories were not what she was good at, she proposed two short books: *Fantastic Beasts and Where to Find Them* and *Quidditch Through the Ages*. Each of these were named for textbooks that Harry used in his years at Hogwarts. *Quidditch Through the Ages* tells the story of the sport and features a warning on the cover and also a list of students who have checked out the book. *Fantastic Beats and Where to Find Them* serves as a glossary of beasts of the wizarding world and is "owned by Harry Potter", as the cover indicates. It also contains annotations from him, Ron and Hermione. Rowling began writing them as soon as she finished with the fourth book, according to her words. As she always says, she writes a lot more about Harry Potter than is published, for personal fun. Much of the material was written before the idea of turning it into a book was considered. Because there was no advertising pressure to release it, Rowling also claims she had more fun writing these two books than the four novels she had already published.

The books were announced on October 16, 2000, and were released on March 16, 2001. The date chosen was for Red Nose Day, an annual celebration organized by Comic Relief to raise funds. However, the books ended up being published in both the United Kingdom and the United States four days earlier, on March 12, 2001 (also, certain US promotional materials mistakenly announced a release date for February). On launch day, Rowling was interviewed on Blue Peter, a BBC children's show. The interesting thing about these two books was that they were the first to include illustrations made by the author herself. Unlike the previous four novels, the U.S. publisher did not adapt the text for its audience to preserve the wording as Harry and his classmates read at Hogwarts.

Although the data provided by the publisher may sound contradictory to other sources, Bloomsbury says that only 400,000 copies of *Fantastic Beasts and Where to Find Them* and 2,000,000 copies of *Quidditch Through the Ages* were sold. However, they apparently kept enough stock, as the Quidditch book was given away to those who bought *Harry Potter and the Order of the Phoenix* through the publisher's website.

Since the books were meant to raise funds for charity, each part of the production chain donated its fees, not just J.K. Rowling. Thus, almost 80% of the price paid by the public for each copy had its end in Comic Relief. In 2009, when the books were reissued with different designs, the organization confirmed that it continued to receive a share of each sale, and that more than £17 million had been raised through them.

During the rest of the year, there were no more publications, but in July, original illustrations for the cover of the first book were auctioned off. In August, Rowling had to make a public announcement that she was not suffering from writer's block. The media had reported that there would be no fifth book in 2001 because the author was suffering from writer's block. Through her agents, Rowling had to deny this in an official statement. In 2002, she would collaborate on the book, *Magic: New Stories*, a collection of stories published by Bloomsbury to help single-parent families. The author wrote its introduction. Also, a legal process would end after two years in which the author Nancy Stouffer claimed that Rowling had stolen the word "muggle" from her book, *Legend of Rah and the Muggles*. The jury not only ruled in Rowling's favor, but also compensated her for punitive damages as Stouffer was found to have falsified documents.

In November of that year, Children's BBC announced that Rowling had donated a postcard where she had penned a ninety-three-word synopsis of *Order of The Phoenix*. It would be auctioned off at Sotheby's for the benefit of Book Aid International. In an unprecedented campaign, the-leaky-cauldron.org website collected $24,000 in two weeks with donations from fans around the world. Its premise was simple: it would be unfair for a millionaire to acquire the letter and keep it secret. All fans had the right to know the content, so the idea was to win the auction and publish it on the Internet. Unfortunately, it took just a couple of seconds after the auction started for the bids to exceed $24,000, the amount that the fansite had raised. The final sum was $44,400, nine times more than the foundation expected to raise, which was *only* $5,000. Melissa Anelli, the director of The Leaky Cauldron, remembers that it left her with a bittersweet flavor, but also assures that, thanks to the move, the project reached the ears of J.K. Rowling who, for the first time, found out what the fansites were capable of.

Three years had passed since the publication of the previous book in the Harry Potter series. The truth is, Rowling did not publish in 2001 because of a decision she made early to produce the best possible book and to maintain her sanity. The author had not had a good time writing the fourth book, mostly because of the problems she encountered in the plot during her writing. When she finally finished it, she did not want to make the same mistakes with the next one, *The Order of the Phoenix*. She wanted to take her time, write relaxed without a deadline to push her. She confesses that she came to think about how she could break her own arm to have the excuse of telling the publisher that she could not write for a while. Both publishers, Bloomsbury and Scholastic, had paid an advance to publish the fifth book in 2001. So, Rowling decided to call them both and tell them she was returning the money. The publishers refused and agreed to give Rowling the time. When Rowling completed the book, they would publish it without any kind of pre-arranged delivery date.

To avoid the problems that she had had with the fourth book, Rowling planned the fifth book too well. In her personal notes, there are sheets and sheets where she outlined chapter by chapter what would happen. For each chapter she detailed the exact month or date in which the general plot took place and what happened with respect to the six common threads that, she believed, were the core of the story: the prophecy, the Order of the Phoenix, Dumbledore's Army, Harry/Ginny/Cho, Snape/father/Harry and Hagrid/Grawp, the latter being the three most important relationships in the book. Another curiosity about these sheets is that Dolores Umbridge was originally called Elvira, although the change kept the Spanish origin of the name. Additionally, the group that Albus Dumbledore had organized to fight against Voldemort was called "Dumbledore's Army", while Harry Potter's secret organization within Hogwarts was the "Order of the Phoenix". Something that not many fans noticed from the planning sheets is that Sirius Black's fate could have been a bit different. It reads "Sirius chooses death rather than Dementor", which gives the idea that Rowling's original plan for Harry Potter's godfather was suicide instead of going back to Azkaban (or taking the Dementor's Kiss).

Bloomsbury's internal files state that the publisher received the manuscript in December 2002, and that the editing process was completed in March of the following year. The state of secrecy for the fifth book greater than its predecessors. Christopher Little, the author's agent, called Nigel Newton, president of Bloomsbury, to meet at a bar. They gathered there and drank a pint of beer. Little handed Newton a Sainsbury's grocery bag, with papers inside, under the table and they said goodbye without talking about J.K. Rowling or any manuscript. Nigel Newton drove home, put other sheets in front of the book so that neither his wife nor children knew what he was reading, and completed reading the material overnight. The next morning, he personally took it to Emma Matthewson, the editor in charge. Matthewson's house had been reinforced in terms of security, and she was prohibited from editing the book on a computer connected to the internet to avoid possible hacks of the material. The process was not very complicated and the only thing to note is that in late April, when the book was already at the presses, they had to do a global replacement of "Prewitt" to "Prewett", Molly Weasley's maidan name. For its part, to maintain the secret that the manuscript was being worked on, Scholastic gave a key name to the book: *The Owl King*. For the fourth book the publisher had also done this, and that code name had been *The Eagle*. This was to avoid leaks to the press, as only people who were specifically working on the original text knew that the material was circulating in the office.

Regarding marketing, this time the title of the book was not hidden as in the fourth one. In fact, Rowling had announced it three years ago. "I am never again going to try to keep the title of a book secret. [...] From my point of view it was enormously stressful, so I would prefer it if we didn't use that marketing strategy again," she would admit (Ballard, 2001). Although she had already released the name in an interview, she needed the publisher to make it official. So, she went on to ask Bloomsbury, "Please will you release the name of the title because I have people outside [my house] searching my trash can looking for bits of paper" (BBC News, 2016f).

The publication date was announced as June 21st on January 16, 2003. The first paragraph of the book was also shared and, for the first time, two hardcover versions would be published at the same time— a “children's” version and an “adult” version which only differed in cover design. The campaign used traditionally aggressive advertising with posters, stickers, bookmarks, and posters with countdowns. Bloomsbury even gave out pieces of stained glass and cardboard boxes that resembled the book (which could not be seen) to show the customers before publication. The English publisher also put advertisements on London buses for the first time with the message, "HIP, HIP, HARRY". Closer to the release date, a phrase from the book was used to create buzz: “It is time for me to tell you what I should have told you five years ago, Harry. Please sit down. I am going to tell you everything.” This announced that the fifth book was the beginning of many explanations that the series was beginning to need.

The Scholastic campaign in the United States used the phrase “Is Harry ready? Are you?”, alluding to the changes that the protagonist would face. For the fifth book, Scholastic ran an original campaign that featured everyday people enjoying their lives, and associated them with concepts from the novels like "Death eaters" and "Quidditch". These posters were the only ones made in the history of the Harry Potter books featuring real models and not with illustrations. Scholastic also distributed 3 million stickers, 400,000 pins, 50,000 posters, and 15,000 event kits for bookstores to use at release parties across the country.

On March 20th, both the British and American publishers revealed the covers of the books. The illustrator of the English edition was Jason Cockcroft, who replaced Giles Greenfield, illustrator of the fourth book. Giles, who could not read the book, started to work on an illustrated flaming phoenix, but had to leave the project for personal reasons. Cockcroft took his place, and following the orders from Emma Matthewson of Bloomsbury, illustrated another phoenix, keeping Greenfield's original illustration as inspiration. Jason, like Giles, did not have access to the manuscript either. Mary GrandPré, on the other hand, did have access to the material since Scholastic editions contained one illustration per chapter. The English cover did not make much of an impact, as it did not show any scenes from the book. However, the Scholastic cover art generated many debates because in it, readers saw the protagonist holding his wand with his left hand (Harry Potter is right-handed). Theories that claimed that he had suffered an accident in his right hand that prevented him from casting spells soon arrived. There were other possible variations: it was the reflection in the Mirror of Erised, or better yet, in a reference to the fourth book, someone left-handed was posing as Harry with the Polyjuice potion. Those who read the book now know that none of this happens, and it was simply a minor detail of the illustration.

Despite all the security efforts that were employed, including the fact that not even the UK illustrator had access to the contents of the book, theft of some copies could not be staved off. The first appearances of stolen copies were in May of 2003, one month before the scheduled release. Donald Parfitt, 44, found two abandoned copies in a field in the small town of Bungay, Suffolk, and quickly contacted *The Sun* newspaper. The newspaper decided to act in good faith and notified the publisher, which began an investigation. But Donald's story wasn't true. He worked at Clays, the printing plant, and found copies of the book in the plant parking lot. He decided to call the newspaper and ask for £25,000 in exchange. The newspaper, in conjunction with investigators, set him up and he was arrested. Parfitt had to complete 180 hours of community service.

A major theft occurred on June 15th, six days before launch. A trailer with 7,680 copies of the book disappeared from Newton-le-Willows, in the north of the Anglo-Saxon country, and was found, the next morning, abandoned 30km from the site. The detectives suspected that the thieves did not know the contents of the truck since it was not possible to know it by the external appearance of the vehicle, and even though the books were a highly desired product, it was practically impossible to sell them all without alerting the authorities. Police warned that anyone who found a copy of *The Order of the Phoenix* before the release date would face criminal charges, regardless of whether they acquired it in good faith.

With all the anxiety about the book and the great risk, the Harry Potter publishing houses and J.K. Rowling's agents achieved a revolutionary change in British law: the legal possibility of imposing a protection against an anonymous or unknown person, simply for their actions. In the United States, this is known as the *Doe subpoena*, a summons for being a defense against any person who is described through his/her actions, without needing to know who he/she is. The protection imposed by the author's team was against "the person or persons who has or have gotten physical possession of a copy of said book or any part of it without the consent of the plaintiffs." This order, which was widely used as jurisprudence in future cases, even outside the publishing world, is known in England as the "Harry Potter order."

In the United States and Canada, it was a little different. A Brooklyn store began selling the book three days earlier, unaware that it was to be kept in the warehouse until June 21st. Wal-Mart also sold copies at a Montreal store. Although the

Canadian publisher contacted the people who bought the book to ask them to return the copies, they refused.

Two days before launch, the BBC had a special segment for the book with a half-hour interview with the author. June 21, 2003 finally arrived and bookstores took advantage of the phenomenon like never before. Shoppers were no longer just the children who regularly read the series. *The Order of the Phoenix* was the first book to be published after the movies, making Harry Potter a global phenomenon that kids who had never read a book before wanted to be a part of. Ottakar's, one of the first bookstores to promote *Harry Potter and the Philosopher's Stone*, changed its name to Pottakar's on launch night. Waterstones, the UK's largest bookstore chain, produced its own promotional material and delivered the books in bags with the caption: "I am taking the magic home." A London store that sold the book at midnight organized events all weekend and a VIP party, with tickets costing £100, which was attended by celebrities such as chef Gordon Ramsay and actress Judi Dench, who attended the event with her children.

However, the luckiest fans were the 36 children who were at the West End branch in Edinburgh. They had been warned that at twelve midnight there would be a surprise. When J.K. Rowling walked in the door, they forgot that they could already buy the fifth book. "It was truly incredible. They saw J.K. coming in and ran towards her. It was magical," recalls Craig Milne, the store manager (Khan, 2003). "When *Goblet of Fire* was published, I was desperate to go into a bookshop at midnight and see children's reactions, so this time I'm really pleased I could," adds the author (BBC News, 2003).

On June 26th, five days after launch, Rowling participated in an event organized in conjunction with Bloomsbury and MSN.com. At the legendary Royal Albert Hall in London,

Rowling read paragraphs from the new book, was interviewed by Stephen Fry and by some of the 4,000 children who attended the event, and thanks to the association with MSN, the event was broadcast live to everyone online.

Bloomsbury printed four million copies of the children's edition and half a million of the adult edition; 1.77 million copies were sold the first day. Scholastic, meanwhile, printed 6.8 million copies, and sold five million in the first 24 hours. It was not just bookstores that took advantage of the momentum. Tesco supermarket chain acknowledged that it sold 220 copies per minute the first weekend, while Sainsbury doubled the number of expected sales. The English publisher, due to the demand of families who buy more than one copy on release date (so as not to have to share copies while reading), also offered family packs. These family packs contained three children's editions of the book; or, two children's editions and one adult edition; or, two children's editions and two adult editions. These packs came in a special cardboard box and cost the same as buying the copies separately. They were labeled as an "Essential Reading Kit."

A month later, the US publisher also published the deluxe edition of the book, which was presented in an illustrated box. Bloomsbury would also publish its deluxe edition in October, with a circulation of 26,000 copies. "J.K. Rowling and Harry Potter have once again reached a new milestone in publishing history with the extraordinary first printing and unprecedented sales of *Harry Potter and the Order of the Phoenix*," said Barbara Marcus, President of the book division for children in Scholastic (Scholastic b). In 2004, Scholastic produced a special edition of the book with a circulation of only 5,000 copies which never went on sale. These copies were for the booksellers who helped spread the Harry Potter phenomenon, and they were given only as a gift at the Book Expo of America, a fair for booksellers, publishers, authors, and other professionals in the publishing world. The cover of this edition does not contain the title of the work or the name of the author and there is no reference to the interior content except for a full-size illustration by Mary GrandPré.

Harry Potter and the Order of The Phoenix was not only a rage in the United Kingdom and the United States, but also in France. One week after launch, the English edition reached the top of the bestseller list. It was the first time that a book in English had done so well. In just a few days, the French sold out of the 16,000 copies that had arrived in the country. Of course, the reason was that fans did not want to wait for the French translation, a consequence of the embargo that Rowling's team had placed. Nobody could have the text before the release date, not even the translators. This not only led to sales of the book in English in countries where it was not the official language, but also to illegal translations by fans that were shared on the internet.

By the end of the year, with the release of the audiobook in English, a curiosity was unveiled. Fans noted that Stephen Fry's recording was missing a paragraph that appeared in the book. Thinking that it was a mistake in the recording, the news reached the BBC, who contacted Rowling's agents, and it was revealed that it was not a mistake. The author herself requested that this paragraph be removed from the book, not only in the audiobook, but also in subsequent printed editions. Today, the new editions of the fifth book do not contain a paragraph from chapter 26, entitled, “Seen and Unforeseen”. The paragraph in question is quite trivial and is not at all substantial to the plot, so the reasons for its removal are unknown.

The sixth Harry Potter book, *Harry Potter and the Half-Blood Prince* would be published in July 2005. Rowling had started working on it as soon as she had finished *The Order of the Phoenix,* between late 2002 and early 2003, during her pregnancy with her son by her new husband, Neil Murray. David Murray Rowling was born in March 2003, so Rowling stopped writing the sixth book to dedicate herself not only to her new son, but also to the promotion of the fifth book, taking it up again after the publication of the latter.

Rowling wrote *Half-Blood Prince* from mid-2003 to late 2004. The opening chapter of the book, the discussion between the Muggle Prime Minister and Cornelius Fudge, was finally included in one of the books. This scene had been considered in *The Philosopher's Stone*, *The Prisoner of Azkaban*, and *The Order of the Phoenix*, but the author felt the scene didn't fit in any of those books. When asked if she was happy with the finished book, Rowling replied, "I like it better than I liked *Goblet*, *Phoenix* or *Chamber* when I finished them. Book six does what I wanted it to do and even if nobody else likes it (and some won't), I know it will remain one of my favorites of the series. Ultimately you have to please yourself before you please anyone else!" (Rowling, 2005c). Rowling knew that the sixth book had to explain a lot of things in the plot, and mainly answer a question that she always expected fans to ask her and had never received: why did Voldemort not die when he received the curse thrown at Harry? Those who remember the sixth book will know that this is where the nature of Horcruxes is explained and why these artifacts allow Voldemort to stay alive.

Interestingly, in *The Half-Blood Prince* readers must wait until the third chapter to see Harry. Rowling wanted to show that the conflict was no longer only his, but was spreading throughout the Wizarding World, and thus affected the entire witch and wizard population. She also confessed that by the end of the fifth book she came to mourn a little over the death of Sirius Black, and at the end of the sixth, she was angry at herself for the events she had to write to make the plot work. Although she never specifically said it, fans can assume she was referring to Albus Dumbledore. Rowling enjoyed the process anyway. "I absolutely loved writing *Half-Blood Prince*, it was an enjoyable experience from start to finish, I would say the two books I have enjoyed writing most, and I have been most relaxed in my life at the time, were *Azkaban* and *Prince*." (BBC News, 2005a).

Writing was delayed by another pregnancy. In April 2004, Rowling became pregnant with Mackenzie who arrived in January 2005. Rowling dedicated *Harry Potter and the Deathly Hallows,* in part, to her. The author recalls that in the past she wrote up to ten hours a day and at night, but due to her pregnancy, for the final chapters, she only wrote around eight hours a day.

Prior to her pregnancy with Mackenzie, in March 2004, Rowling participated in an online webchat for International Book Day where fans from all over the world could ask her questions. She received 16,000 questions and answered 120 of them. It was in that chat that she gave a lot of information about the series which did not appear in the books and that fans wanted to know, such as the middle names of Ron and Hermione, and the houses that the Marauders belonged to. But she was also hinting at what might happen in future books when faced with very elaborate questions. When it was asked if Sirius and Harry's mirror (which plays a very important role in the seventh book) would be seen again, the author only commented that it was a very good question, and that she could not answer it. However, when she was asked if Regulus Black, who was also vital to the story, would be seen in future books, she simply said that he was already dead, so he had been very quiet lately. Any other answer indicating that readers would see him again would have ruined the surprise between the sixth and seventh books.

Rowling continued writing during her pregnancy, and towards the end of November, she delivered the first draft of the manuscript to Bloomsbury. Emma Matthewson served as editor once again. By the end of the month, after conversations between the two, they agreed that approximately 1% of the content should be reviewed and adjusted. An internal Bloomsbury publisher file dated February 27, 2005, was one of the last drafts the publisher produced.

For the sixth and then the seventh book, Scholastic worked hand-in-hand on the material. To help with the seventh book, the team, led by Arthur Levine, was joined by Cheryl Klein acting as continuity editor. Her job was to check and confirm that all the facts of the book were consistent: from the use of capital letters, to the names of each of the spells, to ensuring that details about each character's wands did not change, to the different locations within Hogwarts, and any other details that Rowling might confuse after writing for so long. Her work was especially important in the seventh book, where it was vital that there would be no mistakes in the Elder Wand's history. Although Cheryl had joined the publisher in August 2000, after the publication of the fourth book, she only worked on the last two books and not on *The Order of the Phoenix*. She says that as soon as she had joined the team, J.K. Rowling visited her and signed a copy where it said: "To Cheryl—no doubt you will soon be sick of my name." It was Cheryl who wrote Rowling's biography on the back of Harry Potter books for Scholastic. While she was tasked with spotting continuity errors with the U.S. team, Bloomsbury had also teamed up for that, even with people outside the company. They had organized a file called

"HP Bible", which functioned as a record of everything that happened in the books to maintain consistency. Rowling herself had used something similar in the past—the online fan encyclopedia, "The Harry Potter Lexicon."

The process of publishing Harry Potter books up to this point consisted of three or four readings. This is when most grammatical or typing errors were detected. A specialized team did this. Emma Matthewson and Arthur Levine were in charge of the plot and the mood of the book. For example, in his first reading of the manuscript, Levine left annotations about his reactions in the margins using emoticons like ":)" or slang such as "LOL". Klein checked for consistency and continuity, along with the Bloomsbury team, and then read the book five or six times in order to identify new errors that might have been introduced by the changes. This process took around 4 months.

Even though the file was reviewed several times by both publishers, a line appeared only in the American edition of *Half-Blood Prince* published by Scholastic. In one of the final scenes, in the dialogue leading up to his death, Dumbledore offers Draco Malfoy an opportunity to escape Voldemort's influence. Dumbledore suggests that he can fake Draco's death and hide his family to protect them. Suspiciously, this line was not part of the British edition. The fans, who had already accepted the theory that Dumbledore had faked his death, and that Snape had not actually murdered him, found the confirmation they needed. Rowling included the dialogue but then decided to remove it so that it was not all too obvious. However, the dialogue wasn't removed in the American edition. Arthur Levine, publisher of the book himself, when consulted, confessed that it had simply been a human error. Rowling thought the paragraph was very long and decided to shorten it, but the order had not arrived in time to the printers that had already started to print the book. The fandom did not even believe it when Rowling herself confirmed that Dumbledore was dead. They had to wait until the seventh book to recognize that the extra paragraph in the American version was not a conspiracy or plot error.

Dumbledore's death was also the main topic of another event. In late May, a month before launch, the Blue Square sportsbook seemed to have unveiled which character would lose his life in the sixth book when the Blue Square gambling portal—one of the first to accept bets online—began taking the lead in bets for J.K. Rowling's next book. In late 2004, bets on Dumbledore's death paid £5 each. Shortly before the book came out, a barrage of bets began to favor the headmaster of the School of Witchcraft and Wizardry. This caught the attention of the Blue Square team, and an investigation was started. After looking at addresses and credit card data, the team discovered that all the bets had come from Bungay, a town in Suffolk, England near the Clays plant which was responsible for printing the books. Suspecting that a copy of the book had been leaked, Blue Square decided to lower the value of each bet to less than £1 for each bet and contacted *The Sun* newspaper to write an article for them. Landbrokes, another major sportsbook, decided to stop taking bets on the subject, knowing that there were people who already had the information. Despite the lost money (around £30,000 based on the £6,000 that was wagered, according to the company itself), Blue Square won in the end due to the media attention. Fans who were following the subject believed the rumors were true when the Bloomsbury team itself recommended that these rumors should be taken "with a pinch of salt." Why was the Bloomsbury team only responding to this rumor when there had been dozens of similar stories? Was it because, in this case, it was true? In any case, the pattern around the behavior from gamblers did not create certainty. Around the same time, large sums of money were wagered in favor of Dean Thomas being the Half-Blood Prince.

Rowling's official website played a major role in the announcements. At the time, the website mirrored her desk and one section simply showed a closed door. On special occasions, this door opened after solving a puzzle to make an announcement. In June 2004, the door was first opened to reveal the title of the sixth book, "Harry Potter and the Half Blood Prince", which was later changed to the more grammatically correct title, *Harry Potter and the Half-Blood Prince*. In anticipation of questions concerning the title, Rowling confirmed that the "Half-Blood Prince" was not Voldemort or Harry Potter himself. This announcement also ended rumors of other titles circulating online. *Harry Potter and the Green Flame Torch* was one of the main titles that fans clung to. The green flame was said to be a fire that burned those who had done evil and did no harm to those who were good. Another rumored title, *Harry Potter and the Pillar of Storge*, became so popular that the author denied it on her website, claiming, "I am trying very hard not to feel offended that anyone thought this was possible" (Rowling, 2004b). The author also denied another one that became quite humorous: *Harry Potter and the Toenail of Icklibogg's*. When announcing the book, the author explicitly added that she had considered the title for the second book as well, where she had planned to include much of the plot (especially related to the discovery of the Horcruxes, since the first of them appears in *Harry Potter and the Chamber of Secrets*), but that she had reconsidered and decided that was not the right place.

Just over a month later, Rowling shared an excerpt from the first chapter of the book on her website involving the new

Minister of Magic, Rufus Scrimgeour, whom readers had not met yet; he was a man with the appearance of an old lion and reddish hair. A few months later, in October, on her website, Rowling revealed the title of three chapters: "Spinner's End," "Draco's Detour" and "Felix Felicis," corresponding to chapters 2, 6, and 14 respectively. The manuscript was delivered to Bloomsbury in November and there was correspondence between publisher Matthewson and Rowling in the Bloomsbury internal files dating back to December 3rd. In discussion of Rowling's latest book, Matthewson says, "I do think that revised opening is a masterstroke" (Errington, 2005). J.K. Rowling, for her last announcement on December 20th, wished her followers Happy Holidays and announced that the manuscript had already been delivered to the publisher, and that in the next 24 hours the release date would be announced. That date would eventually be announced as July 16, 2005.

The author also used her website to deny rumors and theories regarding the content of her books, such as Dumbledore being Ron or Harry from the future, Luna Lovegood being the daughter of Severus Snape, the Sorting Hat as a Horcrux, or that the members of the Order of the Phoenix communicated through chocolate frog cards. In February of 2005, Bloomsbury started the promotional campaign, focusing mostly on bookstores. Among posters and banners, one of the items that caught the most attention was a clock-shaped countdown poster made of cardboard. Promotional bags, printed with the cover art of the book were also distributed in bookstores. "All aboard for Harry!" was printed on the side of over 2,000 buses in the United Kingdom and the Republic of Ireland. In March, Bloomsbury and Scholastic shared images of the three dust jackets for the book (Bloomsbury again had a "children" edition and an "adult" edition.)

The Scholastic campaign began on April 7th, announcing the "100 Days to Harry," which included television; radio; and billboards on streets, avenues, and even on domestic flights in the US, all revolving around the question: "Who is the Half-Blood Prince?" In addition to exclusive downloads on the publisher's website, *The New York Times* published an exclusive crossword puzzle alluding to the book's plot. The publisher also announced in May that the deluxe edition would be simultaneously published, presented in a container box, and feature a unique illustration by Mary GrandPré. The circulation of this edition would only be 100,000 copies against 10.8 million in the regular edition. For its part, Bloomsbury had an initial print run of 6.3 million books in its hardcover edition, adding one million in its edition designed for adults (and 26,310 copies of the deluxe edition that would be published in October after launch).

The first American copy of *Harry Potter and the Order of the Phoenix*, signed by J.K. Rowling, had been delivered to the New York Public Library at the courtesy of Scholastic. In 2005, Scholastic decided to give other libraries the same honor by starting up a contest. For this, the publisher decided that all the country's public libraries could participate and thus win the first American copy of the next book, *Half-Blood Prince*, signed by the author. The publisher took advantage of the situation: the book was transferred in a 2 x 1.5-meter chest in the RMS Queen Mary 2, the largest ocean liner built to this day. The media recorded the book while it was kept in the chest and when they carried it with cranes to the boat. They did the same for its arrival in the United States. On the other hand, a week before launch, Amazon announced that book six preorders had broken another record: 1.4 million copies. The number seemed gigantic, but compared to the amount of preorders of the fifth book (which had set the previous record), it didn't seem like much, hardly 100,000 more preorders than *Harry Potter and the Order of the Phoenix*.

The *Half-Blood Prince* launch event took place in Scotland. There, Rowling performed a reading Friday night at Edinburgh Castle, where a crowd waited for her outside with images of the cover art projected on the walls of the promenade. Half an hour before launch, Rowling arrived at the scene in a black car then read for the audience as well as "rookie" reporters, children from ages 8 to 16 chosen to attend at the behest of various media outlets. In order to select these children, each outlet held a raffle or competition to determine who would represent the newspaper or radio/television program. The winning children got the privilege of a special reading early Saturday morning with Rowling before attending the public reading the following afternoon for a round of questions. They then wrote or commented on the event for the medium from which they were sent. Also, that Saturday two television interviews from the children were recorded, one with Owen Jones from Ireland, and the other with Emma Coad from Australia. Both interviews, and the conference for all winners, were broadcasted on Sunday by ITV Network entitled, *Harry Potter at the Castle: Magic at Midnight*. The winning children were not the only lucky fans to be able to ask J.K. Rowling questions that day. Emerson Spartz and Melissa Anelli, administrators of the MuggleNet and The Leaky Cauldron fansites respectively, were invited to J.K. Rowling's house to interview her on Sunday, July 17th.

The reading at Edinburgh Castle was different than the others because Rowling did not start with the first chapter. Considering attacks on the public transport system in London a week earlier that lead to the death of 52 people, the author had decided not to read from the first chapter, where Voldemort's attacks on the Muggle world are described in detail.

For the launch in the United States, a kind of fair with activities for adults and children was held over the weekend in New York at Harry Potter Place, located on Mercer Street behind the Scholastic headquarters. At the event, the copy signed by J.K. Rowling was displayed for the public until the afternoon of July 15th, and the winning public library, the North Asheville Library of North Carolina, was announced. Over 9,000 libraries had previously entered the contest. Along with her signature, Rowling added: "To those who love reading and libraries as much as I do."

Shows and activities followed until midnight when more than 5,000 bookstores in the U.S. began selling copies. In the first twenty-four hours, 6.9 million copies were sold in the United States alone, compared to two million copies sold in the United Kingdom, and average of over one hundred copies per second. That weekend, sales totals eclipsed the numbers for the movies *Charlie and the Chocolate Factory* and *Wedding Crashers* which were in theaters at that time. "When a book beats out movies, we're in great shape. This is a cause for celebration, not just for Scholastic, but for book lovers everywhere," said Lisa Holton, President of Scholastic (BBC News, 2005b).

However, not everything was rosy for publishers. The Canadian supermarket chain, Real Canadian Superstore, mistakenly (they said) sold fourteen copies of the book before the release date. Raincoast, the Canadian publisher, obtained an injunction from the Supreme Court of British Columbia that prohibited those who had acquired the book from reading it. This generated an interesting debate in the media where a lawyer went on to say that, reading "was not a human right" and therefore those who were in possession of the book had no right to read it. The publisher's legal representatives even argued that the "Canadian Charter of Rights and Freedoms" only applied to the government, and that reading the book without permission was like reading other people's correspondence. In contrast, freedom and free expression activists like Richard Stallman spoke out against this, even going so far as to call for a boycott against the publisher. This was not the only problem Raincoast had against the rights of citizens. The publisher warned *The Globe and Mail* newspaper that if a critique of the book by one of its Canadian correspondents was published at 12:00 AM on July 16th, it would be in default for tacitly admitting having read the book before its release date. What the newspaper did, then, was publish a critique on its website but by English journalists, who, by that time had already had the book several hours before. This way, *The Globe and Mail* did not break any law and the next morning was able to publish the critique of its Canadian team.

One of the mysteries left in the plot was the identity of R.A.B., the character who had stolen the locket Horcrux that Harry and Dumbledore had gone to look for in what would be the last adventure for the headmaster of Hogwarts. The mysterious identity of R.A.B. was leaked thanks to the network of translations. Theories had already pointed to Regulus Black, Sirius Black's brother who had been introduced in *Order of The Phoenix,* at the same time that an old locket was shown in his family's house. The confirmation came from Netherland and Norway. The first of these countries translated Black as "Zwarts" at the time, and the second as Svaart. When the *Half-Blood Prince* was published in both countries and the initials were R.A.Z. and R.A.S., it was the confirmation that fans needed.

Half-Blood Prince suffered the same fate as *Order of The Phoenix* and was not exempt from theft of copies. On June, 22 2005, six weeks before launch, Aaron Lambert, who worked at the TNT company warehouse, a book distribution center in Northamptonshire, England, stole two copies. Around 10,000 copies were kept there. Lambert's plan was to sell these copies to the media in exchange for large sums of money. Lambert contacted the newspapers *The Sun* and *The Daily Mirror*, offering them a copy for £50,000 and £30,000 each. As it had happened with the previous scam attempt, *The Sun* newspaper alerted the police and planned a scheme. Journalist, John Askill, met with Lambert, 20, to tell him that he was interested in the book and that he would pay for it. However, the plan was to abscond with the copies and to have the thief arrested by the police. In a series of events that remain unclear to this day (and that neither party want to clarify), the journalist Askill tried to leave with the books which provoked Lambert to pull a gun on Askill. Fortunately, the revolver was only a prop imitation and there were no injuries;the police quickly arrested him.

Lambert was immediately arrested but released on bail. However, he did not seem to regret what he did. He assured Bloomsbury that he had read the book and that if they did not give him money, he would reveal everything that happened in it. He was finally sentenced to 12 months in jail for robbery, 18 months for offenses with a firearm, and 2 additional years for extortion.

The security behind *Half-Blood Prince* was so serious that even the Government Communications Headquarters (GCHQ), the British intelligence agency, was on the lookout for possible leaks. A few weeks before the book's release, the agency found what appeared to be a copy of the manuscript online. They immediately contacted the publisher, who after reading a page was able to determine that it was false. When the agency was asked how they had found the book, their response was, "We don't comment on our Defense Against the Dark Arts" (BBC News, 2016). Nigel Newton, co-founder, and chief executive of Bloomsbury also claimed that certain media outlets offered money to plant employees in exchange for stealing some copies.

Harry Potter and the Half-Blood Prince was the first book published by Bloomsbury in the UK using recycled paper. Thirty percent of the paper was certified by the International Council of Forest Administration, a fact that was celebrated by different organizations such as Greenpeace. Although the Bloomsbury move can be seen as an attempt to preserve nature, the truth is that all the English publishers were receiving pressure to start reusing paper for their publications, so doing it with *Harry Potter* put them one step ahead of Random House and Harper Collins, that so far had done nothing. It was not the first time Bloomsbury had done this, either. The *Harry Potter and the Order of the Phoenix* paperback release had also been printed, in part, on recycled paper. Raincoast, from Canada, had even gone further. Their more than a million copies of the fifth book were printed on 100% recycled paper, making them the only Harry Potter edition in the world that was completely eco-friendly, and this was not only because of the paper, but also because the ink was vegetable based. Raincoast has since published all its editions this way and includes a personalized message from J.K. Rowling: "The forest at Hogwarts is home to magical creatures like unicorns and centaurs. Because the Canadian editions are printed on Ancient Forest Friendly paper, the Harry Potter books are helping to save magnificent forests in the Muggle world, the home of magical animals such as orangutans, wolves, and bears. It is a good idea to respect ancient trees, especially if they have a temper like the Whomping Willow."

Following the book's release, Rowling made no further public appearances until December when she was interviewed for BBC Radio by Stephen Fry. During her interview, she explains certain plot decisions such as why Hogwarts functions as a boarding school. She replies that, "it was essential for the plot that the children could be enclosed somewhere together overnight, [...] the adventure would fall down every second day if they went home and spoke to their parents" (Fry and Rowling, 2005).

Rowling also stated that even though readers, especially children, sent her letters with ideas on how to end the plot, she could not read them because in the case that an idea was good enough (or coincided with Rowling's own idea), she would not be able to use it for legal reasons. She also explained that she was already in the process of writing the seventh book, and that although the sixth had gotten its own plot and outcome, the last two were a great story. "Whereas in six, although there is an ending that could be seen as definitive in one sense, you very strongly feel the plot is not over this time and it will continue" (Fry and Rowling, 2005). Days later, in January, the British magazine, Tatler, aimed at the English upper class, published a long report with the author in which she spoke about the loss of her mother, the Harry Potter series and, the writing of the seventh book. There she emphasizes an idea that she always had in mind: that Harry Potter books are not about magic, but that "My books are largely about death. They open with the death of Harry's parents. There is Voldemort's obsession with conquering death and his quest for immortality at any price, the goal of anyone with magic," and she adds: "I so understand why

Voldemort wants to conquer death. We're all frightened of it" (Greig, 2006).

On the subject of deaths, Rowling said that a few days before the interview she had written the death of a particular character, and that her husband Neil asked her not to. After being questioned about whether she trusted to tell her husband what she was writing, she replied, "Neil is the only person I can talk to about what happens because he instantly forgets." She also spoke of a notebook with notes about the seventh book that she had lost, but she assured, "I am sure it will turn up. I just hope I didn't leave it anywhere. I have been looking everywhere. What I don't want is someone to find it and take it to *The Sun.*" Fortunately, Rowling found it before the magazine was released. She made this update on her website on January 5th. Days before, in December, she had also updated her website to say that she had already finished planning the seventh book and could get fully into writing. "For 2006 will be the year when I write the final book in the Harry Potter series. I contemplate the task with mingled feelings of excitement and dread, because I can't wait to get started, to tell the final part of the story and, at last, to answer all the questions (will I ever answer all of the questions? Let's aim for most of the questions); and yet it will all be over at last and I can't quite imagine life without Harry" (Rowling, 2005e). For the next few months, she kept writing on her website, informing fans about the book's progress, as in February, when she recounted that her plan had not gone as she expected. "Harry can't possibly do all that in just one chapter," she says, acknowledging that what she thought would be two chapters turned into four (Rowling, 2006f).

In June she gave a television interview for BBC's *Richard and Judy,* where she claimed that she had been working on the seventh book for almost twelve months. A month later, she traveled to the United States to participate in an event after six years. On August 1st and 2nd, she spoke at the Radio City Music Hall in New York along with Stephen King and John Irving. The event was named *One Night with Harry, Carrie and Garp*, alluding to the main characters created by each of the authors. It was in support of *Médecins Sans Frontières* and The Haven Foundation, a Stephen King charity for artists and writers who suffered from disability. Tickets ranged from $12.50 to $100, and those who bought one got the ability to submit questions that could then be answered by the authors. There was also the possibility of a family pack for $1,000 which included four VIP seats and three books, each signed by each of the authors. On the invitation, Rowling said that "Stephen pretended to be in suspense about my answer, but frankly, this was easily one of the most enticing propositions ever put to me in an envelope" (Scholastic c). On both days there was a reading of the sixth book and questions from the fans were answered; the main theme was the recent death of Dumbledore. However, the author did not hesitate to make it clear that Dumbledore was dead and that we should not wait for "Dumbledore to make a Gandalf", alluding to the *Lord of the Rings* character who appears to have died but then returns in triumph. During the press conference of the event, the author also repeatedly commented that she had made considerable progress with writing the seventh book. In a few days she returned to British soil, after which there was no more promotions for the sixth book.

The next time Rowling appeared in public, the end of the series would already be printed and bound, available to fans around the world. But for now, all that was still missing, and there would be months to follow full of writing and varying emotions in the room of a luxurious Scottish hotel.

CHAPTER FOUR

The First Ending

"I constantly rewrite. At the moment, the last word is 'scar'."
J.K. Rowling (People Magazine, 1999)

Originally called the North British Station Hotel and reopened in 1991 by Sean Connery, The Balmoral, a landmark for its Victorian architecture, is a luxurious five-star hotel located in central Edinburgh. If you enter the hall and go to the right, you can enter an elevator decorated in gold. Going up to the fifth floor and going down the hall to the right, one arrives at room 552. There is where J.K. Rowling settled in for six months to finish *Harry Potter and the Deathly Hallows* upon returning from the United States after her events with Stephen King.

Not only was Rowling incognito for six months, but very few local employees knew[12]. When she needed to get out, she did it

[12] Thanks to Katy Reilly, manager of Public Relations at The Balmoral, I was fortunate enough to be able to visit the room and to collect some of this data.

through a door in the basement so no one would know. Although called a room, Suite 552 was more of a small apartment consisting of a living room with a fireplace, a television, armchairs, two desks, a room with a large bed, an en suite bathroom, and a dressing room. The walls that were yellow at the time are now light blue, and on the desks are two complete sets of the seven Harry Potter books along with a plaque commemorating that J.K. Rowling wrote the story's end on that very desk.

However, none of those signs live up to the quintessential souvenir of Rowling writing Harry Potter. On January 11, 2007, when the seventh book of the series was finally finished (discounting subsequent editorial changes), Rowling decided that she should leave a mark on her workstation. To do this, she took the marble bust of the Greek god Hermes, which was in a corner of the room, and decided to sign her name on the back of it (not to make it too obvious that she had signed it). She had written, "J.K. Rowling finished writing *Harry Potter and the Deathly Hallows* in this room (552) on 11th Jan 2007", as if it was graffiti art akin to a teenager leaving a mark. When the hotel discovered this, they decided to make use of Rowling's mark. First, they protected the bust in a glass box and placed it facing the wall, so that visitors could appreciate the signature. In addition to decorating the room with book sets on the desks, they also renamed the room, which became the "J.K. Rowling Suite", and a metal owl was adorned on the entrance. Rowling returned to the hotel in 2010 for an interview with Oprah Winfrey. There the author explained the decision as to why she wrote at the hotel. "As I was finishing *Deathly Hallows* there came a day where the window cleaner came, the kids were at home, the dogs were barking and I could not work, and this light bulb went on over my head and I thought, I can throw money at this problem. I can now solve this problem. For years and years and years, I would just go to a café and sit in a different kind of noise and work. I thought I can go to a quiet place, so I came to this hotel because it's a beautiful hotel, but I didn't intend to stay here, but they were so nice to me here and, I think writers can be a little bit superstitious and the first day of writing went well so I kept coming back to this hotel and I ended up finishing the last of the Harry Potter books in this hotel."

The final moment was not easy. Both on her website and in the interview with Oprah, Rowling confessed that when she finished writing the last book, she cried as she had only once in her life, with the death of her mother. "I always knew that Harry's story would end with the seventh book, but saying goodbye has been just as hard as I always knew it would be. Even while I'm mourning, though, I feel an incredible sense of achievement. I can hardly believe that I've finally written the ending I've been planning for so many years. I've never felt such a mixture of extreme emotions in my life, never dreamed I could feel simultaneously heartbroken and euphoric" (Rowling, 2007i). The last words of the book, which she had planned so thoroughly, however, were briefly changed. The last chapter that had remained in a safe since the 1990s, when Rowling had first written it, ended with the word "scar." The author had announced this herself. Revealed after the release of the seventh book, the last sentence was originally going to be "Only those who he loved could see the lightning scar." But Rowling decided to change it to "All was well," because the original sentence gave the impression that, while the scar was still there, Harry had not completely won. "I changed it because I wanted a more—when I came to write it, I wanted a very concrete statement that Harry won. And that the scar, although it's still there, it's just—it's now just a scar. And I wanted to say it's over.

It's done. And maybe a tiny bit of that was to say to people, 'No, Voldemort's not rising again. We're not going to have Part Two. Harry's job is done'" (Vieira, 2007a). Despite Rowling's plan to not have a 'part two' to Harry's story, there was later a continuation in the form of a stage play, *Harry Potter and the Cursed Child.*

Although the book was finished in January 2007, Rowling was thinking of titles as early as October 2006. She already had three in mind at that time. The other two options known were *Harry Potter and the Peverell Quest* and *Harry Potter and the Hallows of Hogwarts*, the latter being the title for years in the author's head. Another of the titles that Rowling also had in mind was *Harry Potter and the Elder Wand*, although this ultimately became the title of chapter thirty-two. As with the sixth book, fake titles re-proliferated among online communities. Although they had already been denied for the previous book, *Harry Potter and the Green Flame Torch* and *Harry Potter and the Pillar of Storge* returned, albeit with less force. The new tentative titles that the author denied on her website were *Harry Potter and the Pyramids of Furmat* and *Harry Potter and the Graveyard of Memories.*

It was in December when Rowling announced the title of the seventh book on her official website. Fans had to solve a small puzzle before facing a hangman game, whose solution was the name of the book. The revelation, made on December 21st as a holiday gift to fans, raised more questions than answers. In the English language, the word "hallows" generated a lot of confusion. "Hallows" is an old English word that is archaic, and today it mainly appears in church names meaning "saint," such as Church of All Hallows. The religious connotation generated many doubts for the readers who theorized about the plot of the seventh book. Would there be saints who would come to save

Harry? What were these mysterious "deathly hallows" referring to? Scholars also explained that hallows were used in mythology to talk about the objects that the saints had used in life and where, once dead, their spirit resided. They were talking about hallows, but they might be talking about Horcruxes as well. Was the title then an allusion to the objects that Voldemort protected? The revelation that Rowling considered using the title *Hallows of Hogwarts* suggested that perhaps, at some point in the writing process, the hallows were the Horcruxes that Voldemort created with the objects of the school's founders; or that perhaps the three relics that we know of did not belong to the Peverells, but to the founders of the four houses.

While fans liked to theorize about the title's possible meaning and symbolism, foreign publishers had a choice to make. It was impossible for them to know what the author was referring to without having access to the final material, but at the same time they had to announce the title in the corresponding language. Thus, in early July, a Swedish publisher, Rabén & Sjögren, revealed, that given the difficulty encountered, they asked Rowling for a suggestion. The author allowed and advised that all translations use *Harry Potter and the Relics of Death*. There were other titles in two other languages that were different, but also approved by J.K. Rowling. In Poland, the book was published as *Harry Potter and the Badges of Death* (*Harry Potter i Insygnia Śmierci*), while in India it was *Harry Potter and the Gifts of Death* (*हैरी पॉटर और मौत के तोहफे*), a title that seems the most appropriate. A few years later, in 2016, Rowling would also explain the inspiration behind the Deathly Hallows symbol, the triangle with a line and a circle. The author claims to have been influenced by the Masonic symbol used in the movie *The Man Who Would Be King* (1975). Rowling claimed to have been watching it the night in

1990 when she received the call announcing the death of her mother, and believed that this symbol was engraved in her subconscious for years later to return and appear in the finale of her novels.

With Rowling having finished the book in February, Bloomsbury and Scholastic began working on it in March. The English publisher used two internal code names to refer to the book and avoid leaks. The first of these, *Edinburgh Potmakers*, was a play on words as "potmakers" can be a way of naming those who work with ceramics, also known as those who make "pottery". The second coded title was, *The Life and Times of Clara Rose Lovett*, and included the subtitle, *An epic novel covering many generations.* The reason this title was chosen is unknown, although it might have been an allusion to Clara Lovett. She was an American educator born in 1853 who, in the late 1980s, made it onto the list of one of the 100 most powerful women published by *Washingtonian Magazine.* The only reference to the full name was in an advertisement created on Ancestry.com in 1999, where a woman named Pam searches for relatives of a certain Clara Rose Lovett.

The official bibliography, overseen by Philip Errington and published by Bloomsbury, also details that work on the manuscript began on March 12th and, after conversations with the author, was sent to production on the 23rd. In April, test copies were generated. In one of several e-mails, editors noted that Rowling had written that Harry had never learned to heal wounds, referring to page 11. However, in *Half-Blood Prince,* Harry had used the Episkey charm.

Cheryl Klein was in charge of these continuity details in Scholastic too, who with the seventh book went through an interesting experience. Mark Seidenfeld was the legal representative of everything related to Harry Potter at

Scholastic. When Bloomsbury shared the news of the finished manuscript with the US publisher, they had to agree on a way for the material to reach the US safely. With the Internet ruled out because of possible hacks, someone had to travel with the manuscript. Seidenfeld traveled back to the United States sitting on nearly a thousand sheets of text for fear of theft or loss. However, after the editorial corrections, and once the final version was reached, someone had to return to England to get the corrected manuscript. This time it was Cheryl Klein's turn. Everything was going well until a security officer stopped her at the London airport to check her. "The woman opens up my bag, and she starts pawing through it. And she says, 'Wow! You have a lot of paper here.' And I thought, oh, God, she's going to look at it, and she's going to see the names Harry and Ron and Hermione. But I just smiled, and I said, 'Yes, a lot of paper!' And she said, 'Uh-huh,' and she zipped it up. That was the end of the scariest two minutes of my life,'" she recalls (Grossman and Sachs, 2007).

Twenty days had passed since Rowling had finished the book at The Balmoral before fans knew the release date of Harry's final moment. On February 1st, Rowling updated her website with a very formal notice: "Harry Potter and the Deathly Hallows will be published on Saturday 21st July 2007 at 00:01 BST in the UK and at 00:01 in the USA. It will also be released at 00:01 BST on Saturday 21st July in other English-speaking countries around the world." Along with the announcement on the official website came the press releases from both publishers. Scholastic announced its regular edition along with its deluxe edition. Bloomsbury added a luxury edition to its children's and adult editions. This was the first time that a luxury edition became available on the release date for Bloomsbury. Warner Bros. took this opportunity to announce that the fifth film would be released on July 13th, just one week before the book release. The media, in response to the hype, decided that July of 2007 would be "Harry Potter Month".

Almost two months later another official announcement came. On March 28th, both publishers released the cover art of their editions. On Scholastic's side, the orange cover was released showing Harry and Voldemort as Harry gets the Elder Wand. The fans questioned the art with vigor. Theories about the plot appeared almost instantly: Where were they? What was that coliseum/amphitheater where the action seemed to be happening? Why did neither of them have a wand? What hung around Harry's neck, the Slytherin locket? Were the hallows suspected to be "saints," the people at the bottom corner?

David Saylor, Scholastic Vice President and Creative Director, who designed the covers, added his description: "The structures around Harry show evident destruction and in the shadows behind him, we see outlines of other people" (Scholastic d). Another detail mentioned was that the cover art was the closing of a circle for the series. The cover of the first book showed, at its ends, two curtains opening, giving way to the work and presenting it. The cover of the seventh book also has two curtains at its ends, this time closing. Those curtains are dirty and torn, implying the passage of time and that the situation was no longer the same as at the beginning. Other, though not so obvious, parallels to the first cover were Harry's outstretched hands (the first to catch the snitch) and the arches representing Hogwarts architecture. Just as Mary GrandPré returned to illustrate the American edition, Jason Cockcroft did the same for Bloomsbury. The regular edition featured Harry, Ron, and Hermione in what appeared to be a treasure trove and a house elf with the Gryffindor sword. Although the location was impossible to guess, readers would learn that Harry, Ron, and Hermione were trying to find the Hufflepuff cup that Voldemort had turned into a Horcrux in that location. Furthermore, almost all fans were sure that the house elf on the cover was Dobby helping the trio of friends. The adult version, on the other hand, was art depicting the Slytherin medallion. The cover of *Harry Potter and the Deathly Hallows* was featured on The Today Show in the United States. Such hype for a book release, like featuring the cover on the second most important morning show in the US, was uncommon before Harry Potter became a sensation. Arthur Levine was featured in the segment and confessed that he cried a lot while reading it, suggesting that the most beloved characters die.

For the promotion, Scholastic launched a multi-million-dollar campaign called, "There will soon be 7", referring to book 7 and the 7 horcruxes. In addition to the traditional advertising that had yielded good results for the publisher, Scholastic added two pillars to their usual campaign. The first was "Seven questions of Harry Potter" which consisted, as the title indicates, of seven questions that fans expected Rowling to answer in the final book. Each of these was released by Scholastic every two weeks, starting on April 12th, and the last one was published on July 7th. The questions were discussed in the publisher's online community and as well as on bookmarks and promotional material that bookstores received and handed out to their customers as they received them. The seven questions were:

1. Who will live? Who will die?
2. Is Snape good or evil?
3. What are the Deathly Hallows?
4. Will Hogwarts reopen?
5. Who ends with whom?
6. Where are the Horcruxes?

7. Will Voldemort be defeated?

The other event in Scholastic's campaign was the National Knight Bus Tour which began its tour on June 2nd, exactly seven weeks before the seventh book's publication. It toured forty libraries across ten metropolitan areas around the country. At each of the stops, fans were invited to board the bus and record a video expressing their feelings and predictions for the seventh book. The videos were then uploaded on the internet. On the website, fans could find out the exact location of the bus during those seven weeks. The bus departed from New York City and returned there for the publication of the book. The bookstores themselves joined in the promotions, such as Borders, which published a book of its own called *The Great Snape Debate*, a text in which debated whether or not Severus Snape was guilty. The book was presented with a cover where he was found guilty, but on its back was another cover that showed his innocence and invited the reader to read it backwards and forwards.

In the United Kingdom, Bloomsbury hired several staff members for their campaign. The Royal Mail (the UK's national post office) issued Harry Potter commemorative stamps in the week of the launch. A template of seven stamps was released, one for each book and with the design paying tribute to each of the covers. The stamps, while they could be used on letters and packages, as they were official, were mostly bought by philatelists who still sell and buy them to these days. Waterstones joined in with the Save Harry campaign, launching an online petition to collect signatures from around the world to present them to J.K. Rowling so that she could continue writing about the adventures of Harry and his friends, no matter what happened at the end of the book. This was because of the fear that Rowling would eventually kill Harry in the last chapter, eliminating the possibility of future stories.

Waterstones' theory was based on what had happened to Sherlock Holmes, who was killed by his author, Sir Conan Doyle, in *The Final Problem*. But under pressure from the character's followers, eight years later, Doyle made him return in *The Empty House*.

On July 6th, Rowling was interviewed by Jonathan Ross on BBC One where she talked about the book's ending. On the same day, she recorded a special for BBC's *Blue Peter*, where she was interviewed by 25 children who had won their spot to ask J.K. Rowling questions. However, this interview was broadcast on July 20th, hours before the midnight launch. These were Rowling's only television appearances in her country.

Just as it could be said that Scholastic focused on the marketing of the book more than Bloomsbury, the British publisher seemed to put all its attention on security to avoid leaks, as had happened with previous books. They invested £10 million, some of which went to satellite tracking systems and security agents across the country. It had been said that contract agents could be paid up to £30 an hour if they worked alongside a guard dog. Printers' employees were threatened with dismissal and legal action in the case of leaks, and there were even rumors that they had to work in the dark to avoid reading the material. Both the publisher and the printers denied this. The trucks, which began to leave the Tuesday before the publication, were monitored to see if any of them deviated from their route. Inside, the books were in sealed boxes with an alarm in case of attempted theft. The plan worked out well for Bloomsbury despite false alerts that they had had to respond to.

In June, on a forum for online security experts, a hacker named Angel Gabriel was reported to have obtained a digital copy of the book thanks to some vulnerability in the system. The hacker claimed that, as Pope Benedict XVI had said, the books were a bad influence on children, and therefore by spoiling the end, they would no longer be worth reading. According to Angel's version of the ending, Snape tried to kill Hermione and Ron who were saved by Hagrid who ultimately sacrificed himself for them. Ron and Hermione then headed to Privet Drive where Voldemort killed Hermione. Harry arrived in time to save Ron and defeat the Dark Lord. This ending was taken seriously by media around the world, which picked up on the news and echoed this possible leak. Bloomsbury made a statement asking the public not to believe the leaks and spoilers that could come out, but never denied any particular detail. Readers know after the reading the book that the leak was false and also because no one with access to the book in Bloomsbury worked on a computer connected to the internet.

All the effort and money that Bloomsbury invested paid off. However, there was no guarantee that issues would not happen with Scholastic in the US. In order to keep the book safe in the US, Scholastic forced bookstores like Barnes & Noble and Borders to keep the books in closed rooms, without access to most of the employees. Even Amazon had to create special sections in their warehouses. But days before the launch, the PDF of the book appeared on the Internet. There were doubts as no one could know whether it was the real thing or a fanfiction. But the file that was claimed to be the book, when decompressed, contained a photo of each of the 759 pages that made up the text of the novel. The photos were a perfect match not only to the book jacket, which had already been shown, but to the design and style that Scholastic used in its editions. Even the author's own lawyers confirmed that certain leaks on the internet appeared to be real. They did not refer to that file directly, but it was clear that they were talking about it. Rowling had already spoken out against spoilers and leaks a few months earlier on her website, elaborating, "I want the readers who have, in many instances, grown up with Harry, to embark on the last adventure they will share with him without knowing where they are ~~they~~ going," and she referred to those who spread spoilers going on to say, "There will always be sad individuals who get their kicks from ruining other people's fun" (Rowling, 2007j). The author touched on the subject again after the book was published, in an interview with *USA Today*: "I felt angry. The [leak of the] epilogue upset me most. I had been working toward that point for a long time. I did have a sense-of-humor failure when the epilogue went up" (Memmott, 2005a). The explanation for the leaks appeared even before the book itself. On July 19th, two days earlier, Scholastic issued a statement claiming that 1,200 copies of *The Deathly Hallows* had been mistakenly sent to customers of DeepDiscount.com. At first, Scholastic claimed that it was human error, and that they would not retaliate. The next day they took legal action. Some of the copies quickly appeared on eBay, offered for $250. Journalists from *The New York Times* and *The Baltimore Sun* accessed the book and read it before the launch by buying one of those hard copies or downloading a digital copy, and they published a review in both newspapers. "I am staggered that some American newspapers have decided to publish purported spoilers in the form of reviews in complete disregard of the wishes of literally millions of readers, particularly children. I am incredibly grateful to all those newspapers, booksellers and others who have chosen not to attempt to spoil Harry's last adventure for fans," Rowling said on the subject (Collette-White & MacMillan, 2007).

Bloomsbury had ultimately been able to protect itself from security problems and leaks, however it could not be saved from the price war. Until 1997, prices in the United Kingdom for the books had been fixed by The Publishers Association, the UK's publishing association. However, this agreement was declared anti-competitive and allowed each bookstore to choose the sales price it wanted. Since the publication of the fourth book, certain shops that managed to sell in large quantities decided that the Harry Potter releases would be "at a loss". They sold the books at a lower price than they bought it in order to attract customers, who would buy other merchandise, to their shops. It worked as a marketing strategy to position the brand. This was not only the case with bookstores, such as Amazon or Barnes & Noble, but also with supermarkets such as Tesco or Sainsbury's in the UK. The problems with the seventh book began when Asda, the British supermarket chain, part of the Wal-Mart group, announced that it would sell the book for just £8.97, half the price suggested by the publisher which was £17.99. Although this did not earn them any profit, since the sale price was what they paid Bloomsbury, they managed to install the brand and get customers and movement in their stores, which led to sales of other merchandise. But that was not all. The chain issued a statement against Bloomsbury accusing it of setting a high price to take advantage of the hype. The publisher did not hold back and counter attacked. In the very week of publication, it claimed that Asda had not yet paid, and was not going to hand over the 500,000 copies the supermarket had requested. The publisher also called for a public apology for the defamation on Asda's part. By the Tuesday before the release, everything had been sorted out, but the supermarket chain played a last card. Perhaps to further infuriate the publisher, the British supermarket chain chose to make the book's price £5. Not even the biggest chain in the country, Waterstones, could afford to sell at that price, nor other supermarkets like Tesco. Both stores had already put up the lowest price they could afford—£8.97. But the biggest losers were the independent bookstores, which could barely offer any discount on the original price of £17.99. However, they could compete against Amazon since they provided the experience of release parties at midnight. The independent booksellers protested and some even decided to buy the books directly from Asda, as the price there was cheaper than from the publisher. For this reason, the supermarket set a limit of two copies per person. Its stock of 500,000 books was sold in the first 24 hours. In Malaysia the problem was similar as the country's four main bookstores refused to sell the book because they could not compete against the price offered by Tesco and Carrefour. It was only three days after the book was released that the stores put the book on sale. The independent booksellers were not only harmed by the competition from the other giants, but also by the publisher itself. Usually, when a bookstore requests for stock, it can return the unsold copies. However, with *Harry Potter and the Deathly Hallows*, Bloomsbury decided to accept only 10% of the books as returns, maximizing the risk for small businesses. However, the bookstores did not want to be left out, and the vast majority organized events, even if this resulted in losses. It might be frowned upon by regular customers that on the big launch night, the long-awaited day for so many years, the bookstores were not there to accompany the readers. But contrary to intuition, some bookstores did better than they planned. The price wars actually benefited the independent sector. “A lot of people seemed to accept that the price was partly paying for the events they attended and were prepared to pay more for it than they could have with other retailers.” said Chris Conway, director of LocalBookshops.co.uk.

The big bookstores also organized events to celebrate the launch. In the United States, Barnes & Noble held events all day Saturday, the 21st, at its New York location and broadcast them live to the entire country. The 280 Waterstones stores celebrated the launch with more than 250,000 fans gathered across the country. At the central London store, Waterstones Piccadilly, the largest bookstore in Europe, was where the main event occurred, and fans lined up from the early hours of Friday the 20th, arriving to spend sixty hours waiting for the book until the sale on Saturday at midnight. The Edinburgh store of Waterstones was also one of the venues for one of the larger events. WH Smith, another English chain, said it sold 15 books per second in the more than 400 stores that they owned. There was a special request from Rowling for all the bookstores that organized an event—put a poster of Madelein McCain in their windows. At the time, she was a three-year-old English girl who had disappeared without a trace during a trip with her family in Portugal. The event had taken place two months before the launch and there was an active worldwide search, so the author made this request to help the McCain family.

It was not only in the physical stores that there was incredible demand, but also online. By May, Amazon had already received 250,000 preorders for the book, and at the time of the launch, the number of orders had risen to 2.2 million, almost 20% of Scholastic's total first printing of 12 million copies. The demand for the books reached beyond the limits of the English-speaking territories. In Germany, more than 170,000 preorders were made in English, and almost 500,000 copies were sold in the first weekend. The madness crossed the barrier of the land and reached the sea as well. The cruise company, P&O Cruises, had planned a trip starting on July 20th from Southampton to the Mediterranean. Those on board craved their copy and they did not want to wait until they got back to the mainland to buy one either. Thanks to an arrangement with Bloomsbury, the company's ships, Aurora and Oriana, were able to keep a stock of the books on the cruises so that they could be put on sale at midnight on July 21st. They also had a themed party on board.

Beyond the sales, events around the world were driven by the imagination of the organizers. In Wilmington, Ohio, the main street took on a Harry Potter theme. The stores changed their names to make them look like something out of the Wizarding World, and fake walls were built in the style of J.K. Rowling's universe. Books 'N' More, the organizing bookstore, handed out Galleons, Sickles, and Knuts (currency from Harry Potter's universe). Fans then bought the book with those coins at the time of the launch. In Oak Park, Illinois, the city was also visually transformed and activities such as a donation of elf socks to donate to charity took place. In Cambridge, Massachusetts, thousands of fans gathered for a concert of “Wizard Rock” based on the novels. The main event in the United States was in New York, organized by Scholastic. As with *Half-Blood Prince*, Scholastic closed one of the streets near its office. The festivities included a 7 meters Whomping Willow, a “Muggle Wall” where fans could leave their messages about the series, the Knight Bus that had toured the country for seven weeks, and entertainers of all kinds: magicians, fire breathers, stilt walkers and more. The event called “Harry Potter Place” began at 8:00 AM with a press conference preceding the introduction of the first copy of the book signed by J.K. Rowling in the states. Lisa Holton, President of Scholastic, summed up the weekend of the launch very well: “The excitement, anticipation, and just plain hysteria that came over the entire country this weekend was a bit like the Beatles' first visit to the US" (Scholastic e). Sadly, many of the events, both in England and in the United States, were affected by people who had read the online-leaked book and decided to go around the bookstores at launch time and shout out the ending to ruin the ending for those who had waited years to read *Deathly Hallows*.

However, the most important event, and the one that all the fans wanted to be at was, "J.K. Rowling and the Moonlight Signing" at the Natural History Museum in London. Rowling read, while sitting in a large red armchair, in front of 500 children and then signed books for an additional 1,200 winners until dawn. The children were chosen at random through the Bloomsbury website. After selecting the 1,700 who would get the privilege of being part of the event, 500 were chosen at random to attend the book reading. Initially, the contest was only for British children, but due to pressure from foreign fans, the published changed the condition and made it only necessary to be a British resident, not a citizen. In Canada, Raincoast held a contest in which a winner was flown to London to attend the event, all expenses paid. Scholastic did the same, but with seven kids.

The lucky 500 who were able to see Rowling read *Harry Potter and the Deathly Hallows* began entering the building at 10:00 PM on Friday, July 20th. For the rest of the winning fans, tickets were issued in different colors, each allowing entry to the museum within a half hour range where the fans had been divided for better organization. Interestingly enough, the cover of the adult edition of Bloomsbury's *Harry Potter and the Chamber of Secrets* shows a photo of the entrance of the London Natural Museum, where this final event for the series took place.

That afternoon, hours before the book was published worldwide, Rowling posted a very emotional letter of thanks on her website for all the people who collaborated, both in the days before the first book was published, and as well to those who had made possible the Harry Potter phenomenon—family members and foreign publishers who bought the rights before the books were widely known. The letter also included a message for fans: "Within hours you will know what happens to Harry, Ron, Hermione and the rest in their final adventure. All the secrets I have been carrying around for so long will be yours" (Rowling, 2007k). She claimed that, "*Deathly Hallows* remains my favourite of the series, even after several re-reads; I cannot wait to share it with the readers who have stuck with me through six previous books." The letter closed with an emotional message for her daughter: "The very last person to be thanked is the most important person of all, the one to whom I owe the greatest debt of gratitude. I wrote the final draft of the first three chapters of 'Philosopher's Stone' while pregnant with my eldest daughter, Jessica. She has never known what it is like to live without Harry Potter. [...] Jessica has never once complained about the attention I devoted to her fictional brother. [...] It has not always been easy to be J K Rowling's daughter. [...] The fact that 'Deathly Hallows' will sit beside Jessica's bed until it becomes dog-eared and falls apart means more to me than anything else, more than the huge print run, more than all the publicity in the world."

The author's testimony did not end with that letter or the event at midnight. Just as the English media had gotten to Rowling before the publication, American television got to her afterward. On July 26th, 27th, and 29th, she appeared in interviews on NBC's *USA Today*, *Today Show*, and *Dateline*. There she confirmed that the seventh book did not change much of what she had in her head at the time of planning it and referred to the deaths of the characters loved by fans. “Fred, Lupin, and Tonks really caused me a lot of pain. Lupin and Tonks were two who were killed who I had intended to keep alive. ... It's like an exchange of hostages, isn't it? And I kept Mr. Weasley alive. He was slated to die in the very, very original draft of the story” (Memmott, 2005b). She also confessed that she was pleased that people believed that Harry could die in the end, because it meant that she had made her story as real as the war itself, where no one was safe. The biggest revelations came on July 30th, in an online chat hosted by Bloomsbury. Fans from around the world submitted their questions and Rowling answered live. Rowling answered just over a hundred questions out of the more than 120,000 that were sent. Due to the nature of those who asked, fans thirsty for more information after finishing the book instead of reporters from mainstream media, the author had the perfect place to expand on and answer unanswered questions of the series that had not been resolved. She revealed that the Potters are distantly related to the Peverells; that the Malfoys did not go to Azkaban after book seven; that Luna married Rolf Scamander, Newt's grandson; that Tonks was killed by Bellatrix Lestrange at the Battle of Hogwarts; that Azkaban no longer used Dementors as guards; that Lily might have come to love Snape if he had not been passionate about the Dark Arts; that Harry made sure that the *Wizarding World* knew that Snape was a hero who was with Dumbledore the entire time; that Dumbledore's boggart is the corpse of his sister, and much more. One fan asked which song from the Muggle world would have played at Dumbledore's funeral. Frank Sinatra's “My Way” was chosen.

The release of *Deathly Hallows* was also the reason that Rowling returned to tour the United States after seven years.

The last time she had been there was in 2000 to promote the launch of *Goblet of Fire*. Although, she had returned to the US for events with John Irving and Stephen King, these had been in New York and were not a part of a tour. They took place in October 2007, just three months after the release of *Deathly Hallows*. The first three were in Los Angeles, New Orleans, and New York on the 15th, 18th, and 19th of October respectively. The publisher selected schools that were responsible for choosing children to attend each event. Rowling read a few chapters of the book, answered questions from the children, and signed copies for everyone. As with the online chat organized by Bloomsbury, the theme of the conversation went mainly through the plot of the book and through some questions that were left unanswered. She had a somewhat critical look at her characters. “Snape is vindictive, he’s cruel. He’s not a big man,” and “Although [Dumbledore] seems to be so benign for six books, he's quite a Machiavellian figure, really. He's been pulling a lot of strings. Harry has been his puppet.” She also claimed that the epigrams at the beginning of *Deathly Hallows* had been in her head since she had been writing the second book.

There was a fourth event on the evening of October 19th, in New York, for 2,000 fans of all ages who won their place through a contest on the official Scholastic site. Rowling revealed dozens of details about the series including that Albus Dumbledore was gay. This admission caused a media frenzy. On October 23rd, Rowling participated in a fifth event in Toronto, Canada where she was questioned about the decision to make one of her main characters gay. The author explained that the decision was not an improvisation, far from it. The sexuality of the Hogwarts headmaster was something she knew even before publishing the first book. When asked why she never shared this fact before, Rowling claims that it was because she was never presented with a question like that. Truth is, she was asked by a fan something similar in a BBC event for the seventh book. A girl called Rose asked "Did Albus Dumbledore ever fall in love?" to which Rowling had replied "Well, in the course of a long life, I think nearly everyone falls in love, but you probably shouldn't read too much into that answer." (Blue Peter, 2007).

Rowling also mentioned plans to write a Harry Potter encyclopedia one day but was not planning to do so soon. It became apparent that Harry Potter had come to an end for the literary world, at least for a few years. There were still a few movies to release, but J.K. Rowling's books and commitment to the story seemed to have faded away once and for all.

However, that was not what happened. In November, just four months after the release of *Harry Potter and the Deathly Hallows*, the BBC announced that Rowling had completed a spin-off of Harry Potter through a special on their website, their television and radio channel (Razia Iqbal, the Arts correspondent for the BBC, had the opportunity to interview the author). Of course, this new book was *The Tales of Beedle the Bard*, which had been completed by Rowling in the last few months. This news was not well received by fans, as the book had not been produced for publication. Rowling made seven copies, written entirely by hand, because she, "wanted to thank six key people who have been very closely connected to the 'Harry Potter' series, and these were people for whom a piece of jewelry wasn't going to cut it. So, I had the idea of writing them a book, a handwritten and illustrated book, just for these six people. And well, if I'm doing six, I really have to do seven, and the seventh book will be for this cause, which is so close to my heart" (Reuters, 2007). The seventh copy she refers to was auctioned off, and the proceeds went to Children's High Level

Group, the charity created by Rowling in 2004. In 2010 it was renamed Lumos. This was the first time that a complete manuscript by J.K. Rowling had been auctioned off.

The Tales of Beedle the Bard included not only five stories (such as "The Tale of the Three Brothers"), but also illustrations. "I imagined there would be about thirty tales of Beedle the Bard, and after I had the idea of writing them out by hand seven times, turns out there were just five," Rowling recalls of her work (Pottercast, 2007a). Each copy was covered in Moroccan leather, not only used in women's clothing, but also formerly used to make luxury books. The paper was vellum, made of animal skin and noted for its thinness and durability, which was widely used in illustrated manuscripts during the Middle Ages. The cover was decorated with five metal pieces, one for each story, and a gemstone, different for each of the copies. They were made by Hamilton & Inches, a house specializing in high-end jewelry in Edinburgh.

Of the six copies, only the whereabouts of two are known. One of those known was for Arthur Levine and the other was for Barry Cunningham whose copy was dedicated: "To Barry, the man who thought an overlong novel about a boy wizard in glasses might just sell ... THANK YOU." In 2016, Cunningham auctioned off his copy, which sold for £368,750 to a private collector (although it could not be confirmed, the book might now be part of the Schwartzberg family collection in New York). The stone of this specimen was a rhodochrosite, curiously the national stone of Argentina. In Cunningham's copy, Rowling wrote that the stone is "traditionally associated with love, balance and joy in daily life." Of the remaining four copies, there are only theories of who their recipients were. Christopher Little, the first agent, is believed to be one of them.

The same goes for her sister Di, who was the first to read Harry Potter and pushed Rowling to publish it.

The seventh copy was auctioned on December 13, 2007 at Sotheby's London. Commonly called *The Moonstone Edition*, for having a moonstone as its gemstone, the book was on display at Sotheby's in New York in late November, and in London in early December where it was on display in an exclusive gallery. Those who went to look at it took a souvenir pin that said, "I have seen Beedle the Bard." In addition to being in public view, on December 10th, there was a private reading that Rowling participated in. Also, an auction of the book took place. With an initial value of £30,000, a sale was expected at approximately £50,000. The final bid exceeded all expectations. Hazlitt Gooden & Fox, a company specializing in the art trade, bought the manuscript for £1.95 million, nearly $4 million, breaking a record for a manuscript of modern literature. Hazlitt Gooden & Fox ultimately revealed that their client was Amazon.com, Inc. on that same day.

Photos of the book and a summary of each story were posted on Amazon's website by Daphne Durham, who at the time was the Editorial Director of Amazon's book section. Summaries of each of the stories were the only way for Harry Potter fans around the world to know what they were about. Although they did not have the rights to reproduce them, nothing prevented them from publishing a review of each of the stories along with the overall plot. They also allowed requested that customers leave their comments and questions to be answered by the editorial team, which had access to the text. To make this process faster, and to make the summaries available online as soon as possible, an Amazon representative took photos of all the pages and sent them to the company's offices in the United States. Durham wrote, "It was one of the most wonderful (and stressful!) moments of my Amazon career. I remember hiding myself away in a tiny phone closet at the office so I could focus entirely on the story. Someone would bring me the stories one at a time as they came in, and I would read quickly and write up my thoughts as I went along. The goal was to give fans a flavor of the stories without giving too much away."

Amazon also promised that the copy in their possession would take a world tour around different libraries, but this never happened. Amazon did run a contest for a fan to win a trip to London to read the book. The rules allowed children from multiple countries around the world to participate, including, of course, children from the United States and the United Kingdom.

Of the five stories, "The Tale of the Three Brothers" had already been included in the last book of the series. The titles of the other stories were "The Wizard and the Hopping Pot," "The Fountain of Fair Fortune," "Babbitty Rabbitty and her Cackling Stump," and "The Warlock's Hairy Heart," the newest story. While discussing the titles, Rowling commented, "If anyone thinks it was easy coming up with a tale called 'Babbitty Rabbitty and her Cackling Stump,' let me disabuse them here" (Rowling, 2007l). Rowling, despite being expected to be unhappy about the recent occurrence, was very grateful and also happy that the book did not end up collecting dust in a collector's safe, but on a tour of children's bookstores, as Amazon had promised. Those who were not entirely happy were the fans, but her gift came on Harry's (and the author's) own birthday. On July 31, 2008, it was officially announced that *The Tales of Beedle the Bard* would be published worldwide. There would be three different editions: two regular editions—one for the United Kingdom by Bloomsbury and one for the United States by Scholastic—and a collector's edition with a circulation of only 100,000 copies would be produced by Amazon.

These new editions, which were published on December 4th, served as an extended version of the original text. They contained fictional comments made by Albus Dumbledore as well as an introduction by the author. The collector's edition was presented in a box that imitated a book that could have come out of the Wizarding World. When opened, in a compartment, was a red velvet pouch with Rowling's signature in gold. Inside the bag there was a copy of the book the same size as the auctioned manuscript, imitating the same shapes, styles, and design of the original. The introduction to the book was also presented in Rowling's handwriting. In a compartment of the box, an envelope with ten sheets with extra illustrations was also included. The sale price was originally $100, although today it is worth three times that value. Out of the 100,000 fans who had reserved the book on the British version of the website, 100 fans received a copy signed by J.K. Rowling.

The text of the published books was not identical to Rowling's seven original versions. It was corrected and edited by Bloomsbury and Scholastic during July and August of that year. It was debated whether *The Tales of Beedle the Bard* should be kept in its British form, as had been the case with *Quidditch through the Ages* and *Fantastic Beasts and Where to Find Them*, or reworked for American English. The latter happened because the publisher understood that *The Tales of Beedle the Bard* was a book of children's fables in the Wizarding World, and it could well be thought that it had been "Americanized" for American children. Bloomsbury's internal files also confirm that Amazon's collector's edition was worked on separately because the texts differ slightly.

For the promotion of the book, Arthur Levine's copy was on display at the New York Public Library during December. On launch day, Arthur Levine read "The Fountain of Fair Fortune," from his own copy, to commence the event and exhibition. The publisher also donated three copies of the book to each of the 87 branches of the New York Public Library. A tea party was held at the National Library of Scotland in Edinburgh where J.K. Rowling served as the hostess, reading passages from the book, signing copies, and chatting with Barry Cunningham, who led the event. The copy that Cunningham had received was also displayed in the National Library during December. The children who participated were chosen from ten local schools and also through competitions and raffles organized by Scholastic, Bloomsbury, and Amazon.

The Tales of Beedle the Bard had not been the last story Rowling had written about the Wizarding World. A few months earlier, between the auction of the handwritten version *Beedle the Bard* and the release of the book to the public, the author had produced an 800-word prequel starring James Potter and Sirius Black, and, like *Beedle the Bard*, it was for charitable purposes, but this time for English PEN, an international association of writers founded in London in 1921 to promote cooperation between authors from many parts of the world. Jorge Luis Borges and Mario Vargas Llosa, among others, were members of the group. Along with Waterstones and Dyslexia Action, an auction was organized with collaborations by authors including Neil Gaiman, Nick Hornby and Irvine Welsh, among many others. Each author had to write what they wanted in a story on an A5-sized postcard, following the topic: "What's your Story?"

Rowling took the opportunity to write a short story about the Wizarding World using both sides of her postcard. "We never dreamed that J.K. Rowling would donate something so precious, and we're incredibly grateful," said the Waterstones' Director (Singh, 2008). Aside from the length, it was only known that Rowling had signed it with, "From the prequel I am NOT working on – but that was fun," so as not to give fans false hope. One of few who had read the story was Philip Errington, the Sotheby's specialist who had been in charge of *The Tales of Beedle the Bard* auction and was now collaborating on this charity auction. The only thing he had leaked was that Harry did not appear, but a Muggle cop did.

The announcement had been made publicly in May 2008, and the auction was finally held on June 10th at Waterstones' Piccadilly, London store. The story sold for £25,000. "I had great fun writing the card and I'm absolutely delighted that it has raised £25,000 for two such worthy causes" (BBC News, 2008). What Rowling's postcard raised was more than the sum of the postcards made by the other twelve authors.

Perhaps because they had learned with *the Beedle the Bard* auction and did not want to make the same mistake and turn the fans against them, Waterstones published a scanned version of the story the next day on their website, so that fans from all over the world could read the adventure of Sirius Black and James Potter in their teens escaping on a motorcycle from a chase by two Muggle policemen. There were also copies of the postcards in the windows of all the stores in the bookstore chain for thirty days. At the end of the month, in August, Waterstones published *What's Your Story*, a volume made up of the stories from all the collaborating authors' postcards. Sales of that book were also for English PEN and Dyslexia Action. The low print run of 10,000 copies and Waterstones' promise to never reprint this volume, which was never edited, makes the Harry Potter prequel an interesting item in the world of collecting.

Unfortunately, in May 2017, the original postcard was stolen from the collector's house in Birmingham. The incident was made public by the local police, asking collectors and Harry Potter fans to report if the stolen copy was offered. Rowling herself joined the order on Twitter, requesting that no one buy it for any value.

Rowling took various opportunities to raise money for charity. Some of them even occurred while writing the original seven books. In 2013, Rowling auctioned off a copy of the first edition of *Harry Potter and the Philosopher's Stone* with annotations, comments on the editorial and creative process of writing the first book, and 22 illustrations, for English PEN. The copy was auctioned for £150,000, an amount that was divided between English PEN and Lumos.

In 2010, Bloomsbury saw its earnings reduced in the first half of the year, but took advantage of the release of the penultimate film, *Harry Potter and the Deathly Hallows Pt. 1* as a justification to relaunch the books. In 2014, sales of Harry Potter books rose 29% on reissues with illustrations by Jonny Duddle. Along with John Green and Neil Gaiman, Bloomsbury's operating profit rose 52% to nearly £3 million in the children's sector. In the same period, the books in the adult section fell in sales. And in 2016, with the publication of the illustrated editions, Bloomsbury saw an increase of almost 60% for the earnings of its children's sector, which translated to an 8% increase of total earnings overall.

Today, the publisher considers itself less of a consumer-focused publisher and one more focused on an academic and professional approach, although that does not mean that it neglects Harry Potter. In addition to the illustrated editions (which come in regular and deluxe editions) printed in 2017, on the 20th anniversary of the launch of *Philosopher's Stone*,

Bloomsbury published eight different editions of *Harry Potter and the Philosopher's Stone.* These consisted of one for each of the Hogwarts houses in both formats: hardcover and paperback. In January 2018, the publisher announced that it would release *Harry Potter and the Chamber of Secrets* in the same format for its 20th anniversary, and they continued with the publication of the rest of the books, although not on the anniversary of each of them. In July 2021, they released the last one, *Harry Potter and the Deathly Hallows*, in this "Hogwarts Edition".

Similarly, Scholastic continues to capitalize on Harry Potter. They also released a 20th anniversary edition of *Sorcerer's Stone* with new covers illustrated by Brian Selznick. Selznick is also the author and illustrator of *The Invention of Hugo Cabret* that was later successfully brought to the big screen under the direction of Martin Scorsese. The film, *Hugo,* was nominated for 11 Academy Awards at *The Oscars*, prompting controversial statements from actor Daniel Radcliffe who complained that *Harry Potter and the Deathly Hallows - Part 2*, a comparable film, had obtained only received 3 Academy Award nominations.

Since 2007, Scholastic has re-released the novels with illustrations by Kazu Kibuishi in addition to an anniversary edition for the 10th anniversary and the recent illustrated editions. Scholastic is not as dependent on the original novels as Bloomsbury because it owns the rights to launch new Harry Potter writings published under the name of J.K. Rowling: *Harry Potter and the Cursed Child* and the *Fantastic Beasts* screenplays published in book form. In response to fiscal year reports, in mid-2017, Scholastic clarified about its fiscal year earnings report (May 2016 to May 2017), "Domestic trade publishing revenues were up 45% on the performance of new Harry Potter publishing," but they expected sales to return to more normal behavior after the furor over recent launches passed (Scholastic f).

Recently, it has been revealed that the seven books of the Harry Potter saga, along with the three derived books, have sold 500 million copies worldwide, both in physical and digital formats, and in 80 different languages. Considering that 7.5 billion people live on planet earth, statistically, one in fifteen people has a copy of a Rowling book. During the COVID-19 pandemic through 2020 and 2021, Bloomsbury sales surged, especially because of the Harry Potter books. People turned back to reading them during the lockdown. Wizarding World Digital, the official online platform for the books, also offered some activities to encourage children to read while they were away from school, under the title of "Harry Potter at Home". Many Harry Potter actors, including Daniel Radcliffe and Eddie Redmayne, recorded themselves (audio and visual) reading a chapter from the first book, with J.K. Rowling reading the last one. Also, J.K. Rowling granted an open license for teachers anywhere in the world to be able to post videos of themselves, reading from the Harry Potter novels, onto schools' online platforms for their students to watch at home. This also helped to increase sales of the Harry Potter books around the world.

But the quality of the books is independent of the numbers, and J.K. Rowling's Wizarding World would still be just as fantastic, even if sales had been low or the books had never been published. Her accomplishments have gone beyond her bank account, getting millions of children to read a book for the first time and discover the joys of reading, and saving lonely teens from depression who made friends and found positive thoughts from reading the books.

Rowling's imagination and writing prowess go beyond her work on Harry Potter. Many have commented on her talent as a writer and her attitude towards the material she is working with. "Jo is a perfectionist and will work really hard to try to make each book as perfect as possible," said editor Emma Matthewson in 2003 (Bloomsbury). "Jo's writing is also very easy to read, which is deceptive because it is very, very hard to write like that. Jo also writes very visually so the reader gets a very clear picture of everything and knows what each character looks like. This makes you feel like you have met them and makes you care about what happens to them, which is important to any story," she added.

It is undeniable that J.K. Rowling has revolutionized the publishing world and that in recent years, her books have been protagonists in libraries around the world. The final question is whether this role will remain over time. Stephen King believes so: "She will indeed stand time's test and wind up on a shelf where only the best are kept; I think Harry will take his place with Alice, Huck, Frodo, and Dorothy, and this is one series not just for the decade, but for the ages" (King, 2009). Rowling does not seem to care much about the subject: "And ultimately, if the books deserve to survive, they will survive, and if they don't deserve to survive, they won't. That's it. History will judge. That ultimately is what matters, and it really helps you put everything else into perspective" (Vieira, 2007b).

More than twenty years have passed since a handful of small independent UK bookstores launched a book about an orphan boy who finds out that he's a wizard, and ten years since thousands of bookstores, chains, and businesses around the world simultaneously launched the seventh novel worldwide on a Saturday in July. Until now, the Harry Potter books have surpassed the passage of time by far and continue to captivate new generations who enjoy both reading the original series and new texts that continue to add to the Wizarding World canon in new formats. It is hard not to agree with Stephen King. It can be said that the Harry Potter books will become classics, and that they were not simply the phenomenon of a decade.

CHAPTER FIVE

Collections & Illustrations

"Keep this copy, it might be valuable one day!"
J.K. Rowling (Signed on a copy of *Harry Potter and the Philosopher's Stone*)

J.K. Rowling is one of the richest authors in the world. However, in the absence of official data, it's difficult to determine which authors possess more money than her. In 2017, *Forbes* ranked the prolific American novelist, James Patterson, above Rowling. In the fiscal year from June 2016 to May 2017, J.K. Rowling earned $95 million in profits (Cuccinello, 2017). The profits were generated from book sales, movie rights/sales, stage plays, merchandising, and theme parks, among other sources. Although this amount may look normal for an author like Rowling, the last time that her annual income exceeded $20 million was in 2008. The increased revenue came in response to the publication of two new stories from the Wizarding World. But despite all of that, there's a market involving Harry Potter in which Rowling doesn't earn a penny, and this market consists of collectors who buy and sell first print edition books, books/media signed by J.K. Rowling, and more from the Harry Potter series.

Book collecting began in the early 19th century[13] when the first edition of *The Decameron,* by Italian writer Decameron Boccaccio, was published and sold in London around 1350. Its value? £2,260, the highest price ever paid for a book. For the rest of the century, collecting centered in England where copies of Gutenberg Bible and Shakespeare's "First Folio" were bought and sold by collectors. During the 20th century, book auctions received more attention and prices for collectibles increased. A first edition of Lewis Carroll's *Alice in Wonderland* sold for $50,000. One of the eleven surviving copies of the *Bay Psalm Book* was sold in November 2013 for a record $ 14.2 million, the highest price for a printed book at the time. The importance of this volume, which was just a collection of psalms, is that it is the first book printed in English in North America.

So, who is looking for Harry Potter books for their collection? There are two large groups of collectors that are easily distinguished. First, there are those who have collections focused on a particular theme or broader subject who look for modern first editions, children's books, English novels, et al. There are also those who collect different editions of Harry Potter books (and works by J.K. Rowling outside of the *Wizarding World*). These two groups intersect in certain

[13] However, as early as the 15th century, nobles were already collecting illuminated manuscripts (that is, hand-written books with painted decoration that generally includes precious metals such as gold or silver). As most of them were made especially by the request of the owner, this type of collecting is usually differentiated from current-day collecting when editions or copies that were made for another purpose are coveted.

interests, such as the first English edition of *Harry Potter and the Philosopher's Stone*. Each group collects books that the other does not care so much about as well. A collector of modern first editions may be interested in editions signed by Ian Fleming, the author of *James Bond*, and a collector of Harry Potter can search for a deluxe illustrated edition of a particular Harry Potter book. It is believed[14] that most Harry Potter collectors belong to the first group, since those are the ones with more capital to invest in books (especially since this group is made of professional collectors). Those who solely collect Harry Potter books usually do it based on sentimental reasons, and they are more amateurish (although there are exceptions to this).

Collecting Harry Potter books began before the phenomenon was known worldwide. The first recorded sale was at the Dreweatts & Bloomsbury[15] auction house, in December 1999, for an "uncorrected proof copy" of *The Philosopher's Stone*, worth £4,200. The following month, at the same location, a first edition of *Harry Potter and the Chamber of Secrets* sold for £1,200. In May, the books went on to appear in London's renowned Sotheby's house. A first edition of *Harry Potter and the Philosopher's Stone* would sell for the sum of £1,762. The price of that book increased over the years as did the values paid for other copies that collectors desired. However, what are Harry Potter collectors looking for specifically?

While some Harry Potter collectors search for editions in a particular language, most of them search for English editions from both the United Kingdom and the United States. Once this

---

[14] It is difficult to confirm information about collectors. Most prefer to remain anonymous, and those who give their identity generally do not disclose much information about what else is in their collection or how much they pay for certain books.

[15] No relation to Bloomsbury publishing.

point is made certain, it can be affirmed that there are four large groups of collectors. The most-well-known group collects first edition copies. Being a fan of Harry Potter, however, is not a prerequisite. Many people understand that the books have great monetary value. So, how does one identify a first edition copy?

Despite being commonly called "first editions," what these books really are, are first print runs. When Bloomsbury first released *Harry Potter and the Philosopher's Stone* in 1997, the first hardcover print run was just 500 copies (of which only 200 went on sale, while the rest went directly to schools and public libraries). Despite that edition continuing to be reprinted for many years, collectors are not looking for just any copy that belongs to that edition (that is, not the edition of the book with that specific cover and text), but rather one of the 500 copies that belong to the first print run. Collecting these copies proves difficult because very few copies have survived since their printing, and of that small number of remaining copies, many are not always in good condition. For a collector, the first print run of a deluxe or illustrated edition has more value than its subsequent reprints. Luckily, books generally have print information on the first page which helps the reader identify which print is being read. Unfortunately, there are those without scruples who won't hesitate to falsify this page to make their copy a first edition and be able to earn money by deceiving an unsuspecting collector.

There are many identifiers to be considered with the first edition and print run of Bloomsbury's *Harry Potter and the Philosopher's Stone.* The best-known identifier comes in the form of a typo on page 53 regarding Harry's school supply list for Hogwarts. "1 wand" appears on the list twice, an error that the editors did not catch before the first print run. However, this error is not a strong enough identifier for a first printing because it continued to be repeated in subsequent reprints from the publisher. Another detail to take into account was a quote by the journalist Wendy Cooling that appeared at the bottom of the cover. In addition to that, the text on the back cover says that Harry is rescued by an owl instead of a giant. Also, the name of Hogwarts appears as "Hogwarts School of Wizardry and Witchcraft" instead of "Hogwarts School of Witchcraft and Wizardry". The first print also does not include a dust jacket.

Books are considered to be a first printing with a line of numbers going from 10 to 1[16] on the copyright page. However, all the points mentioned in the first printing are also part of the second printing (launched just weeks later) in the case of *Harry Potter and the Philosopher's Stone*. This caused many counterfeiters to acquire second printings, add the missing "1", and sell them as first printings. This was almost impossible to detect. Only an error in the sewing of the sheet (since to modify it, the sheet must be removed from the body of the book and re-sewn onto the spine) can confirm that it is not really a first edition. The price for a first edition has been increasing over time, with paperback copies of the first print reaching between £5,000 and £15,000; the hardcover copies can fetch sums up to £125,000, as of 2020.

In addition to *Harry Potter and the Philosopher's Stone*, the first editions and first print runs from Bloomsbury that are also of interest, and are difficult to obtain, are *Chamber of Secrets* and *Prisoner of Azkaban*. From the *Goblet of Fire* and on, the number of copies that were part of the first print run was so many that

[16] The line numbered from 10 to 1 refers to the consecutive sequence of numbers in descending order located at the foot of the legal page: "10 9 8 7 6 5 4 3 2 1" in cases of first printing, while in the second is: "10 9 8 7 6 5 4 3 2"; in the case of a fourth edition "10 9 8 7 6 5 4", etc.

getting one was not so difficult, and therefore the price to pay was not that high.

Some of the 700 copies that Bloomsbury made in the first edition of *Harry Potter and the Chamber of Secrets* can be purchased in a price range dependent upon the condition of the book. If the dust jacket is not in the best condition, and the pages are yellowed, it can be bought for around £500. £3,750 have been paid for a copy in perfect condition (Sotheby's, 2015). As with *The Philosopher's Stone*, *The Chamber of* Secrets also has key identifiers that differentiate its first print runs from reprints. However, it's safest to check the line numbered 10 to 1 on the copyright page.

By June 1999, Bloomsbury had planned a circulation of 2,500 copies for *Prisoner of Azkaban*. However, the demand in the presale caused that number to fall short, and the publisher had to print more books. This new amount was also low, and Bloomsbury had already reprinted the book a second time before its release. However, the publisher had not considered that they were second print runs, so it decided that the two sets were part of a first print run and thus both carry the line numbered from 10 to 1, indicating them as such. However, the interior texts do change, so the first printing of *Harry Potter and the Prisoner of Azkaban* has what are known as two different states.

The first state was considered the true first print, and it is distinguishable because the copyright of the book is in the name of Joanne Rowling (in the second it is in the name of J.K. Rowling) and there is a typographical error on page 7. The second state corrects this typo. There is, however, some confusion about a possible third state. Although some collectors claim the existence of this third state (which is identical to the second state but features advertisements for the previous two books of the series in the final pages), most agree that in reality this is the first printing from Australia. Some clues seem to confirm this theory: there is no printing location details in the copyright page (which would make if it happened to be outside the United Kingdom) and the advertisements in the final pages show the Australian cover of *Philosopher's Stone*. However, this was never confirmed by the publishers, so most of the time it's up to the collector to assign a value to these copies. For a copy in perfect condition from the first state, the cost reaches £2,875 (Sotheby's, 2013) while copies in good condition of the third state (or the Australian first printing) can be found on websites like eBay for 'just' $200 or $300.

Starting with *Goblet of Fire,* whose first print run was 750,000 copies, Bloomsbury decided to stop using a line from 10 to 1 to indicate a first print run and simply added "First Edition" to indicate that that said copy belonged to the first print run. The publisher did the same with the following books in the series. The first edition of *Goblet of Fire* contains the previously mentioned plot error, where James Potter comes out of Voldemort's wand first instead of Lily Potter, when it should have been the other way around. This error was corrected in subsequent print runs. First editions of *Harry Potter and the Order of the Phoenix, Harry Potter and the Half-Blood Prince,* and *Harry Potter and the Deathly Hallows* are not hard to come by.

It should be noted that the characteristics and prices mentioned in the first editions correspond to the hardcover editions. Paperback editions are collected, although to a lesser extent, and in relation to their demand, the price is lower. It is relatively "easy" to get a set of the seven Bloomsbury books in the first print run. All of them are available for less than $100, except for the first book.

The case in the United States is similar. When Scholastic published the books, they were already well-known and there was a greater circulation of copies, and therefore they are not so difficult to obtain. Only the first, *Harry Potter and the Sorcerer's Stone*, which had an initial print run of 35,000 copies, can be assumed to be difficult to find. Its price ranges from $500 to $1,000. *Harry Potter and the Chamber of Secrets* can be found in very good condition for $100, *Harry Potter and the Prisoner of Azkaban* can cost $50, and the remaining four books in the series can be found at any used book sale for less than their original price. One of the interesting details concerning the first North American editions is that the first two books, in their first print runs, did not display "Year 1" or "Year 2" on the spine, indicating that they were part of a series. These labels were added in subsequent print runs to maintain consistency.

Since the price of the first editions of Scholastic is not that high, there are not as many counterfeits. However, there are scammers on websites such as eBay who claim to have a first edition in their possession when in fact they do not. This happens because both Scholastic and Bloomsbury (through the Ted Smart/The Book People company) published the books for book clubs, and those editions differ in small details from the true first editions. For the inexperienced collector, it's very easy to confuse these copies with a first edition and it's possible that he or she end up paying a very high price for a book that's not authentic.

In addition to the group that focuses on first editions, the next big group focuses on uncorrected proof copies. Before the launch of each book, publishers usually produce what are called "uncorrected proof copies" or "advanced reading copies", copies of the book that are distributed among journalists and people from the editorial environment (like other publishers and authors) to start publicizing the book. These copies are usually paperbacks and made with thinner paper and unfinished cover art. The idea is not to present the final book with all its details, but to bring the text to as many people as possible to obtain reviews and critique before launch. The document itself even features a notice explaining that the text may be revised and changed prior to publication, so journalists are asked not to quote parts of the book using this copy. These copies also do not usually include the author's dedication. They are generally printed long before the dedication is added to the book.

The most sought-after proof copies are from Bloomsbury, and the one that is considered most important, without a doubt, is the proof copy for *Harry Potter and the Philosopher's Stone;* it became the first ever printed manuscript of Harry Potter. There was no cover design for this copy. It was all white, with a yellow stripe where the author's name and the title of the novel appeared. It doesn't contain any illustrations. It has an error, naming the author as "J.A. Rowling." Over 200 copies of these were produced, and only some of them were distributed with a test print mimicking the dust jacket proposed for the final cover with art from Thomas Taylor (this cover was changed in the final). Only three of those prints are known to exist, and if they are included with the original proof copy, they increase the price of the copies. Despite their rarity, the price of these proof copies is usually less than first editions.

The proof copies for *Harry Potter and the Chamber of Secrets* are very similar as well. They come in paperback with an unillustrated, all-blue cover with a white stripe for the title and author. Three hundred copies were made, and some of them had a dust jacket (which is the same as the one later released with the first edition except for the change at the bottom). Out of these proof copies with the jacket, only five of them are known to be in circulation among collectors.

There are two different proof copies for *Harry Potter and the Prisoner of Azkaban*. Both were made in paperback. One of them has a violet cover while the other is in green. The violet-covered proofs were distributed first. There are errors in the text that do not appear in the green-covered copy. Even though Bloomsbury claims that 150 copies of each were made, it's estimated that only 50 copies of the violet edition were produced against 250 of the green editions, making the first one more desired and more expensive. However, neither copy was believed to have included a dust jacket like the previous two books had. No collector had seen one until late 2015, when one of the purple proof copies appeared on sale on eBay, surprisingly including one of these dust jackets for the book. The book remained on sale for just a few minutes online. An American collector bought it as soon it appeared.

The case of proof copies in the United States is similar. Scholastic does not call them "Uncorrected Proof Copies," but rather "Advance Reader's Copy." ARCs are low-cost, paperback copies distributed before the book's release. They are given to booksellers before the book is released to familiarize them with the text, and so that they can recommend it to their customers once it arrives. Since Scholastic and Arthur Levine had great faith in the book, they decided to highlight this press copy and chose to print the cover in full color, complete with illustration that would later be used in the final cover. The book also includes a letter from Levine himself with his comments on the novel, which feels much like a prediction made by the Divination teacher herself, Sybill Trelawney: "I predict that you will also face another dilemma: whether to share this with a friend, or keep it for yourself, knowing how much this edition of J.K. Rowling's first book will be worth in the years to come." And his words came true: Today, the Advance Reader's Copy of *Sorcerer's Stone* is worth about $1,000. For the *Chamber of Secrets* and *Prisoner of Azkaban*, Scholastic did the same thing. The modality of the second was identical to the first, and the third followed a similar path. The only difference between these is in the cover as Scholastic decided not to show Mary GrandPré's cover art and used a pattern of purple and black diamonds instead. Both Advance Reader Copies can be purchased for a price ranging from $200 to $400.

Both publishers only made these types of copies for the first three books of the series. They were not produced for the next four novels or companion books (*Quidditch through the ages, Fantastic Beasts and Where to Find Them*, and *The Tales of Beedle the Bard*). The first reason is, that at the time of the publication of these, the series was already known and did not need extra marketing. Booksellers and people in the publishing world already knew who Harry Potter was and what a new Rowling book meant for sales. The second reason was that producing these copies meant a risk in the theft and fraud that the publisher began to monitor. Keeping the secret was very difficult. In fact, publishers publishing J.K. Rowling's new 'adult' novels also did not want to take that risk[17].

Proof copies or Advanced Readers Copies are sought not only because they are the first printed version of the Harry Potter stories, but also because they are the closest you can get to the original text written by J.K. Rowling. The final product differs from what she originally wrote. Neither a manuscript

---

[17] Only media copies of her first novel were produced under the pseudonym Robert Galbraith, as no one knew it was a novel by Rowling herself. Today, those media copies of The Cuckoo's Calling are also sought after by collectors.

nor internal files from the publishing house were leaked, not even galleys[18]. However, there are collectors who have other types of manuscripts by the author to their credit.

That brings us to the third big group of collectors, and it is the one that focuses on rarities. As its name implies, this group is made up of those seeking items of which there is only one unit or a very small handful of copies, such as *The Daily Prophet* that Bloomsbury distributed from July 1998 to October 1999 to Harry Potter Fan Club members. These copies, three or four pages each, are sought after by collectors because they were written entirely by J.K. Rowling. Their price? Unknown. None have appeared for sale in recent years.

Just as proof copies are interesting because they were the first place where the full text of the work was reproduced, *Bloomsbury Autumn Highlights*, printed from June to December 1997, is the first publication with a passage of *Harry Potter and the Philosopher's Stone*. Published and distributed by the publisher with excerpts from its upcoming novels, this book includes the entirety of Chapter 4 from Rowling's first book. It's unclear how many copies Bloomsbury produced.

The above examples are possibly among the few oddities. However, there is other material highly coveted. That material directly involves Rowling herself. The most recent case is from the first edition of *Harry Potter and the Philosopher's Stone* that, for the English PEN and Lumos foundations, Rowling annotated and illustrated in May 2013. The author left comments on 43 pages of the book (about 1,100 words), recalling anecdotes during the writing process, and included 22 drawings. The book sold for £150,000 to a private collector whose name has not yet been released. This person loaned the book to various museums

---

[18] The galleys are first prints of the book for internal use by the publisher.

and exhibitions so that fans could see some of the content. This copy of *Harry Potter and the Philosopher's Stone* is arguably the most important known.

In 2008, Rowling auctioned off the postcard for the short Harry Potter prequel. Also made to benefit English PEN and Dyslexia Action, the 800-word tale was sold to a private collector for £25,000. Although an attempt was made to remain anonymous, the buyer was known to be Hira Digpal, an investment consultant with banks in Tokyo, Japan. Sadly, in May 2017, while Hira was traveling in Bangkok, burglars broke into his Birmingham home and stole his belongings, including the prequel postcard. Rowling went out publicly to request that if any fan or collector found an opportunity to buy the piece, they should denounce the seller. So far, its whereabouts are unknown, and Hira himself believes that, since they also stole jewelry, the thieves probably did not realize the importance of the tale and threw it away or destroyed it.

Rowling's habit of donating manuscripts to be auctioned for charity began in 2002. The first manuscript she donated was not a story, but a simple autographed letter that included the title of her next book at the time, *Harry Potter and the Order of the Phoenix*, and a note with 93 words of details and clues to its plot. The fansite *The Leaky Cauldron* ran a campaign called "Get a Clue" to buy the note at auction and share it with fans, since they believed this was the only way for fans to access the letter's content (and thus learn secrets from the upcoming book). If they failed the campaign, the content would remain secret with the auction winner. Thanks to the "Get a Clue" campaign, the fansite received donations from all over the world. Unfortunately for them, the winner was an American collector who paid $44,400 (£24,000) for the item. All that money went to Book Aid International, a British non-profit organization that works to bring books and the pleasure of reading to the world's poorest children. The money *The Leaky Cauldron* raised was also donated to the organization.

In 2004, Rowling contributed to the 999 Club, an organization that supports the homeless in London, by donating a small miniature book about 2.5cm high. The "mini-book" contained a shortened version of *Harry Potter and the Philosopher's Stone* handwritten by the author herself. It also included some drawings. The item was sold for £11,000. At the end of 2017, it was put up for auction, priced between £80,000 and £120,000, but it was not purchased by anyone (if that had been the case, its current owner would have made a profit of over £70,000).

In March 2005, a two-page, ink manuscript, consisting of passages that were not included in *Harry Potter and the Chamber of Secrets*, was auctioned at the Lyon and Turnbull home. The text corresponds to "The Ballad of Nearly Headless Nick," which was originally included in the novel but was removed in the editing process. It consisted of only 32 lines of text. Ilyas Khan bought the original Rowling manuscript at just £2,000, less than many collectors had paid for first editions or media copies. Khan was a British philanthropist and businessman and allowed the manuscript to be displayed at the Wigtown Book Festival in 2010. The amount paid for the auction was donated to Scottish Language Dictionaries, a non-profit in charge of creating a new dictionary for the Scottish language.

In February 2006, for Book Aid International, Rowling handcrafted "The Noble and Most Ancient House of Black", the Black family tree. It includes characters from the Harry Potter series and the relationship between them. It was auctioned for £30,000 (a price closer than what collectors often pay, compared to "The Ballad of Nearly Headless Nick,") and ironically, the buyer was Daniel Radcliffe, the actor who played the Harry Potter throughout the eight films of the series. “This should put paid to anyone who says that Daniel doesn't like reading,” said his mother about it (BBC News, 2006).

But Rowling's greatest manuscript for sale was one of seven copies of *The Tales of Beedle the Bard*, which Amazon bought for £1.95 million. Its selling price is currently a record price for any modern literature manuscript and book. Curiously, the estimated price that Sotheby’s (who was in charge of the auction) had set was between £30,000 and £50,000. The money was donated to the author's own charity, Lumos.

Unlike with other authors, Harry Potter publishers have never made limited editions of J.K. Rowling's books. But of course, for different circumstances, there have been copies that have been made in small quantities. In 2012, to celebrate the fifteenth anniversary of the publication of the first book, Bloomsbury ran a contest to find the most fanatic Harry Potter fans in the UK and Ireland. The prize for the winner? A special edition of *Harry Potter and the Philosopher's Stone*, bound in leather, numbered, dedicated, and signed by J.K. Rowling. Fourteen other winners would also take a copy of this numbered special edition, but without the author's signature. Even though there are fifteen copies of this edition in the world, none of the winners have published a photo of the book anywhere, so its appearance remains a mystery.

In August 2017, Lumos campaigned heavily to receive donations. Depending on the amount donated, an incentive intended for Harry Potter fans, such as t-shirts or posters, was received. If someone donated $2,500, he or she would receive one of ten copies of the script for *Fantastic Beasts and Where to Find Them,* signed by J.K. Rowling and presented in a special suitcase-shaped box. These ten unique copies were sold out in less than 24 hours. Although, after a few days, they were available again. Lumos did not clarify whether more were added or if any of the donations were rescinded[19].

The University of Exeter published two articles by J.K. Rowling in its annual journal for the Department of Ancient and Classical History called *Pegasus*. The first was in number 41 (1998 edition), when Rowling was invited to submit an article. Rowling had recently become famous for the success of her first book, and she submitted an article called *What was the Name of that Nymph Again? or Greek and Roman Studies Recalled*, humorously, with anecdotes from her years at university. In the article, she confirms that Professor Binns, the History of Magic professor at Hogwarts, characterized by his monotonous and boring classes, is based on a professor from Exeter. The University did not reprint this journal, so the number of original copies circulating is not high and its price, in the world of collecting, is close to $800[20]. The second article was in issue 44 (2001). In 2000, the author was given an honorary title at a ceremony, and the publication contains the speech given in her honor and Rowling's subsequent response to that speech (in a similar sense to that given years later at Harvard and published in *Very Good Lives*). Since Rowling was better known by the year 2001, the university printed more copies of this journal, so the quantity that circulates today is greater than the other and, therefore, its price is lower. It can be obtained for about $200 in an acceptable condition.

---

[19] It would be a problem for Lumos to admit that more copies were added from the original ten. Some of the $2,500 donors could have done so just to have one of the ten existing copies. In the case that there would be fifteen, twenty, or even more, the price of the book could be considered lower, as its rareness decreases, and there could be a matter of advertising deception by Lumos.

[20] In 2006, a reader letter published in Pegasus suggested reprinting a special edition of the journal with Rowling's texts plus a new one to raise money to continue producing future issues.

Considering that collectors not only want books, but also any publication that contains some of Rowling's writing (such as these journals or Bloomsbury fan club editions of *The Daily Prophet*), they also want newspaper and magazine clippings where the author was featured in columns or interviews. While the case of the former is better documented, the trace of all the interviews in print media is more complicated, especially in the author's early years of fame. It's unlikely that more than a few people held onto a newspaper that was published twenty years ago without a specific reason.

The rarities go beyond written material. On the fifth anniversary of *The Tales of Beedle the Bard*, the Lumos Maxima bracelet, designed by the author and manufactured by Scottish jewelry Hamilton and Inches, was auctioned in December 2013. The bracelet, almost 20cm long, was made of gold, gems, and diamonds. Its price was £20,000, which went directly to Lumos.

Years before, just after the publication of *Harry Potter and the Goblet of Fire*, Rowling donated the wooden chair she used in her Edinburgh apartment in the mid-1990s to the National Society for the Prevention of Cruelty to Children. Before delivering it, she decorated it and left the following messages on the wood: "I wrote Harry Potter while sitting on this chair" and "You may not find me pretty, but don't judge on what you see". The auction reached £15,000, and the chair disappeared for years. In 2009, it reappeared, when it was sold on eBay for £19,555. In 2016, the Heritage Auctions house auctioned it off in New York City, estimating its retail value to be around £45,000. Its current owner paid £278,000.

The price paid for the items that fall into the rarity group are not items that the common fan or regular collector may be in possession of. In fact, sometimes these items are acquired by wealthy people who are often not lovers of the series or don't even own a collection; they typically see the items as an investment. It is common that people prefer to protect their heritage by investing in objects whose resale value will be maintained or even increased, such as Rowling's chair which increased its value by more than 1000% over time.

This introduces us to the fourth group. The most accessible and, at the same time, the most desired item by the regular fan who does not collect is a copy of a book signed by J.K. Rowling. These copies are the most accessible because the number of books that the author has signed over the years far exceeds the first editions, proof copies and obvious rarities, and their price is often lower. And they are the most desired copies, because any follower of the series, even if he or she is not interested in collecting, wants to have an autographed copy by Rowling on their shelves. Because these books are desired by many fans, they attract potential buyers who are not well-educated in this area. They are very easy to counterfeit. This combination is a dangerous cocktail.

In fact, it is estimated that more copies with fake signatures are circulating than copies with authentic ones. Cases are known where some eBay users have bought used Harry Potter books, forged the signature, and then sold them for a higher price. Rowling herself, through her website, publicly complained about these cases of counterfeiting in 2006. She went on to say that "For every (as far as I can tell) genuine signature there are six to ten fakes" (Rowling, 2005d), and that obviously there is no relying on "certificates of authenticity", as they are just as false as several of the signatures[21]. Rowling's

[21] Certificates of Authenticity are certificates issued by a third party that guarantee that the book signature is authentic. They are not trustworthy, as most of the time the third party has an unknown reputation, and as with signatures, these certificates are easily falsifiable.

complaint went not only against those who sold books saying they were signed when in fact they were not, but also against eBay, which allowed these types of trades. Rowling's underpinning was that, just as professional auction houses made sure they were offering genuine signatures before the auction went on, eBay should do so as well, considering it was earning a sales commission.

Rowling's anger came not only because of this, but also because eBay had authorized illegal sales of digital books and audiobooks. Rowling's complaints led a group of fans to organize to create the *JKR's Army* and urge eBay to be more responsible with the signed books it allowed to be sold. After several months, an agreement was reached. JKR's Army fans monitored the site, and upon finding a book containing a forged signature, they notified eBay, which promised to take the listing down. This method worked well for some time, and even Rowling thanked the group of fans who carried out the task. But after a few years, it was dissolved, and eBay stopped acting on the claims, causing the books with false signatures to pour into the online portal.

Nowadays, it may be risky to buy a book that was supposedly autographed by Rowling without knowing where it came from. To avoid further counterfeiting, Rowling's office has designed a hologram of authenticity that is included in each book that she officially signs, that is, at an event or for her publisher, which she will then distribute in different bookstores or award in competitions and giveaways. However, this is impossible with older books as the hologram system was implemented in 2007 with the release of *Deathly Hallows*.

In the case of wanting to buy them at auction, it is always convenient to do it in places with a good reputation. Although, there is no guarantee. Some collectors say that, more than once, established auction houses have sold a signed book that was a forgery (but it was so well done that it was almost impossible to notice). Other possible auctions are from charities that Rowling helps by donating a set of autographed books so they can raise money. In those cases, the signed copies come with the authenticity holograms and a letter from Rowling's office that legitimizes them.

Acquiring them in those places carries a higher price. To pay as little as possible, one should target websites like eBay, but with cheapness also brings the insecurity of the autograph one acquires. It is wise to buy from sellers or other well-known collectors who can be trusted, but sometimes signed books that have an affordable price come from sellers with no reputation. In these cases, it's wise to always try to use as many techniques as possible to ensure the veracity of the signature. First, ask the seller to share all possible evidence information about when and where it was signed. Vague or inconsistent answers should trigger an alarm. However, the decisive test is the signature itself. There are specialists in Rowling's firm who study her signature to analyze it and give a verdict. Not only that, but Rowling's signature has changed over the years, so a signature, with the stroke and style of 1999 in a 2005 book, is a clear alert that there is something amiss. Fortunately, these specialists share their wisdom online, writing guides so that any fan can learn. They also denounce the publications that they believe are false on sites like eBay or AbeBooks[22].

Just as with the first editions, the older the book is, the more it is desired. The same happens with signatures. For example, the 1997 autographs are worth more than the autographs from 2007, the year Rowling held signature events in the UK and

---

[22] Site specialized in selling books worldwide.

toured the United States. Regarding what accompanies the signature, that depends on the collector. Some prefer a signature without a dedication over one with one, unless it has a history. For example, a first edition of *Harry Potter and the Goblet of Fire* that Rowling signed and dedicated to her father[23] was sold for £27,500 in December 2003, and similar amounts were paid for first editions that Rowling dedicated to people who worked in Bloomsbury and assisted her in publishing her first book. To know a signature's value, it also depends on the book. If Rowling autographs a book from one of the groups mentioned above, its price can double, triple, or even more. A proof copy of *Harry Potter and the Philosopher's Stone* with a signature from Rowling from her early years (1997) can cost ten times more than the normal market value. In November 2017, when Bonhams Auction House made a first edition of *Harry Potter and the Philosopher's Stone* available in excellent condition that was signed and dated by J.K. Rowling, it sold for £106,250 (a record at the time). But it's not just the J.K. Rowling signatures that collectors look for in their books. Collectors also look for signatures from the illustrators.

Thomas Taylor was 23 years old in 1996 and worked in a children's bookstore in Cambridge, England. The previous year he had completed his postgraduate degree in Children's Illustration at the Cambridge Art Department. He learned from his contacts where he worked that Bloomsbury was creating a division of children's books and decided to bring his portfolio. He knew they were looking for illustrators. He was commissioned by the publisher to cover a forthcoming book, *Harry Potter and the Philosopher's Stone*. That same year, Bloomsbury sent to him the manuscript, which made Taylor

[23] Rowling did not like that her father auctioned the books that she had given him, so they quarreled and went a few years without speaking.

one of the first people to read it, and to give Harry his first public face. The initial project included black and white illustrations that would become headers for each of the chapters. After some tests and sketches, the publisher decided that it would only require the cover art. Taylor had no contact with Rowling since the scene to be illustrated (Harry on platform 9 3/4) was chosen by the editorial team. Taylor had become the first illustrator of Harry Potter, and collectors want not only his autograph on copies of the first book in the series, but also his signature with a small sketch. When the collector wants even more, Taylor makes pencil or watercolor illustrations on demand (which he charges for) that can be included in the books themselves or as separate plates. In 2002, the luxury house, Asprey, took a first edition of the first book signed by J.K. Rowling, rebound it with Moroccan leather, and included twelve watercolor illustrations made by Thomas Taylor. The copy was auctioned at Sotheby's in 2012, with an expected price of £40,000, but no one bought it.

While working on the front cover, Barry Cunningham asked Thomas Taylor to include an illustration of a wizard on the back cover. Thomas Taylor drew a young, brown-haired wizard who was not a character in the book. For a few months, readers of the book sent letters to the publisher asking who the character was on the back cover. Was it a young Dumbledore? Was it Quirrell? The truth is that he was nobody. Taylor had been inspired by his father to draw this character that did not exist in the novel. Due to pressure from the publisher, and he had no clear explanation to give, Taylor was asked to make another similar illustration, but this time using Albus Dumbledore, which is the one included in subsequent reprints of the first book. The original back cover illustration (of the unknown character) was auctioned at Sotheby's in 2013. A collector paid

£10,000 for it. The original illustration of Albus Dumbledore had also been auctioned at Sotheby's in 2001, although it only sold for £3,525. The original illustration of the complete cover art was also sold at the same auction for £85,750. The only regret Taylor has is not having any first edition copies of the book. According to him, the publisher promised him a copy signed by Rowling, but the copy never came into his hands.

Bloomsbury decided not to stick with Thomas Taylor for the next book. They considered his style to be very childish, and so they went with Cliff Wright, a more experienced artist who had been working on children's books and nature scenes since the late 1980s. There is a rumor that the change in style was also because the editorial team had changed, with Barry Cunningham having left and Emma Matthewson (who continued with the remaining six books) took charge. Wright, who in 1986 had earned a degree from the University of Brighton School of the Arts, also had no contact with Rowling and worked directly with Matthewson, with whom he exchanged faxes with sketches of the covers. As in the case of Thomas Taylor, Cliff Wright's signature on the books bearing his cover is sought after by collectors who also look for prints that include small pencil or watercolor sketches.

Cliff Wright worked on the second and third books in the series, and refused to continue with the publisher, despite being offered a job on the fourth book. The problem was that the publisher had lost the original and back cover illustrations for *Harry Potter and the Prisoner of Azkaban* and offered the illustrator £10,000 in compensation. Cliff Wright had to accept the offer if he wanted to work on *Harry Potter and the Goblet of Fire*. In addition to that, the new deal would be different. While the copyright of the illustrations he had produced so far belonged to him, that would not be the case with future works.

He did not accept the new deal and decided to initiate legal actions for the loss of his original. To meet the costs, he auctioned off the originals of *Harry Potter and the Chamber of Secrets* which sold for a total of £18,800. With that money, Cliff Wright litigated in court and was victorious. Regarding the original illustrations of *The Prisoner of Azkaban* that the publisher claimed to have lost, Cliff Wright never recovered them, but he did sell pencil sketches he had made for the job. A cover sketch (showing Harry and Hermione on the hippogriff but from a different angle than the final version) was sold for £5,000, while front and back cover sketches sold for around £10,000 each.

The artist designated to continue the job was Giles Greenfield. He had already worked with Bloomsbury on the books, *Chaucer the Cat* and *Owen and the Mountain*. After the problems they had had, it was reasonable for the publisher to choose someone they already knew and trusted. Even though Greenfield maintained the copyright of his work, the original of his cover is in the possession of Bloomsbury (although there are rumors that, as with Cliff Wright, the original art was lost by the publisher[24]). Greenfield sold a preliminary pencil sketch he had made for the back cover at £4,700. Regarding works for fans, he is one of the most active illustrators in this sense. He makes pencil and watercolor illustrations of the copies on request.

Greenfield's relationship with the publisher was not good, but he still decided to work on *Order of The Phoenix*. However, in early 2003, his six-month-old daughter, Sasha, was diagnosed with a terminal genetic disease, so he decided to abandon the project. Instead, Bloomsbury again chose someone in-house, and it became Jason Cockcroft's turn. He had already been

---

[24] When it is said that the art was lost, what is suspected is that the publisher or an employee illegally sold it to a collector.

working on illustrated books. Cockcroft took the watercolor illustration that Greenfield had started, showing a burning phoenix, and decided to continue with it. Albeit, in his own way, it served as a tribute to the work the previous illustrator had done. The Greenfield originals based on Cockcroft's work, both pencil and watercolor, were auctioned off at Sotheby's soon after, but failed to sell. Cockcroft, who agreed to give the rights to use his illustrations to Bloomsbury, continued to work on the remaining three books in the series. The illustrator did not have access to the material before publication, so the publisher had to give him all the details of the scene to be illustrated, including the color palette, since Cockcroft was painting blindly. His originals hang in the Bloomsbury office, so he was never able to profit from the auctions of his work.

Scholastic's case was different from Bloomsbury's. Mary GrandPré served as the illustrator for the entire series. The copyright of her illustrations belongs to Warner Bros., and in this case, she did have access to the books before their publication since she had to read them because the United States editions include a small illustration for each chapter. The originals were never auctioned, nor were any preliminary sketches. Mary GrandPré did sign copies, even at book launch events in the United States, and occasionally added a small pencil or pen drawing next to her signature. She does not make color illustrations on demand for collectors, although there are exceptions. For the launch of *Goblet of Fire*, she made twenty-five copies of an almost full-page illustration of Harry Potter. The price of one of those copies today can reach $10,000.

Any writing on a book is considered a deterioration in its condition save for autographs from Rowling or illustrators. Over the years, old first edition books have appeared, but collectors do not want them as much because they have an inscription, often from a family member to another who gave the book as a gift. In other cases, the signature may be from someone famous, but even so that does not mean that the value of the book increases, as when the signature is from the actors or directors of the films. In those cases, the signature on an item related to the films, such as a poster or a DVD, is better, but not on the books, since celebrities were not involved in the book series.

The Harry Potter collector will try to have everything. When they get the first editions, proofs copies, and rarities, he or she will want J.K. Rowling to stamp her signature on them. Then, the illustrators do the same, and if possible, add their own drawing. If it is in color, the better. One will also want, along with the book, to have related promotional material: bookmarks, posters or any items related to its launch. The passion, in these cases, has no end.

A Note On Collecting

Collecting is a fascinating activity that any fan can start doing today. It is not necessary to spend a fortune, nor is it obligatory to follow the current trends. The only thing that matters is that the collector enjoys what he or she is buying. They can be old editions, broken books or copies that only interest us for some personal reason. What is important is having patience and being informed. Before making a purchase or acquiring a book, you must educate yourself and understand what you are buying. The internet is full of people who do not mind scamming you by selling you something that is not authentic. And patience is pertinent in order to wait for the moment when the book you want is available for the price you can pay.

The most important tip is probably the one that sounds the weirdest: you always must convince yourself that your collection itself is the best one out there. Constant comparison does not work. Collecting is not for those who have more or better things, but for the enjoyment of the search for the book—walks at used book fairs, stalls and parks, or hours surfing the internet until you find that book. Hopefully this chapter will spark a bit of curiosity in the fans to start collecting, starting with the most basic and simple, until one day they feel the pleasure and the need to have that rare copy of *Harry Potter and the Sorcerer's Stone* that Scholastic distributed to certain schools in the United States.

CHAPTER SIX

From Shelves to Cinemas

"The greatest power you have as a writer or novelist is to sell the rights to the people you believe will make the best film, and I believe I have done that."
J.K. Rowling (JK Rowling chat, 1999a)

David Heyman, the son of film producer, John Heyman, and Oscar-nominated actress (and producer) Norma Heyman, was born in London in 1961. He obtained a degree in Art History at Harvard, and following the line of his parents, became a part of the film industry. He worked as a production assistant, and in 1986, he joined the production team at Warner Brothers. In the 1990s, he decided to embark on the production of independent films and produced *Juice* (1992) and *The Stoned Age* (1994), which became a cult film. In 1996, he returned to London where he opened Heyday Films, a small, independent production company that was funded by Warner Bros. Heyman struck a first-look deal. Warner Bros. took care of the company's expenses and was first to see anything Heyman selected.

Heyman hired Tanya Seghatchian and Nisha Parti, and the three began searching for material that could be adapted for the big screen. Heyman had the idea to work on book adaptations, so the company was very attentive to upcoming releases, and that is why in early 1997, they received a proof copy produced by Bloomsbury of *Harry Potter and the Philosopher's Stone.* "The book arrived via J.K. Rowling's agent Christopher Little. It was sent to us at the same time it was sent to a handful of other production companies in London," Parti recalls. However, the text ended up in a pile of similar material. It stayed there for three weeks until, one Friday, Nisha Parti took it and read it over the weekend, as she used to do. She hoped to arrive on Monday and say it wasn't worth it, "But on this occasion I remember reading it at home and was totally gripped from the get go." On Monday, at the meeting with Heyman and Seghatchian, Parti said she loved the book and that they should consider it. Heyman was skeptical—the title was not eye-catching, and the idea of a boy going to a magic school seemed unusual, but, "he was taken aback because I never liked much and it was the first time I really felt strongly about something." Heyman took the proof copy from her to discard it after reading the first pages, but he could not put it down. It reminded him of his childhood, teachers, and classmates, especially because he attended a British school like Hogwarts where students lived at the institute during the school year. But at the same time, he thought that, at best, the book could become a modest British film, no more than that. Seghatchian would work as an executive producer on the first four films in the series, but Parti would separate after the first, to open her own production company. Today, she continues to have a good relationship with

Heyman, whom she considers her mentor, and they stay in contact, even giving each other advice.

Lionel Wigram, also British, was Heyman's childhood friend, executive producer at Warner Bros. in Los Angeles, and David's direct contact with the company. From childhood they dreamed of working together on a film project. When Wigram received the early copy of the book, he also found it fascinating. Now all that remained was to convince the rest of the Warner Bros. team to give the project the green light, a task that became somewhat difficult, because they did not share the same enthusiasm. The story was riddled with nods to British customs that are very foreign to the average American, so it was a question if the film would be well received. After a few twists and turns, Warner Bros. relented, but on the condition that not much money should be spent. Negotiations for the rights were not easy, and took several months to acquire, until an agreement was finally reached in early 1998 (Disney also attempted to buy the rights). The sum, which was kept secret, is rumored to have been over $2 million (from which Rowling received 80% due to her contract with Christopher Little) for the rights to adapt the seven books into movies. Among the concessions to be fulfilled by Warner Bros. was that actors had to be British or Irish, at least in the first films (some exceptions occurred in the later films, especially when foreign characters appear, such as students from France, or from Nordic countries). Warner Bros. also could not make related films or use the characters for other stories without the author's strict permission.

With the rights already acquired, all that was left to do was start working on production. There was a lot to decide in those early stages. Would each movie be a book? Were the special effects available enough to recreate the Wizarding World? Was it better to make an animated movie instead of a live-action movie? These questions had to be answered at that time before taking any action. Once they answered all those questions, Heyman and Wigram began looking for someone to adapt the book into a script, but all the writers rejected the offer. They decided to wait until September, when the book was published in the United States by Scholastic and Harry Potter's name became known to the country. The wait paid off. After the book took off, writers lined up to write the adaptation and many directors expressed interest. However, none of the early names stuck.

J.K. Rowling was out of the running to write the script, too busy with upcoming books to publish. Heyman approached the duo Richard Curtis and Mike Newell, who had written and directed the critically acclaimed English film, *Four Weddings and a Funeral (1994)*, but they both decided to pass on it. The possibilities were increasingly limited, so Heyman began welcoming the possibility of an American adapter, since the film also had to attract that audience. Finally, the options were reduced to two: Steve Kloves and Michael Goldenberg (although only one of them would adapt the first book, both of them ended up working on the franchise).

Steve Kloves had a portfolio of interesting and very good adaptations, but his style was not childlike as Harry Potter demanded. Despite that, Kloves read the book and accepted the challenge. Only Rowling's approval was missing, so everyone traveled to Los Angeles. Heyman, Kloves, Rowling, Wigram and other Warner Bros. executives had lunch together, and it was there that Rowling realized that Kloves was the one to turn her novel into a screenplay.

The complete script was delivered in late 1999, when the Harry Potter name was already well-known. As is normal in these cases, after the script was presented to the producers, it underwent some changes. For example, Kloves' original idea was for Harry, Ron, and Hermione to enter the Forbidden Forest on their own and find the unicorn there. But Rowling believed that the concept of punishment was important to the characters, as well as seeing Harry and Draco together and alone in a dangerous environment. This was corrected in the next version of the script, where Kloves returned to the original scene in the book.

The next step was finding a director. Steven Spielberg was the first to show interest in the project. He first met with Heyman for two hours to share his ideas for the project, and then with Rowling and Heyman together. Apparently, Spielberg, who was rumored to want to make a fully animated movie, dropped out of the project on his own: "I really believe that as I grow up I have a responsibility to tell stories that are a little more authentic. I purposely didn't do the Harry Potter movie because for me, that was shooting ducks in a barrel. [...] There's no challenge in that" (The Guardian, 2001).

Terry Gilliam was J.K. Rowling's and Heyman's favorite. Gilliam was a part of the Monty Python group and, in 1995, he led the critically acclaimed film *12 Monkeys* (1995). He seemed to be the perfect candidate because of his track record of movies on fantastic worlds, his humor, and the sensitivity of his characters. But the people at Warner Bros. were not comfortable leaving their new jewel in the hands of someone as unpredictable as Gilliam. There were meetings with other candidates, such as Jonathan Demme (*The Silence of the Lambs,* 1991) and Brad Silberling (*Casper,* 1995).

Chris Columbus, who had worked on some great hits of the 80s such as *Gremlins (1984)* and *The Goonies (1985)*, and had gained his recognition as a director thanks to *Home Alone*

(1990) and its sequel, and *Mrs. Doubtfire (1993),* ultimately showed interest thanks to his daughter, Eleanor, who, having already heard about the book, mentioned to him that it was surely going to be a great movie. Chris was not motivated by the children's theme of the novel, but after reading the book, he felt the need to direct it. He contacted his agent, who commented that there were already at least twenty other directors interested in the film, but Chris still asked his agent to get him a meeting with Warner Bros. He had only one condition: to be the last to be interviewed by the large studio. This came from his experience in actor castings. The last ones to be interviewed are the ones that are most present in the memory. Being last also gave him more time to prepare.

He had twelve days, after receiving the script from Kloves, to demonstrate his vision of how the film should be, and to be able to show how interested he was in getting the job. He rewrote the script as an exercise to get deeper into the material. All of Columbus' efforts surprised Warner Bros., mainly Heyman. "It was so exciting to discuss *Harry Potter* with him," (McCabe, 2011) recalls the producer. Columbus' enthusiasm and vision got him the job, and so he signed on to direct the first two films. But even though his signature was already on a contract, he knew he still had to meet Rowling. He traveled to Edinburgh, and in a two-hour meeting, he explained the type of film he wanted to make. When finished, Rowling said, "That's fantastic. That's exactly the same sort of film I'd like to be made of my book" (McCabe, 2011).

A physical location was needed to start production in the United Kingdom. The most famous studios Pinewood and Shepperton, did not meet all the requirements that were sought: large venues that the technical team could fully own without interfering with other projects. This was why the Leavesden

Studios in Hertfordshire, over 30km north of London, was chosen. The Leavesden Studios would become the home for the eight Harry Potter films and, eventually, the *Fantastic Beasts* films. The Studio Tour Exhibition would also be built there many years later.

With the studios already chosen, Heyman and Columbus knew that one of the key points of the films would be the world and sets; they concluded that the experience of seeing them on the big screen should be just as magical as the experience of reading them on the pages of books, or even more so. For this, they contacted the production designer, Stuart Craig, eleven-time nominee and three-time winner of an Academy Award [*Gandhi* (1982), *Dangerous Liaisons* (1988) and *The English Patient* (1996)]. Craig got a call to fly to Los Angeles and meet with the producer and director, but he still did not know about the book. He bought it and read it on the flight. When he landed in California, he knew that the job was for him. Stuart Craig oversaw the stage designs of important locations from the books such as Diagon Alley. At the time of producing the first film, the production team could not afford to build large stages (as it would in the later films in the series), but instead it had to find locations that were as close as possible to the author's ideas.

Craig began by imagining Hogwarts as if it had existed for thousands of years, as if it were the oldest educational institution one could imagine. The connection with the Universities of Oxford and Cambridge quickly emerged, and then with the different cathedrals that exist in Great Britain. Thus, Hogwarts ended up being a mix of a Christ Church in Oxford, Durham Cathedral, and Gloucester Cathedral. Craig's work throughout the entire series was acclaimed by fans, his colleagues and, mainly, by J.K. Rowling herself. He was nominated multiple times for the British Academy Film and

Television Arts (BAFTA) Awards and the Art Directors Guild, some of which he won. Craig also worked at the Universal Studios theme park, designing it entirely at the author's request: "And the key thing for me was if there was to be a theme park that Stuart Craig, who was the production designer on the films, would be involved, I mean, more than involved. That he would pretty much design it. Because I love the look of the films, they really mirror what's been in my imagination for all these years" (Pottercast, 2007b).

Having a set, a great production designer, and a director like Columbus were just the first steps. The next step was to fill the cast. The first actor hired was "the tallest." Robbie Coltrane was chosen for the role of Rubeus Hagrid, and he was not only the studio's choice, but also of Rowling herself (there was also a rumor that the character in the book was written with the actor in mind, but that has been denied). Continuing with the Hogwarts staff, next up was headmaster Albus Dumbledore. The first candidate was Irishman, Richard Harris. Although Harris was David Heyman's godfather (and represented by Heyman's father), he did not want to participate in the film. But when his granddaughter, Ellie, called him and said that if he did not accept the role, she would never speak to her again, he did not have any other choice.

Alan Rickman's case was similar. However, he had no children pressuring him to accept the role. Nonetheless, this did not take much pressure, since J.K. Rowling's writing attracted him from the beginning: "You're gripped from the first page and must keep turning the pages; you get involved with the characters and want to see what happens next" (McCabe, 2011). Rickman also knew about Harry Potter, but he only read the first book after reading the script. Maggie Smith was the first choice for the role of Minerva McGonagall, and when she was contacted, the response was positive. Smith was already a fan of the books and she considered them as a great tool for kids to become more interested in reading, so it did not take too long to convince her.

While the main trio of actors were still missing, Stuart Craig continued to expand his team. Stephenie McMillan joined as a set decorator, in charge of decorating the stages that Craig created, along with costume designer, Judianna Makovsky, who had previously worked with famous directors such as Francis Ford Coppola and Ridley Scott. Makovsky was responsible for one of the decisions for the first film that spread to the rest of the films: the use of Hogwarts' uniforms. They are not mentioned in any of Rowling's books, but have become a symbol for the franchise.

Susie Figgis, casting director, was still searching for the trio of children. The casting had started months prior, with advertisements in different media, which brought on thousands and thousands of requests for the casting team to review.

Emma Watson was born in 1990 in Paris, but at the age of five she moved to Oxford with her mother and brother due to her parents' divorce. She loved poetry and used to recite it at school events, because she liked to be in front of an audience. On weekends, when she visited her father, he would read the Harry Potter books to her before going to sleep. (Though after *Prisoner of Azkaban*, she read them alone.) When she found out that the production company was looking for girls from all over the UK for the role of Hermione Granger, Emma decided to participate in the casting.

Rupert Grint was two years older than Emma Watson and was the oldest of five siblings. He was born in Essex, but his family had moved to Hertfordshire, very close to Leavesden Studios. He acted in school plays, and one morning he saw the advertisement for the role of Ron Weasley in the *BBC Newsround* children's segment. His sister read the books and had told him that he resembled Ron Weasley, so he also participated. To express interest, actors were instructed to send a photograph and a personalized letter to the casting team. However, Rupert Grint thought he would be more original, so he filmed himself, disguised as a theater teacher, explaining why he should be considered for the role. As if extravagance was not enough, he created a rap to list off his personal merits. Creativity captured the attention of the casting team, who then contacted him.

While Rupert and Emma followed the typical casting processes, finding someone to play Harry Potter remained an issue. Tom Felton, a year older than Rupert Grint, attended the casting. He had more experience than most children, having acted in commercials, but knew nothing about Harry Potter (a schoolteacher had read a chapter in class which Felton thought was boring). So, when he was in the queue for the audition, the casting team asked each of them which scene in the book they would like to recreate. Felton had no idea and repeated what the boy right in front of him just said. The staff quickly noticed the lie, and perhaps they felt that Felton was a bit of the Draco Malfoy they were looking for. At the same time, the casting of Neville Longbottom and Ginny Weasley, Matthew Lewis and Bonnie Wright's roles, were finally secured.

But the protagonist with round glasses was still a problem. Thousands of children had auditioned and none of them convinced Columbus. The director wanted to try one child named Daniel Radcliffe, who had acted at age nine in the television adaptation of *David Copperfield*. However, Daniel's parents, who were from show business (both actors who had become a casting director and literary agent), did not want this project for their son. They thought that the films would rob Daniel of the best part of his life and preferred that he enjoyed most of his childhood and adolescence without working. It was in June 2000, two months before film photography began, that the matter would change. One night, David Heyman and Steve Kloves decided to go to a theater to see the *Stones In His Pockets* where Radcliffe would perform. There they met Alan Radcliffe and the Radcliffe family. Heyman, who had only seen Daniel Radcliffe on screen, was fascinated. Next morning, Heyman called Alan to convince him, but it was not necessary: Alan believed that the casual encounter was a good sign. Thus, the boy was able to be part of the auditioning process, although he only needed four sessions to land the part.

Emma Watson was the first to get the role, although she didn't know it at first. "It would have saved many sleepless nights," she says (McCabe, 2011). She acted in front of Heyman and Columbus with different groups of actors who were doing their Harry and Ron parts. Heyman and Columbus wanted to see the chemistry between the three of them. They wanted the three of them to look like real friends. Finally, David Heyman and Chris Columbus made the decision, and they chose the three children who would be the leads for the Harry Potter films.

On August 22, 2000, Rupert Grint and Emma Watson were called to the Leavesden offices, thinking they had been called for another audition, but they were told they had obtained the roles. Daniel Radcliffe joined them in the afternoon (he had had confirmation the night before when Heyman called his home). With the three of them in Leavesden, a photo was taken and within five minutes the press release was online, available to everyone. Five minutes later, there was media at Emma Watson's front door. The three actors were taken to The

Landmark Hotel in London where they would spend their days during production. That same day they had a photo shoot, and on the next day, they attended a press conference where they were introduced. The press came to call the three "the one in glasses," "the girl", and "the other boy."

The trio formed by Daniel Radcliffe, Emma Watson and Rupert Grint joined a cast made up of the great actors of British cinema. In addition to those already mentioned, Ian Hart (as Quirrell), Richard Griffiths and Fiona Shaw (as Harry's uncle and aunt), Julie Walters (as Mrs. Weasley), Warwick Davis (as Professor Flitwick) and John Hurt (as wandmaker Ollivander), among others, joined the case. Even Rowling herself was asked to play the role of Lily Potter, both in the flashbacks and in the scene from the Mirror of Erised, but she declined. A rumor spread that Rowling appeared incognito in the film as one of the many witches who greets Harry on his arrival in The Leaky Cauldron, but it was also proven later that this too was not the case.

Just a month after casting wrapped up, on September 29, 2000, filming began. At the North Yorkshire train station, the technical team, 150 extras, the trio, and Robbie Coltrane, in his role as Hagrid, along with Martin Bayfield, his body double, were present. There, on the first day of filming, the last scene of the film, where the Gryffindor students say goodbye to Hagrid before boarding the Hogwarts express, was filmed.

To mimic Hermione Granger's big front teeth, Emma Watson wore fake teeth on the top row, but they kept her from speaking clearly, so she did not use them again. For attentive observers, the teeth can still be seen in the last scene of the film since it was not reshot. Another problem there was with Daniel Radcliffe. His character's green eye color is important to the plot, so the team decided that he should wear contact lenses since his eyes are blue. But he had such an allergic reaction to the lenses, that they discarded the idea. The tech team decided it would be better for Harry to have blue eyes in the film adaptation. It was not the only allergy Radcliffe had during shooting. In the first weeks of recording, Radcliffe had small spots around his eyes due to an allergy to the nickel from his glasses.

Apart from the Leavesden studios, and mainly for the first films, production had to be relocated to different places to use them as a film set, such as Alnwick Castle, where the flight class scene took place, or the cathedrals from Oxford and Gloucester, which served as the interiors of the School of Witchcraft and Wizardry. While Radcliffe and Grint were with their respective parents, a guardian oversaw Watson. Being away from home also implied a change in their education. The three actors, like the rest of the children who were part of the cast, had different teachers who taught them on set. Minors, by law, cannot work more than a couple of hours per day and must spend at least three hours in classes. Despite the age differences, the children shared teachers and attended the same lessons, which also helped their relationships in an area outside of filming itself.

Aside from the scenes at Hogwarts, another one that was filmed on a different location was the interior of Gringotts, for which the Australian Embassy in London was used.

Warwick Davis played several of the elves in the Harry Potter films, acting as one of the Gringotts workers. However, in the first film, the role of Griphook, the goblin that takes Harry and Hagrid into the underground chambers, is portrayed by Verne Troyer, best known for his role as "Mini Me" in the *Austin Powers* series. People often think those scenes were acted out by Warwick Davis. However, Davis only provided his voice.

While the Hogwarts hallways were shot outdoors, Stuart Craig thought the Great Hall was too important for the film and decided to build it entirely at Leavesden Studios. No money was spared for this set. The floor, even though it would have been cheaper to do it in resin or some imitation material, is real York stone, the most popular paving stone used in all of England. The decision, as Craig assures, was correct. The stone, after several years and with heavy use, did not wear out and remained in perfect condition to be reused in each subsequent film. The floor was not the only real thing on the set. An attempt was made at first to make the floating candles actual candles on thin wires, but on one occasion, one of the candles melted the wire it was hanging from and fell on children. No injuries occurred, but the production team noticed the risk and decided to remove them, opting to add them digitally in post-production.

Peeves was played by the English comedian Rik Mayall. The scenes were cut from the final version of the film. Peeves, despite having an important role in some of the following books, never appeared in any of the films. When asking Heyman about the reason for this decision, he says, "When you see the first cut of any film it is inevitably too long and you have to make choices about what remains in. Peeves felt like a detour in the film, not essential to the story we were telling."

Something similar happened with Richard Bremmer, who portrayed the Voldemort that appeared on the back of Professor Quirrell's head. While he went through several hours of makeup and rehearsal, the effect was ultimately done digitally. And because the title of the book differed from the United Kingdom and the United States, each scene where "the Philosopher's Stone" was mentioned had to be recorded twice, using the American name, "the Sorcerer's Stone."

The first promotional poster was released in the first days of December 2000, in the middle of production. It showed an owl carrying a letter to Harry Potter, and announced that the film would be released soon, as the exact date had not yet been decided. After the holidays, on March 1, 2001, the trailer was released. With hardly any dialogue and non-definitive special effects, it was the first time that the world saw Harry Potter in live-action. The score that John Williams created for the franchise, which became a staple for the Harry Potter film series, was also heard for the first time. The film finished filming just a few days later, in late March, although a couple of scenes were reshot in July.

The original release date was set between July and August, but due to calendar issues, it was moved to November 16th in the UK, US, Ireland, and Canada. On November 4th, Rowling attended the world premiere event with the producers, director and a large part of the cast at the Avant Premiere in Leicester Square in London. The premiere celebration in New York took place on November 11th, just two months after the attacks on the Twin Towers. The film grossed $32 million in the US and Canada on the day of its release which broke the record for *Star Wars: Episode I – The Phantom Menace* (1999). The film exceeded $90 million in its first weekend worldwide, breaking the previous record by *The Lost World: Jurassic Park* (1997).

With nearly $975 million raised globally, *Harry Potter and the Philosopher's Stone* remained the highest-grossing film in the series until 2011 with *Harry Potter and the Deathly Hallows – Part 2.* Critics had positive responses to the film, and it was nominated for three Academy Awards and seven BAFTA Awards but failed to win any.

This film could also have influenced the Harry Potter books. On the first chapters of *The Goblet of Fire,* Rowling mentions that the Great Hall has chairs, while from half of the book to the end of the series, she mentions there are benches instead of chairs. This modification could have been caused by what she saw on the movie set for the Great Hall (where the students sit on benches instead of chairs), and that could have affected what she was writing (which, at the moment she visited the set for the first time, it was the fourth book).

Success came to the big screen for Harry Potter, and the streets were awash with its posters and products. The toy stores had dozens of shelves dedicated to action figures, clothes, stuffed animals, and video games from the wizarding world. But that did not mean that the team could rest. In fact, they had already started working on the second movie. In March, Steve Kloves had finalized the script, which he previously had to make some changes to. He had guessed at events that contradicted what would happen in future books. Rowling noticed these issues in the approval process: "I anticipated a few things and that was a lot of fun because I anticipated something [...] She said, 'That's great, but you can't do that because something's going to happen in Book 5 that makes that impossible to happen,'" remembers Kloves (Linder, 2001). Filming started a few weeks earlier for the main actors, who were already in Leavesden in September, and the official filming began just three days after the premiere of the first film.

Chris Columbus, who had returned to direct the second film of the series, had not been satisfied with the special effects of *The Philosopher's Stone*. He attributed this to the pressure Warner Bros. had exerted to release the movie as quickly as possible. Therefore, Columbus decided to film the scenes that needed computer effects first, reverse the original production plan for *Harry Potter and the Chamber of Secrets*. This way, the post-production team had several months to perfect the special effects. The first scenes filmed were related to Quidditch, the basilisk, and the flying Ford Anglia that Harry and Ron crash into the Whomping Willow.

The new movie brought new actors to the cast. Emmy Award-winning actor and director Kenneth Branagh joined to play the role of the conceited Gilderoy Lockhart. Although Kenneth undoubtedly fit the role perfectly, at the time there was a candidate who would have been better—Hugh Grant. Not only did he did fit in very well, but he had a unique approach to the character. According to rumors, he signed a contract, but then had to rescind his commitment because of conflicts with other projects that he had already agreed to work on. Acclaimed by the press both on screen and in theatre, Branagh was another one of the legendary British actors like Harris and Rickman who joined the world of J.K. Rowling.

Jason Isaacs, who in *The Patriot* (2000) played the villain of the film, auditioned for the role of Gilderoy Lockhart as well, but he was offered the part of Lucius Malfoy. At first, Isaacs did not want the role, having already signed on to be Captain Hook in a new adaptation of *Peter Pan*, and he did not want to play two villains at the same time, and so he communicated this to his agent. But after a weekend where nephews, godchildren, and even his parents, begged him to accept, he made the decision for which he is now eternally grateful. He was so fascinated by the role—which he would continue to portray in subsequent films—that he declared, "If Jo called me and went, 'I want to do a Lucius Malfoy spin-off film', she wouldn't get to the middle of her sentence before I've said yes and left my house!'" (Alexander, 2017). The final scene in *The Chamber of Secrets,* involving Lucius and Harry speaking to each other outside Dumbledore's office, has one of the most memorable lines from the films. However, this line was not part of the script. "Well, let us hope that Mister Potter will always be around to save the day," was improvised by Isaacs, while Radcliffe's response, "Don't worry, I will be," was also improvised, and surprised Isaacs.

Gilderoy Lockhart and Lucius Malfoy were not only recognizable by their scenes, but also by their iconic wardrobe. Responsible for this was Lindy Hemming, the new costume designer. Originally, Hemming had envisioned Malfoy in a suit with a striped design, but then envisioned the character wearing clothing that had been in the family for generations, giving him the look that we all recognize today. Newcomers, Isaacs and Branagh, were also joined by Mark Williams (as Arthur Weasley). Julie Walters (as Molly Weasley) and Miriam Margolyes (as Professor Sprout), expanding their roles, and having titles of the Order of the British Empire, returned alongside the newcomers to add to the number of renowned British actors.

Although the friendship between the main trio was growing, the actors did not share as many scenes together in this film because Hermione Granger spends much of the film petrified. "It was a bit disappointing. I wasn't really in the second one very much," recalls Emma Watson (McCabe, 2011). It was during this filming that Watson realized that she was attracted to Tom Felton. Although it is something that at the time made her very embarrassed, she could not hide it, since Felton himself and also Radcliffe and Grint informed her that it was obvious.

Two different versions of the Whomping Willow were built for the scene involving Harry and Ron arriving at Hogwarts—one with a hydraulic motor when the Ford Anglia crashes into it, and the other with the branches that attempts to smash Harry and Ron. The production team worked with sixteen different cars, although only a couple of them completed the entire filming, as most were damaged to serve specific scenes.

Just as the filming included the creation of sets such as The Burrow and the Forbidden Forest, the set of The Chamber of Secrets itself also had to be built and still holds the record for being the largest set built, even greater than the Great Hall, measuring 76.2 meters long by 36.5 meters wide. For the Chamber of Secrets and the path that leads to it, Stuart Craig took inspiration from the sewer system from the city of London, which he visited on different occasions.

Beyond the locations and props, what will remain in the memory of the fans is Dobby. The house elf, who has appearances throughout the film, was originally intended to be made as a resin puppet, which would guide the actors' performance and interaction with the character (mainly Daniel Radcliffe, who shared most of the scenes with the elf). But after some tests that option was ruled out. However, Dobby's puppet was built and used in some scenes where he is focused from behind, but for those where the magical creature has movement or dialogue, a version completely made by computer graphics was used. The puppet now rests in Chris Columbus' office in San Francisco.

Shooting finished in July 2002, and it was around that time that Chris Columbus communicated to David Heyman and Steve Kloves that he would not direct the next film, expressing that the Harry Potter films were too demanding. Columbus sensed that the first film would take approximately ninety days to shoot, but they ended up shooting for one hundred and fifty days. It was not only the physical and mental fatigue that informed his decision, but also the lack of time to spend with his family. Columbus had calculated that if he directed the seven Harry Potter films, he would not see his children grow up. After communicating that to Rowling, he decided to tell Daniel Radcliffe, Emma Watson, and Rupert Grint. According to the director himself, it was a difficult moment for him.

With the departure of Columbus, Heyman and the production team had to decide who would be the next director to take to take over the Wizarding World. M. Night Shyamalan, Guillermo del Toro, and Marc Foster were the first three directors to reject the film. Kenneth Branagh's name was mentioned in conversation, but ultimately, he was not offered a position. Finally, Alfonso Cuarón took on the responsibility of carrying out *Harry Potter and the Prisoner of Azkaban*. The offer came mainly from his success with *Y Tú Mamá También* (2001). Despite having a clear contrast with the family-friendly Harry Potter films, the film had an interesting take on adolescence. *A Little Princess* (1995), the second film of Cuarón's to note, was a favorite of Rowling's because there is a juxtaposition of the real and fantastic world. The production team wanted him, but the decision at first was not entirely clear, because Cuarón had not even seen the two films already made. He quickly called his friend, Guillermo del Toro who recommended him to read the books. Cuarón did so, and the story captivated him. There was still the question of how he could approach a material that was already quite formed. How could he add his vision of the Wizarding World without destroying everything that had already been built? He considered it and even consulted Guillermo del Toro again who recommended that he approached the project with humility and without thinking about his own ego.

Unfortunately, Columbus' departure was not the only blow to the Harry Potter film series. The premiere for *Chamber of Secrets* was dated for November 3, 2002, again in London's Leicester Square. Sadly, on October 25th, Richard Harris, who played Albus Dumbledore, passed away at age 72. In August, he had been diagnosed with Hodgkin's disease, and he spent his last days at London University Hospital. David Heyman went to visit him, and the producer did not find him well, but Harris kept his humor and said, "Don't you dare recast me" (Williams, 2010). It was then necessary to find another actor for the headmaster of Hogwarts. Harris' family suggested Peter O'Toole, a friend who fit the role well. The studio considered it, but decided not to hire him, since O'Toole was already at an old age and there was a risk that, over the years, his health would prevent him from participating in all the remaining films. Another alternative was Sir Ian McKellen, who had already finished filming *The Lord of the Rings* trilogy in the role of Gandalf. He declined the role because he believed it was disrespectful to take Harris's post.

Eventually, Cuarón, who had already started working on the third film in September, and Heyman, were drawn to Michael Gambon who was Irish like Harris; a seasoned actor in film, TV, and theater; and a BAFTA award recipient. Gambon did not mind replacing another actor, a normal custom for him. With theatre, it's normal for the casts to rotate and for several actors to take over the same character. Gambon preferred not to read the books which explains why his interpretation is not very close to J.K. Rowling's Dumbledore, but Cuarón himself is also responsible for that.

Gambon wanted a more physically active, running and not walking Dumbledore, and this was reflected in his new outfit. Jany Temime and Laurent Guinci oversaw the design, and their new tunic not only changed in appearance, but allowed freer movements.

The production of *Harry Potter and the Prisoner of Azkaban* continued while *Harry Potter and the Chamber of Secrets* premiered worldwide on November 15, 2002, a year after the first film. Commercially it did very well, earning $879 million dollars worldwide, but did not exceed *Harry Potter and the Philosopher's Stone's* numbers. In that same year, *Philosopher's Stone* competed against *The Lord of the Rings: The Two Towers* (2002) among others.

The filming of *Prisoner of Azkaban* began in February 2003 and lasted until October, extending the times compared to the previous two, since it was discussed that the deadlines had not allowed enough work to produce a great film. This broke the rhythm for a Harry Potter movie release each year, with 2003 being the first year with a film absence. However, fans were not so upset because the *Harry Potter and Order of The Phoenix* book was released that year. Even though Cuarón knew that he did not have to take over the Wizarding World and just direct one film, he knew how to leave his mark on each of its characteristics.

The dark colors, the desaturated images, and an angrier Harry are all stamps that were introduced in the series by the Mexican director. These were replicated in future films. Cuarón is also responsible for changes in the actors. From the beginning of the project, he tried to make the actors connect more with their characters, especially those who were already teenagers. It started with a simple exercise for Emma Watson, Daniel Radcliffe, and Rupert Grint. He asked them to write an autobiographical essay as their character. Emma Watson took on the task seriously, and submitted a multi-page brief, as did Daniel Radcliffe, who also obliged. Both recognized that the work helped them see their characters in a different way and understand emotions. Rupert Grint, however, did not present anything, because according to him, it was what Ron would have done. Cuarón realized that Grint already understood his character. The director left them more lessons on the set, giving them liberties to propose possible reactions and emotions for their characters in each scene. Watson fondly remembers Cuarón, and even asserts that she learned the most from him as the director.

As in every new movie, the cast continued to grow. This time, more established British actors were added: Emma Thompson in the role of Trelawney, Gary Oldman as Sirius Black, and David Thewlis as Professor Remus Lupin. For the role of Trelawney, the London actress Tilda Swinton had been considered. She did not accept the offer, and years later, confessed that she was against films like Harry Potter because they romanticized the idea of boarding schools like Hogwarts where children go to live during the school year—very cruel places in her opinion, because children need to live with their parents.

Oldman acknowledged that he felt that the character fit perfectly with him, but that it was a challenge, since he had to start as a threat, but towards the end of the film become the father figure of the protagonist without losing his essence. Something similar happened with Thewlis's character Lupin, whose true nature we don't know, and it's not even until the end of the film that we learn about his position. Originally, for Cuarón, Lupin was homosexual, although this was never hinted at in the film. However, the idea that the lycanthropy that Lupin suffered from is a disease was featured in the film. This is clearly seen in how the wolf version of Lupin looks (unlike other Hollywood films, the audience doesn't see a strong or large werewolf, but a thin and frail wolf). Initially, the transformation into a wolf was attempted with makeup and later with actors specialized in movements within the costumes, but the result was not what was expected, so they decided to do everything with CGI technology. It was one of the few things that Cuarón agreed to do with special effects.

The director knew that the more effects used, the less realism was imposed on the film. Despite the advanced level of computers, the resources were still not quite right, and that was why Cuarón always preferred to do things "for real." Only in the case of Buckbeak and the Dementors is when he had to use CGI as a last resort. For the hippogriff, animatronics was first tried, but in post-production computer visuals were added. In the case of the Dementors, it was a little different. The director initially tried to make them with puppets, so he called the renowned puppeteer, Basil Twist, who then created puppets of Dementors that were filmed underwater, and then reproduced at different speeds. In practice, it was impossible to film all the scenes that involved them in this way, but the tests and recordings were exactly what the special effects team needed to see, and they used them as a base and then created the creatures with computer graphics.

In the case of the Knight Bus, no special effects were used. A double-decker bus was modified, adding a third floor, and drove at a normal speed while cars around it drove almost zero kilometers per hour. In this way, when the speed of the film was increased, it seemed that the cars were going at normal speed and the bus was avoiding them very quickly. More surprising in the use of resources was the scene with Aunt Marge. Different costumes with balloons inside to simulate inflating, a little makeup, and threads and cables to simulate the suspension were used for the scene. The result made for a memorable scene.

Cuarón is also partly responsible for the geography of Hogwarts, which in the previous two films was almost non-existent. When meeting with Stuart Craig, the director explained that he wanted to give Hogwarts a sense of external and internal location. He wanted the viewer to understand the paths that the protagonists took to get from one point to the other—the location of the different classrooms inside the castle, but also outside. He also introduced the great green land that surrounds Hogwarts, where he included a touch of Celtic monoliths. He moved Hagrid's hut (formerly at the entrance to the forbidden forest, now at the bottom of a small hillside), and even proposed a small cemetery where Harry and Hermione would hide at before saving Buckbeak. This last idea was discarded by Rowling, because that cemetery could have a fundamental role in the next books. At that point, not all of the books had been released, and it can be assumed that that cemetery would be the possible burial place for Dumbledore who dies at the end of *Half-Blood Prince.* Cuarón's intuition, although it was suppressed in that case, worked in others. When Rowling saw the film, she claimed that the director had put things that would seem like clues to future books, but in fact they had been his total invention. She was referring to the scene between Lupin and Harry where the professor talks about the importance of the similarity of the eyes with his mother, who plays a vital role, especially towards the end of the seventh book. "I really got goose bumps when I saw a couple of those things, and I thought, people are going to look back on the film and think that those were put in deliberately as clues" (Puig, 2004).

Prisoner of Azkaban, despite having extensive source material from the book, resulted in a shorter movie with a running time of 141 minutes. This cut in time caused the film to have many scenes left out. The backstory of Sirius Black himself is barely explained, while there is no mention of the Marauders' Map origin. Because of this, viewers who have not read the books would not know the importance of the map to Harry's father. Although Harry Potter's feelings for Cho Chang were removed (the character does not even appear), more emphasis was placed on the relationship between the protagonists themselves, even more emphasis being placed on the relationship between Ron and Hermione. Even so, with these vital differences with the book, *Harry Potter and the Prisoner of Azkaban* is one of the films preferred by fans, and by critics, who reviewed it in a very positive way.

Released on May 31st in the United Kingdom and June 4th in the United States, *The Prisoner of Azkaban* failed to surpass the box office numbers of the previous two movies. Despite a wide release, including in IMAX theaters (the first in the series delivered in IMAX) and once again breaking records on launch day and the weekend, the film grossed $796 million worldwide, again almost a hundred million less than its predecessor. At the time, the trending contention was that the Harry Potter films could be saturating the market and perhaps it was not appropriate to finish making all of them. Warner Bros. had acquired the rights to only the first four films, and while the first had cost only a bit more than $100 million to make and had earned more than $900 million worldwide, subsequent films cost more and failed to match the numbers of *Philosopher's Stone.*

The one that came to save continuity was the fourth movie, *Harry Potter and the Goblet of Fire*. "The box office of the second film was less than the first and the third less than the second. The third film made almost $800m so was very successful, but I did not know what would have happened had the films continued to decrease at the box office as each film was costing more," Heyman confesses.

Cuarón, who even made a cameo in the scene from The Three Broomsticks, wanted to focus 100% on finishing *Harry*

Potter and the Prisoner of Azkaban without any distraction. For this reason, he decided not to direct the fourth film, forcing David Heyman to go in search of another director. The producer turned to someone who had already been approached with the proposal to direct Harry Potter. Although, at the time, Mike Newell had to refuse to be part of *The Philosopher's Stone* due to other commitments, he did not hesitate to accept being part of *The Goblet of Fire*, becoming the first British director for the series. Steve Kloves adapted the script again. The length of the book (more than 700 pages) and its more complex plot compared to the previous ones brought complications that affected the story on the big screen. "We always thought it would be two movies, but we could never figure out a way to break it in two. So it will be a different experience from the book," (Los Angeles Daily News, 2004), Kloves said, anticipating that *Goblet of Fire* should have been divided into two halves. This strategy ultimately wasn't used until the adaptation of the last book in the series, *Harry Potter and the Deathly Hallows*.

Filming started in May 2004. While another part of the team finished with the third film, the main actors began their work in late June, when the promotion of the film had ended. Just as the magical universe expanded in this fourth film, the cast did too. David Tennant as Barty Crouch Jr., Brendan Gleeson as Mad-Eye Moody, and Miranda Richardson as Rita Skeeter joined the cast, among others. The role of Rita Skeeter had been offered to Rosamund Pike, who ended up rejecting it because she was not comfortable with the commitment involved in participating in future films, as was the original idea. Ultimately, the role of Skeeter was removed in the following films. Clémence Poésy as Fleur Delacour, Stanislav Ianevski as Viktor Krum, and Robert Pattinson as Cedric Diggory completed the Triwizard

Tournament champions. Pattinson would later jump to fame with the *Twilight* saga. Despite expanding the cast on one hand, it was shrunk on the other. The Dursleys were removed from this film, and Richard Griffiths (who played Uncle Vernon) was disappointed not to appear in *Goblet of Fire*. Even fans around the world started an online petition gathering signatures for the production to re-enter Harry's family into the film.

Brendan Gleeson was living in Dublin when Newell arrived to offer him the role of Mad-Eye Moody. The actor admitted that he did not know anything about the series, but his son did. Indeed, when Gleeson told his son about the character he would play, he recommended his father accept it only if he was 100% dedicated to work. The son, Domhnall Gleeson, would later join the Harry Potter cast as Bill Weasley. Brendan studied the character and believed that "Moody is a gunslinger with a wand. He's obviously suffered terrible trauma [...], he is on the verge of being paranoid" (McCabe, 2011). This analogy with the gunslinger suited Jany Temime, a costume designer, who used the old spaghetti western style to inspire the character's attire. Temime depicted Mad-Eye wearing a large overcoat where he kept all his possessions, since she imagined the character without a fixed home, with a nomadic life. Regarding Richardson's character, Rita Skeeter dresses for the occasion. It's no coincidence that, during the first tournament task, she wears a green outfit as if she were just another dragon. Temime was also responsible for the dresses worn at the Yule Ball, one of the most important events in both the book and the movie when it comes to character development. Just as it took more than a hundred extra workers who had to redesign the Great Hall for the ball, the costume team worked for six months to create more than a hundred different dresses for the gala.

Hermione Granger's dress alone took three months of design and more than twelve meters of gauze was used.

Any dance needs good music. John Williams, who composed the soundtrack for the first three films, was not available for the fourth, so it was Patrick Doyle, who had already worked with Newell, who took over the task. Initially Doyle was going to work on what Williams had already done, but he ended up using only "Hedwig's Theme," the brand's iconic song. Doyle invited Jarvis Cocker, singer of the British band, Pulp, to write a song for the Wizarding World. Radiohead's Jonny Greenwood and Phil Selway joined Cocker, and the three composed and recorded some tracks for the soundtrack and made cameos as the band members of The Weird Sisters. A band with a similar name in Canada initiated legal actions against Warner Bros. and for this reason, the name of the musical group in the film is not mentioned. In a deleted scene they are presented as "the band that needs no introduction."

The Triwizard Tournament was a challenge for the production team. There were entirely new creatures and scenarios, so attempts were made to reuse as much as possible. The Hungarian Horntail, a Harry Potter obstacle in the first task of the competition, had to be created twice. The first time, for the scene where Harry looks at him in the woods, the basilisk from the second movie was recycled. The team added wings and fire through his mouth. The second version which Harry faces in the task, however, was all made with CGI.

The creation of the set was quite a challenge, and it became one of the largest built for the entire series. The inspiration came from the Spanish bullrings. But the arena was too small for the dragon, and the decision was made that the action would go throughout all Hogwarts. The final scenes of the task were very demanding for Daniel Radcliffe, who was hanging or climbing the exteriors of Hogwarts. Even though the stunt team did its job perfectly, Radcliffe was not ashamed to admit that during certain moments he was afraid of falling and that a harness might fail.

But if the first task seemed difficult, the second was even more so. Three attempts were necessary to create the largest aquatic tank in Europe, which was 20 meters long, 6 meters wide, and 6 meters high. Not only did the underwater set allow several actors to participate in the same scene at the same time, but also submerge the technical equipment and cameras necessary to film. Radcliffe took six months of diving training before beginning to record his part, which did not make things completely easy. He had to record his scenes underwater imagining creatures that would later be added digitally, and all while holding his breath, without even releasing air bubbles that could compromise the scene. Contact with water also made it difficult for makeup. His scar had to be constantly redrawn after each shot. Rupert Grint and Emma Watson did not go through the same thing. It was decided that the students that the champions had to rescue would be dolls. To have actors submerged underwater and tied to the ground was very dangerous.

For the third and final task, it was decided that the enemy to overcome would be the maze itself and there would be no other difficulties within it. In original conceptual arts, the maze was much larger and extended beyond the horizon, giving a feeling of infinite branching. In taking this path, the maze must have its own personality and attempt to hunt down the contestants. Real walls, up to 8 meters high, were built and moved with remote controls. John Richardson, responsible for this, assures that all the necessary safety measures were taken to avoid accidents, but that he still feels that the actors involved were afraid and that the faces that appear in the film were not performances, but genuine fear.

When Harry and Cedric reach the center of the maze itself, they are transported to the cemetery, which reveals Lord Voldemort for the first time. Mike Newell specifically wanted Ralph Fiennes in the antagonistic role. The actor had already been recognized for his roles in *Schindler's List* (1993) and *The English Patient* (1996), which had earned him Academy Award nominations. But Fiennes was not convinced to participate, and asked Newell if, before signing the contract, if he could see some of the film, to know what type of work he was joining. Finally, two things convinced him: his nephews, and a photomontage made by the production team to dramatize the final appearance that Fiennes would have as Voldemort. However, there were internal differences in how Tom Riddle should look in his new form. On the one hand, the director did not want too much makeup, as he was convinced that any effect on Fiennes's face (digital or not) would overshadow his emotions. On the other hand, David Heyman wanted to be as faithful as possible to the characteristic look of the books. Thus, an intermediate point was reached. Heyman managed to get Fiennes' nose removed digitally in post-production, but not use red eye contacts, as described by J.K. Rowling in the novels. The reason is that the eyes of such a striking color overshadowed the emotions that Fiennes knew how to display very well. To maintain hostility between the characters, neither Fiennes nor Radcliffe spoke to each other during the filming of the final scenes. Furthermore, between the cuts of the shots, Fiennes insulted Radcliffe to make him angry and that he could interpret his role more emotionally, which Daniel knew how to appreciate. "It was a challenge to be really horrible with Harry

Potter, because everyone loves him," recalls the seasoned actor (McCabe, 2011).

The first trailer of the film was released on May 7, 2005 on ABC during the network debut of *Harry Potter and the Chamber of Secrets*. The trailer was released online the next day.

Harry Potter and the Goblet of Fire was the first movie in the series to be rated PG-13 in the US for containing “sequences of fantasy violence and frightening images.” It premiered on November 18, 2005, with an Avant Premiere in London on November 6th. For the event, the animatronic Hungarian Horntail used in the film stood next to the red carpet. The film, contrary to the trend of its predecessors, was a success. It grossed $896 million worldwide, surpassing the second and third films in the series. It was the most successful film of the year, and it became the eighth-highest-grossing film worldwide. This was the confirmation that Warner Bros. and Heyday Films (David Heyman’s production company) needed to see to continue with Harry Potter films going forward.

However, many questions remained to be resolved. Should the same director who managed to revitalize box office numbers continue? Should Steve Kloves continue to be in charge of book adaptations? And more importantly, should teen actors continue to lead their characters, or were their age ranges no longer appropriate?

CHAPTER SEVEN

Success on the Big Screen

"I know the movies will be very different. I know they can't be the books, and I don't want them to be the books."
J.K. Rowling (Martin, 2009)

Warner Bros. and Heyday Films had only acquired the rights for the first four films of the series back in 1998. At that time, Rowling had only gotten to work on the first three books, and although the last four books had been planned, there was no certainty that they would eventually be published barring some unforeseen event. It was also unknown if the adaptations would be successful in the film industry, something that was only confirmed with the release of *Harry Potter and the Goblet of Fire* in 2005, directed by Mike Newell. "It's a very odd way of working, and not a way I enjoyed at times," (Gritten, 2005) said the director about the difficulties of working shorter days due to child labor laws, and the complications of a big-budget film like Harry Potter, something that he was not used to. Maybe this was why Newell did not return for the fifth film. With the franchise already established, Warner Bros. and Heyday Films had secured the film rights of the remaining three adaptations (*Deathly Hallows,* however, was yet to be published). With the departure of Newell, David Heyman set his eyes on David Yates.

Yates, from Lancashire, England, had only directed one television film and one mini-series for the BBC. Although none of the projects seemed like Harry Potter, Heyman was convinced otherwise. He saw *The Order of the Phoenix* as a totally political film, about the adolescent rebellion and the abuse of power, something in complete harmony with what he had already directed. "This is a world on the verge of war. [...] The politics of Hogwarts and the wizarding world are very much at play here" (McCabe, 2011), said the producer, who was so sure that Yates had already convinced Warner Bros. that he was the right choice. The studio was also comfortable with the idea, as it wanted to add spontaneity to the series.

Although the directors changed throughout the first four films, and the announcement of a new one was not surprising, the case of Steve Kloves was different. Kloves, who had adapted all of the first four scripts, preferred to take a break after spending nearly eight years working in the Rowling universe. Adapting the fifth book (almost 800 pages in its British edition, and 900 in the North American edition) was a huge task, and Kloves preferred to work on another adaptation: *The Curious Incident of the Dog in the Night-Time*, which would also be produced by Heyday Films (to this day, the film has not been produced). Kloves had started working on *Order of The Phoenix* before dismissing it after finishing the first 30 pages. This scrip included a very emotional scene between Petunia and Harry.

Ultimately, the responsibility for *The Order of the Phoenix* fell into the hands of Michael Goldenberg, who had also been a candidate to adapt the first film. Goldenberg had a vision very similar to Heyman's: "It's about a situation that recurs in history about the abuse of power and what happens when citizens being oppressed by that power are forced to fight back" (McCabe, 2011). Despite being the longest book, *The Order of The Phoenix* was adapted into a short script and the film became the shortest so far (*Deathly Hallows Pt. 2* became the shortest in the series). The challenge was accomplished by maintaining the spirit of the book's story, rather than the passages themselves. The writer decided to cut everything that was not crucial to the journey that Harry was going through as the protagonist, which is why the Quidditch scenes were removed (which disappointed Rupert Grint, who was eagerly awaiting them), as well as the scenes involving St. Mungo's Hospital, Firenze's classes, and some Ministry of Magic rooms in the final battle (the Brain Room, for example). Others, like Severus Snape's worst memory, were condensed and rewritten to keep the spirit of the book but shown very briefly. Oddly, the character of Kreacher was not going to appear in the film, but when J.K. Rowling read the script, she advised that he should be added, since he was going to be of vital importance in the seventh book. With the addition of Kreacher, Dobby was removed from the film, using other characters to complete younger house elf's actions. Although it should have remained a secret between the author and the production team, the importance of Kreacher in the seventh book was leaked before its publication.

In late June 2007, almost a month before the publication of the final book, and two weeks before the film's release, the team and the actors held a press conference in London. There, David Heyman commented on this anecdote without mentioning the character, and when he was asked who he was, the director said he could not mention him. However, David Yates confirmed this to MTV News, announcing that the house elf, who once knew himself to be from the Black family, would play an important role in the *Deathly Hallows* book, this interview taking place before the book's release (Vineyard, 2007).

Just as Warner Bros. had the rights to the first four movies, the actors had also signed on to the first four films. When the time came to start production for the fifth film, it was necessary to renew Daniel Radcliffe, Rupert Grint, and Emma Watson's contracts. In the case of the first two actors, it was not difficult to retain them, but Watson was not so willing. The actress felt overwhelmed by the responsibilities and demands of shooting these films, and the restrictions on other activities that she wanted to do—dance, play hockey with friends, take classes and exams to enter college. Finally, with certain concessions made by the studio, Watson agreed to return as Hermione Granger for the fifth film.

Filming began in February 2006 and lasted until December, with a two-month hiatus in May for Radcliffe and Watson to take their exams that would allow them, depending on the grade earned, to enter a university in the United Kingdom. Shooting with a new team led by David Yates was another change for the teen actors. "It was the first time I ever felt insecure about whether a director thought I was any good or not," recalls Watson of Yates' way of working (McCabe, 2011). Although he did not communicate it, Yates was happy with the actress' work, and even considered her for other responsibilities. Watson knew the world of Harry Potter too well, so she was a sort of pocket guide for him. Radcliffe and Grint also welcomed the new director. For Felton, who after so many years playing Draco Malfoy seemed tired and no longer felt the passion for the world of cinema as before, the arrival of Yates changed everything. It was the director who restored his desire for acting.

The fifth film begins the story of Luna Lovegood's character, and with it, of Evanna Lynch. For months, the casting team saw thousands of girls, but none of them were convincing. It was decided to do an open casting in London, which was attended by more than 15,000 girls. Among them was Lynch, who had flown from Dublin with her family the night before. She was already a fan of the series and felt like Luna Lovegood so much that she had written a letter to J.K. Rowling in the past expressing that sentiment. When she finally got the role because of her resemblance to Luna physically and behaviorally, Heyman communicated it to Rowling who, according to the Heyman, remembered the letter and was happy to have found Luna for the screen. After the release of the seventh movie, the author confessed that she pictured Evanna Lynch when she was writing the books after her casting. “The only exception, actor-wise, to my sort of ‘didn't intrude’ rule was Evanna Lynch who plays Luna. And I hear her voice when I write Luna,” said J.K. Rowling (Creating the World of Harry Potter Part 7: Story, 2012).

The cast was also joined by Natalia Tena in the role of Nymphadora Tonks, George Harris as the auror, Kingsley Shacklebolt, and Imelda Staunton in the role of the new Defense Against the Dark Arts teacher, Dolores Umbridge. Imelda was familiar with Rowling's books because of her children, who were reading them, but had not yet reached the fifth book when a friend recommended that she should audition to the role of Umbridge, which would be perfect for her. When Staunton read the description, she wasn’t flattered, but understood the idea. And being part of a production like Harry Potter was something unique. “I’m in this top job with all the top people,” she said, referring to colleagues such as Michael Gambon, Maggie Smith, and Emma Thompson (McCabe, 2011).

One of the most anticipated scenes was the kiss between Harry Potter and Cho Chang (Katie Leung). The scene was awaited by both the actors and producers who had seen Daniel Radcliffe grow. They believed that it was a key moment in the actor's career. The original filming date had to be postponed due to Radcliffe being under the weather, but when the time finally came, everything went well. While the actor’s most rabid fangirls may have disliked seeing him kiss a girl on screen, there were two other parts of the film that became somewhat controversial. One of them was the appearance of Lord Voldemort dressed in an elegant way in King's Cross, very different from how he is portrayed in the books.

The other scene that was not well-received was the death of Sirius Black, which occurs in an abrupt and anti-climactic way and the director himself understands the audience. Although the director believes that Harry's reaction to death is done correctly (both in the acting and in the story within the film), he feels that the relationship between Sirius and the protagonist was not fully developed, especially due to the problem of having had to adapt so much story into a single movie. In fact, David Yates shot a three-hour movie, but he had to cut it down to two hours and fifteen minutes (135 minutes), so many scenes were cut out. Michael Goldenberg devised the mechanism to quickly tell the story's progress through the headlines of *The Daily Prophet*. This mechanism was still used not only through the rest of the films of the series, but also in the *Fantastic Beasts* movies years later.

Sirius Black's death came at the hands of Bellatrix Lestrange, played by Helena Bonham Carter. However, the actress who was originally going to play the part was Helen McCrory. Rumors of McCrory's involvement began in mid-2005, and in February 2006, when filming began, these rumours were confirmed. However, in April, McCrory was dropped due to a pregnancy that would not allow her to film the final battle scenes in September and October. Her replacement ended up being Bonham Carter, which was announced promptly in May, and McCrory was left with the role of Narcissa Malfoy, who she would portray in the following films.

Helena Bonham Carter's Bellatrix Lestrange and Gary Oldman's Sirius Black are both a part of the Black Family Tree (making them cousins by blood). A tapestry of this family tree covers an entire wall in the Black family home. The tapestry is mentioned without too much detail in the books, but it had to be included in the film, so one day David Heyman called Rowling asking if there were more details so they could design it correctly. In less than fifteen minutes, Rowling faxed the producer the complete family tree, including up to five generations, with the characters' names and dates of birth and death.

The climax of the film occurs at the Ministry of Magic. The Ministry Atrium, designed by Stuart Craig, was inspired by the London Underground and by the front of a Burger King restaurant located on Tottenham Court Road in the English capital, which imitates a Victorian style that fit exactly with what was sought. The set of the atrium was the largest built for the series up to that moment, more than 60 meters long, almost 40 meters wide, and 10 meters high. For the Hall of Prophecy, Stuart Craig wanted to do something similar, however, creating 15,000 crystal balls for the prophecies was an impediment, especially if the scene had to be reshot. So, something happened that Craig did not really like, but had to accept: His sketches and designs were not transformed into real props, but into digital ones created by CGI, a resource that was also used for Grawp (Hagrid's giant brother) and the thestrals.

For the first battle at the Ministry of Magic, in the Death Chamber where Sirius Black dies, both stunt and dance coordinators joined to choreograph the movements that the actors had to do when casting the spells in duels. David Yates wanted to differentiate how adolescent amateurs cast spells (simply saying the word and waving their arms), from how experienced adult Death Eaters or Order of the Phoenix members did. Jason Isaacs fondly remembers his fight against Sirius Black as they had to rehearse various moves. Isaacs also emphasizes that, while Black has a more street style, Malfoy's movements are more elegant, implying that the distinction of classes also affects the choreography of spells. In the case of the second battle between Dumbledore and Voldemort, Yates wanted to make it more visceral, so the duel begins with effects like what happens at the end of *Harry Potter and the Goblet of Fire*, but quickly the weapons used change to common elements: fire, water, and glass (turned into sand). Yates wanted to impact viewers with familiar elements, which not only made the fight more credible, but also created more real fear.

During filming, the recording of *Harry Potter and the Queen's Handbag* took place. To celebrate Queen Elizabeth II's 80th birthday, a party was organized for the country's children on the grounds at Buckingham Palace. The theme was British literature. In addition to the assistance from Rowling (who did a reading and signed books), there was also a pantomime (made of short stage plays and pre-recorded clips). The story consisted of different villains, offended at not having been invited to the party, organizing to steal the queen's handbag containing her glasses, and thus the queen couldn't read her commemoration speech. Several characters in literature try to help the queen, and one of them is Harry Potter, along with his friends Ron and Hermione. In a nearly three-minute short, Harry, Ron, and Hermione receive a letter from the Muggle Prime Minister asking for help with the situation. After trying to retrieve the handbag using the accio spell (and after Neville's appearance), Hermione sends a letter to Buckingham Palace to grant temporary magic power to locate the stolen item more easily. Leaving aside the fun part of it, this short film did not make any sense in the canon of the Wizarding World. Ron Weasley names Voldemort by name, something that never occurs in the books, and even Harry Potter makes a reference to Peeves, a character that never appears or is named in the film series. The short was shown on a giant screen at the event and was televised on BBC.

Filming for *Harry Potter and the Order of the Phoenix* ended in December of 2006, but by mid-November, the first trailer for the film was released with the film *Happy Feet*, and on the November 20th, the trailer was available online.

There was controversy when it came to marketing the film in mid-May 2007, when a poster for the film was released with the teen lead actors. In a poster advertisement for the IMAX 3D experience for the film, Emma Watson had been digitally retouched. Her bust had been enlarged and her waist had been shrunk in comparison to other posters. This caused strong criticism in different online media, especially since the character who was being sexualized was only fifteen years old. Warner Bros. quickly went on to say that the poster version was not final and that it had been uploaded to the movie's website by mistake. Beyond the controversy, this news worked to announce that the fifth film in the saga would be the first to have 3D scenes in its IMAX version (although it would only be for thirty minutes of the total film). The premiere in London took place on July 3, 2007 (J.K. Rowling attended, despite being busy with the imminent release of the last book), and five days later its counterpart event took place in Los Angeles. The film premiered on July 11th in most western countries, but not Australia, where the film was planned to be released in September. After complaints and many signatures from fans, the release date was moved up to the same date as the rest of the countries. The world debut of *Harry Potter and the Order of the Phoenix* in theaters was a success. It quickly outperformed all its predecessors in the series save for *The Philosopher's Stone*, and thus became the second-highest-grossing Harry Potter film to date, following the new trend that started with *The Goblet of Fire*. With a box office of almost $940 million, it became the sixth-highest-successful film in history until 2007, and the second film in the series to overcome the barrier of $900 million.

Accompanying box office success, positive reviews from media outlets arrived. Everyone agreed that this new film was the best to date—darker and with first-rate performances, highlighting Imelda Staunton and Helena Bonham Carter. Fans, however, were not so happy, especially since they noticed a poor adaptation with too many differences from the original text, missing scenes, and modifications to the actions of certain characters. This might be the reason why the studio decided that Steve Kloves should return as a screenwriter for the sixth film. By then, Kloves had already regretted not adapting *The Order of the Phoenix*: "They asked me on the wrong day. They asked me for the last time on the wrong day. Had they asked me the next day, I probably would have said yes" (Martin, 2009).

David Yates returned to direct the sixth film; the offer came as *The Order of the Phoenix* details were being finalized and production for the sixth film was due to start soon. It was not difficult to convince him. Yates liked the idea of making these great productions with total freedom and wanted the challenge of overcoming what was achieved with the fifth film now that he had the experience. Between the two, Kloves and Yates outlined what the adaptation would be like. They decided that while the opening chapter of the book, where the Minister of Magic pays a visit to the British Prime Minister, could be a great scene, it was more interesting to show how Voldemort's attacks affected the Muggle world, rather than recounting it through a conversation. Just like in *The Goblet of Fire*, the Dursleys were removed, placing Harry in a train station showing a clear interest in the waitress. For that scene, Steve Kloves had originally written that Dumbledore would comment on the girl, comparing her to a woman from his youth, but when Rowling read it, she explained to Kloves that Dumbledore was gay, whereupon the screenwriter was one of the first to know the secret and the dialogue was removed.

The other big change from the book was the notion of removing the final battle at Hogwarts prior to the headmaster's death. The reason was that the team thought that it would become repetitive, since in the last movie there would be another battle at Hogwarts, and it would be more important. To maintain a duel between the Death Eaters and the Order of the Phoenix in this film, an attack scene in The Burrow was added, implying that there was no longer any safe place to hide. Voldemort's followers could attack anywhere. Regarding the scene of Dumbledore's death, Kloves added a different touch. While in the book Harry hides under the invisibility cloak and Snape does not know of his presence, in the film Snape sees him and asks him to remain silent. Kloves' idea was to make that simple encounter haunt Harry later, making him feel a little guilty: "While I was writing, I just had a notion about a moment between him and Snape, something Harry could look back on and question as to why he didn't act differently" (Martin, 2009). It was also decided to not include Albus Dumbledore's funeral, because they considered it was not in tune with the rest of the final product.

The fact that only two childhood moments are shown from Voldemort's past—which plays a fundamental role in the novel—was the decision of David Yates. Steve Kloves had not only included all of them in his first sketch of the script, even those related to the Gaunt family—but had added his own to dramatize more, including the death of Tom Riddle's mother.

Along with Yates and Kloves, Stuart Craig, Tim Burke as special effects supervisor, and Nicholas Hooper as composer also returned. However, with the actors, there were still uncertainties. Rumors that the main trio of teens would not return was stronger than ever.

In March 2007, different media outlets reported that Emma Watson had rejected an offer of £2 million to act in each of the remaining films, but it took just a few weeks for Warner Bros. to confirm that the actress would not only participate in the sixth movie, but she had also renewed her contract to play Hermione Granger in the last two films. The return of Daniel Radcliffe and Rupert Grint for the last two parts of the series had been confirmed a few days earlier. Jim Broadbent joined the cast as the new Potions teacher, Horace Slughorn, and Helen McCrory joined to portray Narcissa Malfoy. For the young versions of Voldemort, Frank Dillane played the teenager, while Hero Fiennes-Tiffin, Ralph Fiennes' nephew, played the child. Christian Coulson was originally considered as he had already played Tom Riddle at school age for *Harry Potter and the Chamber of Secrets*, but at the time of filming *Harry Potter and the Half-Blood Prince*, Coulson was almost thirty years old, and was out of the running. English actor, Bill Nighy, came very close to joining the cast. He had already worked with David Yates on one of his television films. When he learned that Yates was working on the Harry Potter franchise, Nighy joked that he would stop being the only English actor who was not yet part of the series, but they did not call him for the sixth film. According to Yates, he had already thought of Nighy for the role of Rufus Scrimgeour, but by removing the character from the adaptation, Bill Nighy was left out. Nonetheless, the director would finally use the actor, and Nighy would play the Minister of Magic in *The Deathly Hallows*. Shooting began just months after the release of the fifth film, in September 2007, and lasted until May 2008. However, some of the main actors began filming in December (such as Emma Watson) and others, like Alan Rickman and Helena Bonham Carter, in February.

The film could have had a very dark side, but David Yates preferred to add hints of a romantic comedy, and for that, one of the common threads is the jealous relationship between Ron and Hermione. While the latter uses Cormac McLaggen (Freddie Stroma) to make Ron jealous, Ron goes a little further and begins a relationship with Lavender Brown (Jessie Cave). Just as Daniel Radcliffe had had his kiss in the previous movie, this time it was Rupert Grint's turn. "It was embarrassing because our first kiss was in a room full of people, not like Dan's. He was sort of his own in the Room of Requirements" (McCabe, 2011), remembers the actor, referring to Harry Potter's kiss in *Order of The Phoenix*. This time Radcliffe had to repeat a first kiss with Ginny Weasley (Bonnie Wright).

In contrast to the other teens, Draco Malfoy is chosen by Voldemort to carry out one of the most important tasks for his victory. Tom Felton, who plays Draco Malfoy, acknowledges that his role ceased to be one-dimensional, and went from making grimaces or comments in the background to having a bigger impact on the story. He and Yates set out to show the most vulnerable side of Draco Malfoy. Both of them knew that, if at the end of the film the viewers felt sympathy for him, they had achieved their goal. It seems that their goal was met (even more so than in the book, since at the end of the film there remains the question of whether Malfoy is really a victim or a victimizer). Special attention to detail was taken into account, and different means were used to express different messages, such as Draco's black suit in the film: despite being physically at Hogwarts, not wearing a uniform translates into his focus on his plan and not on school.

All the attention paid to Malfoy's character did not earn him an award, but earned him the approval of Rowling. She sent a letter to his house congratulating him on the performance, especially for the scene prior to the murder of Albus Dumbledore. The actor who was not satisfied with that scene was Daniel Radcliffe, who said that after so many deaths scenes, he did not know how to show a different reaction to it.

Special effects were used extensively in the scene where Dumbledore and Harry search for Tom Riddle's horcrux in a cave. The entire internal stage of the cave was made by CGI, a decision made because the set was too big to build, and because Yates had had a good experience with the Hall of Prophecies in the fifth film. The only thing that was not done on the computer was the exterior, which was filmed on the Cliffs of Moher in Ireland and is the only filming location in the entire Harry Potter series outside of the UK. The Inferi, the creatures that guard the horcrux inside the cave, were also created by CGI. David Yates did not want them to look like zombies, but he wanted the audience to feel compassion for them because, ultimately, they were victims of Voldemort. Conceptual art was first designed, analyzing corpses that were submerged in water for a long time, and from that, sculptures were created. These sculptures were scanned and combined with the movement of actors. Bruno Delbonnel, born in France, joined the team as director of photography. In the first reactions from Warner Bros., the film was too dark, so he was asked to add a little color, and Delbonnel and Yates had to do this in post-production. Because of his work, *Harry Potter and the Half-Blood Prince* was the only film in the series to be nominated for an Academy Award for Best Cinematography.

The film was originally going to be released in November 2008, but Warner Bros.' decision was to move it to the following year. The cause was purely financial. In July, the studio released *Batman: The Dark Knight* (2008). Directed by Christopher Nolan, the film was a resounding success in theatres. "Spending" on Harry Potter in a year when Warner had already exceeded its goals seemed silly. But this decision generated a bit of controversy among fans, and in the media. *Entertainment Weekly* magazine did not receive the news in time, and in one of its August 2008 editions, *Harry Potter and the Half-Blood Prince* was the cover story for its release on November 21st. On the same day that the magazines reached the newsstands, the announcement of the new date was made public.

Harry Potter and the Half-Blood Prince was released on July 15, 2009. To keep the film from leaking, Warner Bros. and Heyday Films kept the film on six separate reels until nearly a month before release, and they were finally reunited days before distribution began.

The film was released in its regular edition and in IMAX 3D worldwide simultaneously, except in the United States, due to conflicts with *Transformers: Revenge of the Fallen* (2009). Since

IMAX had given *Transformers* exclusivity for a month, the sixth Harry Potter movie was released on IMAX 3D only on July 29th. Globally, it grossed $935 million, the second most successful film of the year, behind James Cameron's *Avatar* (2009). It surpassed all the Harry Potter films so far except *The Philosopher's Stone* and *the Order of the Phoenix.*

With six films released, and the last two with unquestionable success, only one book was still missing to be adapted. The book, *Harry Potter and the Deathly Hallows,* had been released just two years prior, but the production team had already started to work on it. The last novel resolved not only the fate of Harry Potter, but also of all the characters, answering the outstanding questions that had been generated throughout the saga. David Heyman knew that it would be a difficult task to condense what was happening and solve all the loose ends in a single movie.

The idea of making two films had already been considered during *The Goblet of Fire,* but Heyman was still not convinced. The suggestion had come from the other producer, Lionel Wigram, who had been involved since the beginning of the series, and had been endorsed by David Barron, who had joined the production team during the fifth film. They knew that at that point, no details could be left out. Making two films also involved renegotiating certain contracts, such as David Yates, who had agreed to direct the adaptation of the seventh book but had never confirmed that he would film two more films. Finally, they all agreed when Steve Kloves confirmed that two movies should be produced to tell the story well. He even suggested that perhaps three were necessary.

Making two films involved a great commitment from the entire cast and crew. The decision was to film the two at the same time, which called for a shooting schedule twice as long as the typical Harry Potter film: eighteen continuous months of filming, from February 2009 to June 2010. It was an experience that, although David Yates remembers as interesting, he would not like to repeat. He filmed scenes mixed between different films, which generated confusion and constantly changed context, both for his team and for the actors involved.

Although it had been decided to divide the book into two parts, the breakpoint had not yet been chosen. Dobby's death had originally been thought about, but the previous three films had already ended with the death of a character close to Harry, and Yates did not want to repeat himself. The ending idea was brought forward to the moment when Harry is captured and taken to the Malfoy manor. Another idea was to cut with a cliffhanger, a suspenseful ending that would leave the viewer wanting more. When Yates did the editing, he noted that although the suspense goal had been achieved, the first part was not emotionally concluded. It was a movie, after all, and not a TV series episode, and the story had to be closed somehow.

The end was then again made around Dobby's death, but the scene of Voldemort getting the Elder Wand was now included; in this way the viewer was left with the question of what would happen next. Although the exact cut was not clear to Yates, the conceptual division of each of the films was. For the director, Part One of *Deathly Hallows* was more of a road trip movie where what mattered was the human relationship and, above all, the trio's internal relationship, while Part Two was much more dramatic with big battles, much more action, and the expected return to Hogwarts.

Filming, especially for Part One, was a great physical challenge for Radcliffe, Grint, and Watson. They had to do a lot of takes running in the forest, chased by the Snatchers. David Holmes, who had been Daniel Radcliffe's stunt double, was filming a scene where he had to be thrown and hit a wall. The cables that made the move to simulate the reaction to an explosion threw him against the concrete, and the blow was more than he could bear. Holmes fell and knew something was wrong when the coordinator took his hand and told him to squeeze his fingers. Holmes was unable to do so. He suffered a spinal injury that left him paralyzed from the chest down, without arm or leg mobility. He spent six months hospitalized at the RNOH (Royal National Orthopaedic Hospital), where Daniel Radcliffe and Tom Felton, who had become friends with him, visited. The two actors organized auctions to raise funds to cover the medical expenses. Today, Holmes is in a wheelchair, and is an Ambassador for the RNOH, where he helps people who have suffered from similar accidents.

Aside from the physical demands, the main actors also had to endure the cold. For the scene in London, after escaping from Bill and Fleur's wedding, the production closed the Piccadilly Circus area of the English capitol to film at dawn. Although Radcliffe and Grint could wear thermals under their clothing, Emma Watson was still in her red dress, and suffered from the low temperatures.

The film required a great commitment from the actors, and this was seen during scenes involving the Polyjuice potion. In Part One of *Deathly Hallows*, Harry, Hermione, and Ron become employees of the Ministry of Magic to enter incognito. Radcliffe, Grint, and Watson first performed those scenes, while Steffan Rhodri, Sophie Thompson, and David O'Hara studied their movements in detail. Then, these three interpreted the scene imitating the original, as if they were Harry, Ron, and Hermione in the body of the employees.

Something similar happened in Part Two when Hermione becomes Bellatrix Lestrange to enter Gringotts. Although it seems confusing, the result is Helena Bonham Carter acting as Hermione Granger with the appearance of Bellatrix. Bonham Carter not only imitated Watson's movements when filmed, but also captured the discomfort that Hermione's character would feel in Bellatrix's body: the hesitation to speak, the complexity of walking in heels and the tight corset against her body.

Emma Watson and Rupert Grint endured a bit of discomfort when they filmed their expected kiss in the Chamber of Secrets. Unlike the previous kisses, the actors had known each other since they were ten, which made the situation a little more awkward. "Neither of us was looking forward to it. [...] It didn't feel right," Grint recalls as Watson adds, "Rupert and I were nervous that it might look disingenuous, as we were so desperate to get it over with" (McCabe, 2011). In the final version of the scene, they both laugh after the kiss.

Stuart Craig felt his role changed considerably for *Deathly Hallows Part One*. Whereas the previous films mainly took place within Hogwarts and the occasional Wizarding World setting (which was to be created), in the case of the first of these two films, Craig had to find outdoor locations for most of the shooting, especially for all the scenes in the woods. Still, he had several sets to design. For Bill Weasley and Fleur Delacour's wedding, Craig wanted to imply that the party had been paid for by the French family and added French flair to the moment. The boathouse is another set that does not appear in the books, but where one of the most crucial scenes occurs—the death of Severus Snape. Thanks to that set, Stuart Craig received one of his biggest compliments, as Alan Rickman thanked him for his work, because he helped him interpret the death of his character.

The change in location for Snape's ending was not the only difference from the books. Steve Kloves, just as he had done for

Half-Blood Prince, where he preferred to show instead of tell, wrote the scene where fans see Hermione erase her parents' memory to demonstrate the sacrifice her character made when embarking on the journey with Ron and Harry. Another addition was the brief meeting at Hogwarts between Harry and Snape prior to the duel between professors Snape and McGonagall.

Another difference that gave the audience a lot to talk about was the dance that Harry and Hermione shared in the tent, during one of the many days when they were without Ron. Director Yates is convinced that the emotional and sexual tension between them had to be shown, and that scene achieved it. Nick Cave's song titled "O' Children", that is heard on the radio while the characters dance to it, was chosen by the director himself, and is the only song on the soundtrack that was not written for any of the movies in the series. As soon as the music ends, the magic of the dance and the characters' good humor breaks, returning them to the difficult reality that they must face. In that way, it works as a temporary escape and a moment where Hermione and Harry forget about the problems they're carrying.

The criticism from the fans was not because of the concept of the scene, which was welcomed to convey that message, but because it seemed outside of the Wizarding World canon and something that Rowling's characters would not do. The instrumental soundtrack, in both films, was overseen by Alexandre Desplat. He had also overseen the soundtrack for *Twilight: New Moon* (2009), and for the Oscar winner, *The King's Speech* (2010).

What did cause a bit more of a stir was the entire outcome. The final fight between Harry and Voldemort is as far as possible from what happens in the book. Yates not only wanted to make use of the special effects and show an "epic" duel between the two—the ending that the series deserved, but also to express a bit of symbolism. Voldemort was clearly more powerful and magically superior to Harry, but Harry was not afraid to die. The scene that illustrates this is when they are both on the edge of the precipice, and Harry takes Voldemort down into the void with him. In that same effect the two become entangled as one. The effect of fading into ashes, also applied to the death of Bellatrix Lestrange at the hands of Molly Weasley, is something that differs from the books entirely and was never explained or justified by the team. The trio are then seen walking across the Hogwarts Bridge, and as Harry breaks the Elder Wand, the three look at the horizon to end the seven-year adventure. But this scene not only does not occur in the same place as in the book, the office of the late Dumbledore, but it misses an important point. Harry does not repair his wand. For Yates, it was enough to show that Harry had all three Deathly Hallows, something Dumbledore had always fought for, but did not want to shoulder that responsibility and wanted to get rid of them (and no one could take them) as quickly as possible. David Heyman asked Rowling if this was the best ending and received the author's approval.

Interestingly, the first of the two *Deathly Hallows* films includes three minutes of animation for a scene in which "The Tale of the Three Brothers" is narrated. "David Yates and David Heyman wanted to make sure this sequence would stand out from the rest of the movie," recalls Ben Hibon, animation director who oversaw the short film. "The choice to use a different visual style for the sequence also reinforces the cinematic separation between the world of fantasy Harry inhabits, and the world of fables and mythologies that exists within it," he adds.

At the first meeting between Hibon and Yates (who was also joined by production designer, Stuart Craig), the animation director came up with the idea for the tale to have a style similar to shadow theatre, inspired by work by the German filmmaker Lotte Reiniger. Yates approved the idea, and under Hibon, the special effects studio, Framestore, brought the story to life. It took six months of development and a team of more than thirty people to make this happen. "We had a recording of Emma's voice-over well before we started production - which gave us a great sense of what the pace and tone of the sequence would be. Emma's voice and delivery indirectly dictated how the final sequence came together - a personal and intimate imagining of this ancient tale - her version of it," says Hibon.

One of the biggest difficulties in recording this movie was how emotional the process was, because it was the last time it would happen. A large part of the team had worked together for the past ten years, and the lead actors had grown up on set among all those people. Many had lived their best days as professionals in the film industry for ten years, working on one of the most successful film franchises of all time.

The first farewell was with the Dursleys, filming one of the first scenes of *Deathly Hallows*. It was the last scene for Richard Griffiths, Fiona Shaw and Harry Melling in the entire series, and as Radcliffe remembers, it was painful to say goodbye to the actors who had been around since the first film. The final farewell was on June 12, 2010, the last day of shooting when Daniel Radcliffe, Emma Watson, and Rupert Grint, along with Peter Mullan (the Death Eater Yaxley) filmed their escape from the Ministry of Magic.

Perhaps it was not the most interesting scene, but it did manage to thrill all the witnesses of that historic moment. The actors present admit that it was a complicated moment (although not for Yates who would still work on the film in post-production for a couple of more months). When recording the scene was finished, all the actors and all the people, who in some way or another worked in the place, gathered in front of screens to see, for the first time, the trailer for *Harry Potter and the Deathly Hallows - Part 1*. As soon as it ended (it had already caused more tears in some), another clip of just three minutes began, a recording that contained a small fragment from each of the 261 days of filming, where the guest of the day, a friend who was visiting, appeared, or someone special for the occasion. As if that was no longer enough, Daniel Radcliffe said some emotional words, and David Heyman joined him to say some final words as well.

Despite the emotional ending, the celebrations, and the speeches, shooting was not finished. One of the most difficult scenes for everyone to film, although it had no special effects, was the epilogue. It had originally been recorded at King's Cross (permission had been obtained, and a platform had been closed for production) in May. Because it was filmed in a public place, some photos were taken by spectators and leaked online. Fans criticized the appearance of the characters. While Harry Potter had to look 37, the techniques that had been applied to both Radcliffe and Grint made them look closer to 50, while Emma Watson didn't even appear to have aged and still looked like Hermione who had just left school. The post-production team noticed the same thing as the fans when they saw the reel and tried to fix it with effects, but there was no CGI that worked. Almost as if it were a play of fate forcing them to make the epilogue the last scene to film, in December 2010 they brought the actors together again in King's Cross to reshoot the scene: this time they used just a little makeup, which was then edited and retouched with digital effects.

Warner Bros. knew that both parts of *Deathly Hallows* were going to be a success, and it bet heavily on marketing. Initially, the promotion started with both films at the same time. The first official poster, released in July 2010, showed the Hogwarts castle on fire with the slogan "It all ends" (which was going to be reused to promote only Part Two), and the release date of the two films. The first trailer for the public claimed that the premiere was the "Motion Picture Event Of A Generation", which caused a bit of discussion, especially in other fandoms that did not share Harry Potter as something so important and revolutionary in the film industry.

Part One premiered on November 19, 2010, worldwide, with the usual premiere in London on the 10th, and in New York on the 15th. Days before launch, it had sold out more than 1,000 theatres in the United States, making it the fifth highest-grossing film ever. However, two days before the premiere, the first 36 minutes of the film was leaked on the Internet. Many suspected that the footage had been purposely leaked from the production company itself to generate even more press.

Harry Potter and the Deathly Hallows - Part 1 was a complete success. The premiere at midnight in the United States grossed $24 million, making it the third highest-grossing release in history at the time, behind *Eclipse* (2010) and *New Moon* (2009) in the *Twilight* saga. Globally, *Deathly Hallows - Part 1* grossed $330 million in its first weekend, and in its entire stay in theatres around the world it reached $960 million dollars, surpassing all previous Harry Potter films, except for *The Philosopher's Stone*. The press reviews were very favorable. All agreed that it was the best film in the series based on story, performances, emotion, and special effects. *The Deathly Hallows - Part 1* was nominated for two Academy Awards: Best Special Effects and Best Art Direction.

Even though part two had already been filmed, editing was underway, and the material was available, Warner Bros. preferred to pause before starting the promotion of *The Deathly Hallows - Part 2*. It was in March 2011 when the first clips and the first official poster came to light. While for *Part 1* the slogan had been "Nowhere is safe," Part Two focused more on the concept of closure and hovered around that idea: "It all ends," alluding to Harry's adventure, but also to the series.

The eighth and final film was released on July 15, 2011, worldwide, with two Avant Premieres. The first in Trafalgar Square, in the city of London, on 7th. Fans from around the world traveled to the event, some of them waiting at the venue a week before it to be as close as possible to the actors, and obviously, to J.K. Rowling, who also attended.

The first to arrive was Rupert Grint, after four in the afternoon, and he began signing autographs for the fans. The red carpet started in Trafalgar Square, but it extended to Leicester Square, where all the previous releases were and where this film would be screened as well. The distance between the two squares is over a kilometer, making this red carpet the longest in history. At about six in the evening, Emma Watson joined. An hour later, Daniel Radcliffe, at the same time as J.K. Rowling, arrived at the scene.

The actors signed autographs and spoke to the press. A stage was also set up where the three main actors and J.K. Rowling said a few words. The author was moved by the screams of the almost 8,000 fans, according to the organization, who watched and listened from the stands. "Maybe I'll just write another one," Rowling began her speech, implying that she would miss the love of the fans. "That is a joke," she quickly clarified. Tearfully, she dedicated words to the producers and directors who passed through the series, as well as to the cast. "Of the actors, I can only say I could never have dreamt the talent we'd have in these films, but there are seven that in private I refer to as "The big seven", and that's Dan, Rupert, Emma, Matt, Evanna, Bonnie, and Tom. And they cannot know how much I love them, what amazing things they did for my favourite characters," alluding to the teenagers who played Harry, Ron, Hermione, Neville, Luna, Ginny, and Draco. Finally, to close while still deeply moved, Rowling mentioned the words that were recorded not only for the fans who had the opportunity to see her live, but also for those around the world who would later listen to them in recordings or reports: "No story lives unless someone wants to listen. So thank you, all of you, thank you for queuing for the books all these years, thank you for camping out in a wet Trafalgar Square. [...] Dan has already said it, but the stories we love best do live in us forever. So whether you come back by page or by the big screen, Hogwarts will always be there to welcome you home."

Harry Potter and the Deathly Hallows - Part 2 broke all expectations. In the United States and Canada alone, it raised more than $380 million, and globally it exceeded the $1.34 billion. It was the highest-grossing Harry Potter film, the 2011 highest-grossing film of the year, and became one of the top 20 highest-grossing films of all time. It also held the records for fastest film reaching $500 million (6 days), $900 million (15 days), and $1 billion (19 days). In the UK and Ireland alone, it raised nearly $15 million on the day of its release. All the media agreed that it was the end that the series deserved. *The Daily Telegraph* even printed "This is monumental cinema" (Womack, 2011). The only critique was that the film felt like a grand finale that could not be detached from its predecessor, and not a self-sustaining film. It earned three Academy Award nominations: Best Art Direction, Best Makeup, and Best Visual Effects. The film won a BAFTA Award in the latter category.

It took a while for the legacy of the Harry Potter film series to be recognized. In retrospect, it has undoubtedly influenced the world of cinema. It has been one of the first franchises to establish the idea, copied by other studios, that a succession of films belonging to the same fantastic world is a success. The Harry Potter series was the first to split an ending into two films, a policy that was adopted by *The Hobbit* (2012), *Twilight Saga: Breaking Dawn* (2011), *The Hunger Games: Mockingjay* (2014), and *Avengers: Infinity War* (2018). It was also a clean-up for the adaptation of youth literature to the big screen, adding to those already mentioned is *The Divergent Series: Allegiant* (2016).

Its monetary success has been resounding. Harry Potter is the second highest grossing series in history, only behind the Marvel Cinematic Universe (MCU). The world of Harry Potter has an advantage. Eight films were produced, while Marvel has twenty-three to date. Rowling's world surpasses franchises such as *Star Wars*, *James Bond*, *Batman* and *Jurassic Park*, among others.

Although fans generally place books one step above movies, it is undisputed that films were the fuel the Wizarding World needed to assert itself globally in the Muggle world. With their differences and mistakes, they managed to make the series become popular and reach more people, growing the passion for the phenomenon. Even if prequels or sequels continue to be produced, canon or not, it will be impossible to relive the years when the world of Harry Potter was formed through books and movies. Those years did not end in 2007, when the seventh book was published, but in 2011, with the eighth film. J.K. Rowling herself says that she did not cry at the launch of the last book, but she did at the premiere of the last movie. She, like most, knew that it was the end.

CHAPTER EIGHT

Expanding the Universe

"I no longer write for money. I do it for my own satisfaction and loyalty to the fans."
J.K. Rowling (Treneman, 2003)

Books and movies are the mainstays of the Harry Potter phenomenon, but merchandising is the third wheel that also helped the brand go further. In 2011, the sale of all kinds of products related to the Harry Potter brand exceeded the profits of the movies and books. Warner Bros. reported revenue of $7 billion from merchandising, while movies generated $6.4 billion, and books "just" $1.2 billion (Kruhly, 2011). This wave of related products has its origin in 1999, when Warner Bros. acquired the rights to the Harry Potter films and to market its products. The company was part of Time Warner, a media conglomerate that the following year was bought by AOL, turning it into AOL Time Warner. In this way, AOL Time Warner could advertise the brand in the different media it managed to give it more reach such as an article in *People* magazine, a segment on CNN, or even a commercial on Cartoon Network.

It was in the year 2000, when the films were announced and people began to know about them, that Warner Bros. began to sign licensing agreements with Mattel, Hasbro, Electronic Arts, Coca-Cola and Lego, among others. However, the products these companies made needed to be approved by J.K. Rowling. When negotiating the rights to the films and merchandising with Warner Bros., the author agreed to maintain creative control in exchange for receiving less money in the agreement. The writer personally vetoed having Harry Potter as part of McDonald's Happy Meals because she felt it didn't seem like the right place for her character. Coca-Cola was another case where Rowling was able to prevail. Although the company acquired the rights for its products to promote the Harry Potter films for $150 million, there were a couple of important conditions. First, the soda company had to donate money to community projects, and $18 million to *Reading is Fundamental*, a non-profit organization that promotes children's reading. Second, no Coca-Cola product could appear in the Harry Potter movies. Finally, Coca-Cola could not reference or use images of Harry Potter (either from the books or the movies) in its own products that were not part of the movie campaign. Fans might remember the Coca-Cola cans with images from the first film, and the glass bottles with stills from the second film, the last one in which the company participated. Its promotion also included plastic cups with images from the film and even owl stuffed animals. However, some fans were not happy with Coca-Cola representing the brand and *Save Harry* was born, a campaign launched by the Centre for Science in the Public Interest that claimed that Coca-Cola was unhealthy for consumption by children and was a bad example for them. The campaign, which eventually created its own website, invited fans to write letters to Rowling to end the contract and donate their earnings, estimated at $15 million, to nutrition campaigns. While *Save Harry* generated a lot of noise in the mainstream US media, it never achieved its goal. However, it's hard to tell whether the movement was the reason that Coca-Cola did not continue to participate in the publicity of the following films.

One of the keys to merchandising success was not flooding the market with products. Just as the tactic of not giving the fans everything they wanted worked with the launch of the books, where secrecy generated anxiety and desire, something similar occurred with the licensed products. For example, in 2004, the year that *Harry Potter and the Prisoner of Azkaban* was released, there were more *Spider-Man 2* and *Shrek 2* products on the market than *Harry Potter* (not only from the third film but from the franchise in general). In 2006, between the fourth and fifth films, and between the sixth and seventh books, the number of licensed products of the animated film, *Cars,* doubled *Harry Potter.* Not saturating the market also made everything that went on sale demanded by fans.

The first batch of merchandising is nostalgic for older fans, as it was made entirely from pre-movie illustrations, without being contaminated by images of the great Hollywood productions. In these illustrations, made by Fred Bode and Chet Phillips, fans could see how the wizards are dressed in jeans underneath their robes, for example. Still, Bode and Phillips were in contact with Rowling herself to be as faithful as possible to the novels. "On one occasion I was fortunate to receive guidance from J.K. Rowling in regards to the look of the Sorting Hat. Warner Brothers team had put forward a puffy, rounded cartoonish version of the hat. She preferred a more traditional pointy witch's hat version that she supplied to me via fax", remembers Chet. The illustrations were part of the merchandise for 2000 and 2001, until the film was released. They were used mainly in stationery items such as notebooks, diaries, and pens, but board games and even action figures were also made. With the release of the films, they gradually disappeared. A year after the release of the second film in theaters, Panini released a sticker album in 2003 of *Harry Potter and the Chamber of Secrets* with these illustrations instead of film scenes. The explanation is that it was the first year where Panini had no reason to put out a Harry Potter album. In 2000, they released the first album based on the art from Bode and Phillips. In 2001 and 2002, an album based on the movies was released, and in 2003 there was nothing left on the market. This was why the company made the decision. After this, Panini only published albums from the films and not from illustrations.

Warner Bros.' thirst also affected the books. Translators from different parts of the world, who oversaw the foreign language editions of the Harry Potter books, were requested by Warner Bros. to keep the original names in English for the characters, places and other proper names. The reason was that children and adults quickly identified the different Harry Potter brands that appeared in the merchandise. A clear example is Dumbledore, who in Italian is Albus Silente. Children did not associate the Headmaster of Hogwarts with Albus Dumbledore when they saw that name on the packaging of the action figures. Keeping everything unified and under the same standard, Warner Bros. secured trademarks worldwide.

Additionally, all Harry Potter translations that were produced after 2000 have the same cover art as the American edition produced by Mary GrandPré. The reason for this is that a few months after acquiring the rights to the films, Warner

Bros. also acquired the trademarks of the world of Harry Potter, such as the names of the characters or made-up names like Hogwarts and Quidditch. Not only that, but they also acquired the illustrations created by Mary GrandPré and even the title design, which made their first appearances on the Scholastic covers, and were later used as the official logo in all the films. The copyright page clarifying that Warner Bros. owns the rights to the entire art and related works can be seen in reprints of Scholastic books starting in the year 2000. If someone wants to publish Harry Potter in a language that currently doesn't have a translation, they must purchase the rights to do so and get permission to reproduce the cover art.

Of course, too much merchandising needed a larger outlet. In December 2012, The Harry Potter Shop at Platform 9¾ opened, serving as an official store with all Harry Potter related products: books, DVD sets, official merchandise, and limited collectibles. The store is located in King's Cross, London. Hundreds of fans take photos inside the station, in front of a brick wall with the poster of the platform where a cart, midway through the wall was placed. There is a professional photographer for most of the day who takes photos that can later be bought from the official store next door. At peak times there are lines of up to a hundred people to take their photo in front of the wall.

In November 2016, at the premiere for *Fantastic Beasts and Where to Find Them*, another official store was opened but this time in Heathrow, London's main airport. It was placed there to serve the more than 16 million passengers who use Terminal 5 of the airport annually. For many years people preferred to bring souvenirs from The Beatles or Sherlock Holmes, but little by little Harry Potter began to occupy that place, especially for the new generation. In 2021, a store with three floors opened in

Manhattan, The Harry Potter New York Store. Spanning over 1,800 square meters, the store offers exclusive merchandise, photo opportunities, and virtual reality experiences. However, the largest Harry Potter store is not in New York, or in London, or in Edinburgh, but 35 kilometers from the British capitol in Leavesden.

Just a year after the start of World War II, Leavesden Aerodrome was built in conjunction with the Air Ministry[25] and de Havilland company. By the end of the war, the place had become the largest factory in the world (in terms of production). The British government lost interest in the place, and de Havilland obtained full control over the factory. Through the years there were many owners, but it finally fell into the hands of Rolls-Royce, who used the factory to manufacture engines for airplanes and helicopters. In the early 1990s, following the Black Wednesday crisis, the manufacturing industry fell, so Rolls-Royce tried to sell the airfield. They were unsuccessful, and by 1994 they planned to convert the 80-hectare site into a golf course and hotel. Fate intervened in another way.

EON Productions, the studio behind the James Bond films, was producing *GoldenEye* (1995) at the time. Pinewood Studios, which had been the home of the previous films, was already occupied and could not be used to shoot this new movie. The production company quickly went out to look for alternatives and found the abandoned Leavesden grounds. Empty hangars were perfect for making film sets, and factories were transformed into buildings and offices, so EON Productions decided to rent the location. The success of *GoldenEye* prompted other productions to be interested in filming there.

---

[25] Although it may sound like a Ministry of the world of Harry Potter, it was a real ministry belonging to the British government during the WWII.

In 1996, *Star Wars: Episode I – The Phantom Menace* (1999) worked there for two years, and then Tim Burton's *Sleepy Hollow* was filmed in 1998. When *Harry* Potter's turn came in 2000, Warner Bros. also decided to rent the location for the first production of the series.

Due to the large number of locations used, most of the sets were occupied by *Harry Potter*, although some other movies were also filmed at the site through the years: *Sweeney Todd: The Demon Barber of Fleet Street* (2007) and *Sherlock Holmes* (2009), which leveraged the Victorian tone of the *Harry Potter* sets, and other movies such as Nolan's *Batman* trilogy and *Charlie and the Chocolate Factory (2005).*

Around 2010, when the production of the eight *Harry Potter* films was ending, Warner Bros. decided to buy the lot from the company MEPC, which owned it at the time. The company had to wait for the approval of the local council, and eventually Warner Bros. was allowed to take over the property with the promise of investing $161 million to remodel and improve the place. Currently, Warner Bros. shoots its films there, but also rents the studios privately for other productions.

In addition to the existing studios (A through I), Warner Bros. decided to create two more: J and K[26]. These studios would be used to create a permanent exhibition of Harry Potter so that fans could visit the film sets, see the costumes and props, and learn about the special effects created for the film. *Warner Bros. Studio Tour London - The Making of Harry Potter* was announced in 2010 and tickets went on sale in October 2011. It was opened to the public in March 2012.

In the permanent exhibition, the main set is the Great Hall with the long tables that are seen in the films. Fans can

---

[26] A simple coincidence with the author's initials.

appreciate the props and architectural details, and other sets such as the Gryffindor common room, the dungeons where Snape teaches Potions classes or Dumbledore's own office, among others. Other locations are the exterior of Privet Drive and the Potter house in Godric's Hollow. Towards the end of the tour, there is a 1:24 scale Hogwarts model that was used for all the aerial shots seen in the movies. This room, which has lighting that alternates from day to night and back again so that visitors can appreciate the castle at different times of day, is the icing on the cake, and possibly the favorite place for fans who visit. The exit leads to an impressive store with all the Harry Potter products, including the new objects belonging to the *Fantastic Beasts* films. From clothes, stationery, ornaments, toys, collectibles, paintings and even books, it's possibly the most complete store of all, only matched by the recent New York flagship. There's even a wand on display signed by J.K. Rowling.

The attraction, which created 300 jobs in the area, receives around 6,000 visitors per day. To continue attracting those who have already been, temporary exhibitions and specific events are held, such as *Breakfast at Hogwarts*, where visitors can have breakfast on the set of the Great Hall—just like a Hogwarts student. The events are with limited capacity and include a special tour.

The entire studio remodeling was completed in March 2013, a year after the attraction opened to the public. On April 26, 2013, Prince William, along with his wife Kate and his brother Harry, went to the facility and made the opening official. They took the Harry Potter tour: "Harry is just excited to see a real-life talking owl. I haven't yet told him Harry Potter is fictional-so please don't let the secret out just yet," William joked about his brother, then added, "The journey today began most obviously after the legendary story by inspiring author J.K. Rowing. Translating her phenomenal imagination on to paper in the form of the Harry Potter series. But in another sense the journey today began way before, since this country has a long and proud literary and visual arts history" (Perring, 2013).

For those who wish to visit the Great Hall, walk the corridors of Hogwarts, see the entrance to the Chamber of Secrets, get on the Ford Anglia and the Knight Bus, walk through Diagon Alley, and for a few moments, feel part of the world of the *Harry Potter* movies, there is no better option than visiting the *Warner Bros. Studio Tour London - The Making of Harry Potter*. However, for those who want to immerse themselves in Hogwarts and feel something closer to magic, there is another alternative.

The first rumors of a Harry Potter theme park began in 2003, when only five books had been published and two movies had been filmed. In a meeting with his employees, Bob Gault, the president of Universal Orlando, told them that Disney had already reached an agreement with the Harry Potter brand, and that Universal would look to *The Lord of the Rings*. The rumor did not seem so crazy: Disney, through its ABC channel, had acquired the rights to broadcast the first two Harry Potter films on television, in a deal that was around $140 million. It was expected that later Disney closed another deal with Warner Bros. to add Harry Potter attractions to their parks.

However, Disney did not have these rights, but Gault and his team believed they had them. The confusion came from Universal's own team. The company was very interested in adding Harry Potter to its parks, as it was shaping up to be the franchise of the future, and the time for negotiation was now. For that, they prepared a proposal for a show with real actors and stuntmen. The idea was to fill the stage with all kinds of effects, like cauldrons that would overflow liquids and steam, and magic brooms that would fly through the air. But the best was the end of the show, where Harry, Hermione and Ron would finally face Voldemort. The final battle would culminate in the triumph of the trio against Voldemort, who would die and disappear as he was consumed by the flames of the spells that have been cast on him. Even using stuntmen, this was very dangerous, so the Universal Creative team worked with an animatronic replacement that would be Voldemort in the final act, with a robe made of a material that would ignite quickly and show more flames.

The team went with this show proposal which was not based on any of the books but was a separate story that tried to capture the essence of the series, and presented it to J. K. Rowling's team. However, when they contacted the representatives to schedule a meeting, they received a decline. *Thank you, but the rights have already been acquired*, was the message they received. Thus, the people of Universal assumed that Disney was the one who had beaten them, but they were wrong as it was Warner Bros. itself which had also acquired the rights to develop Harry Potter attractions.

Despite being wrong, Bob Gault was not so far from the truth. Disney was very interested in adding the Harry Potter franchise to its parks, and over the next few years it tried. But Rowling's requirements were nearly impossible for the Mickey Mouse company to meet. Among some of those that were rumored to be true in public, Rowling requested that Hogwarts Castle be as large as possible to be like the one described in the books, which would mean building a larger structure than the iconic Cinderella Castle at Magic Kingdom Park, something Disney refused to do. Ultimately, Universal received the rights, but not before having to agree to Rowling's terms.

The company wanted to offer pizza and hamburgers to its visitors, but the author allowed only British food. On the other hand, Coca-Cola had an agreement to sell all its products in every corner of Universal's parks, but Rowling would not allow a bottle to be sold in The Three Broomsticks. After so many comings and goings, Coca-Cola finally accepted that it could not market any of its products in the Potter area. The folks at Universal were also reluctant to sell the Weasley family sweaters, considering that no one would buy one in July in Florida. Rowling insisted that they should be offered, and finally ended up being right, since they are one of the most sought-after products by fans.

It was in early 2007 that rumors of the deal began to appear on the internet, but the contract between Warner Bros. and Universal wasn't signed until May. In the document, it was clarified that Universal would have the rights to use content from *Harry Potter and the Deathly Hallows*, which had not yet been published, and the next films yet to be released. A few days after the agreement was signed, on May 31st, the news was officially communicated to fans around the world. "The plans I've seen look incredibly exciting, and I don't think fans of the books or films will be disappointed", Rowling said about it (Universal Studios, 2007). The announcement informed fans that the park would be ready by 2009, and that it would be a "Theme park within a theme park" (Universal Studios, 2007), meaning that The Wizarding World of Harry Potter would be a special section within the park of Universal's Islands of Adventure in Orlando, Florida. One of the most important things about the announcement was that Stuart Craig, who was in charge of the movie sets, would also be involved in the design of the park, so that the different sets were as faithful as possible to what people saw on the big screen. Among attractions that fans could enjoy, there was Hogwarts Castle and Hogsmeade. The latter served as a place to buy merchandise and eat foods mentioned in the Harry Potter books.

Although construction for the park began within a few months of the announcement, the promised date was not reached, and it was quickly pushed back to 2010. As the Islands of Adventure area where the Harry Potter section would be located was closed to the public, the organization placed posters around it pretending to be from the Ministry of Magic, following the design style of the films with captions that read "Magic at Work. Your patience is requested", so as not to spoil the atmosphere of the place.

The work was completely finished at the beginning of June 2010 when the soft opening began. The event took place on June 16th and included the actors, crew members from the films, J. K. Rowling, and representatives of Universal Orlando. The ceremony ended with a performance by the Orlando Philharmonic Orchestra, led by John Williams (composer of the films' soundtrack). Two days later another event was held only with the actors. The theme park was then presented to the public and certain television channels made a live broadcast.

All of Universal's effort to secure the rights to Harry Potter was not in vain. Attendance at the park was up 66% the first year, surpassing the attendance at the Animal Kingdom and Hollywood Studios parks of its competitor Disney. "Things have really reversed: Disney used to lead. Now Disney's following Universal," said Gary Goddard, who worked for both companies designing sections of the parks (Leonard and Palmeri, 2017). Today, Disney is trying to regain its leadership with sections in its theme parks of major film franchises such as *Avatar* and *Star Wars*. However, Universal continues to extend its Harry Potter reach. In July 2014, at the Universal Studios

Japan, in the city of Osaka, The Wizarding World of Harry Potter was also inaugurated. It contains the same attractions like Hogwarts Castle. It also contains a Great Lake, the lake that sits just outside of Hogwarts Castle.

The Wizarding World of Harry Potter expanded further in Florida, though not within the same park. On July 8, 2014, The Wizarding World of Harry Potter opened a new park at Universal Studios Florida in addition to Islands of Adventure, adding Diagon Alley and Gringotts. Both sections are connected by the Hogwarts Express, which visitors can board and watch a movie through the windows as if they were traveling across the British meadows. While many fans were happy with the announcement (as there were more Harry Potter attractions to enjoy), others complained, because it meant paying for two tickets, one for each park. Sales and the number of visitors did not decrease because of the complaints, but resulted in quite the opposite. Every day more fans travel to Orlando to feel like they are setting foot into Hogwarts.[27]

But it's not just Hogwarts that fans of the series want to visit. Just as Elvis Presley's fans go to Memphis to visit the mythical Graceland mansion, Harry Potter fans also want to see those places where the series was conceived in person. The best-known places are the cafés where Rowling wrote the first books in the series in Edinburgh. The Elephant House, located at 21 George IV Bridge, is possibly the best-known café. It has signs outside announcing it as the "Birthplace of Harry Potter" and inside there are photos of when Rowling was writing there, newspaper clippings mentioning the place, and even a book signed by Rowling herself. With fans coming to the venue from

[27] Not just Orlando. In 2016, another version of The Wizarding World of Harry Potter opened at Universal Studios Hollywood, in Los Angeles, California, being the third that exists worldwide.

all over the world, The Elephant House sells souvenirs such as postcards, cups and t-shirts.

The Nicolson's Café is the other Edinburgh building famous for hosting Rowling while she wrote *Harry Potter and the Philosopher's Stone* and *Harry Potter and the Chamber of Secrets.* Located at 6th Nicolson Street, it was run by the author's brother-in-law for many years, until it was sold and changed into a Chinese food restaurant called Buffet King. In 2009, the owner of the place, Eddie Ng, put it up for sale, and tried to sell it to Rowling herself for a million pounds, an offer that she declined. It was bought by Moira McFarlane, who ran the Spoon Café a few blocks away, and what was once the Nicolson's Café became Spoon Café Bistro, a café more like the place Rowling visited. Contrary to The Elephant House, it does not take advantage of its fame and there is only a plaque at the entrance that says: "JK ROWLING wrote some of the early chapters of HARRY POTTER in the rooms on the First Floor of this building."

Aside from the cafés, Rowling is known to have finished writing the Harry Potter series in suite 552 at the Balmoral, one of Edinburgh's most luxurious hotels. However, to enter the room and sit at the desk where the story of Harry Potter was put to an end, the price is a little more expensive than a cup of coffee. A night in the suite comes out a little over £1,000.

Of course, there are other places to visit in the Scottish capital related to Joanne's life. At number 7 South Lorne Place, meters from Leith Walk, is the first apartment where she lived with her daughter, Jessica, who was just a baby. With a simple typewriter, Rowling typed the letters she sent to literary agents to offer her book. It's not a very good area, and Rowling herself confessed that even drunks broke one of her windows with a stone one night. When the money began to come in from the sales of her books, she moved to 19 Hazelbank Terrace, into a quieter neighborhood away from the city center. Both addresses are visited by fans who want to see the places where Rowling lived when she conceived the story.

There are also tours that claim that Rowling was inspired by the George Heriot's School to create Hogwarts and Victoria Street and Candlemaker Row for Diagon Alley, but there is no evidence of these claims. What did inspire Rowling is the Greyfriars Kirkyard Cemetery, a few meters from The Elephant House. The author used to roam the cemetery reading the tombstones in search of names for her characters. Thomas Riddle is the most famous name of the place, which inspired Lord Voldemort's real name, but there is also McGonagall, Scrymgeour and even one belonging to Anne Potter (although Rowling claimed that she used Potter from her childhood neighbors, perhaps the grave triggered her memory of the surname).

It is also possible to visit locations that were important in Rowling's life before she started working on the Harry Potter books. From time to time, fans come to the houses from her childhood, in Yate, in Winterbourne and especially in Tutshill. The house there is adjacent to St Luke Church, a church Rowling visited often and where she left her signature on the guest book several times before she was 10 years old. This book was in public view, but faced with the danger of being stolen, it was removed and is now locked away. Of course, it was replaced by another guestbook, which is full of fans mimicking Rowling's signature in attempts to confuse future visitors. The Church Cottage, as the home where the author lived in her childhood, went on sale in 2011 and sold for almost £400,000. Thanks to the news of the sale, we were able to know details about its interior. There are two facts that will sound familiar to those who read *Harry Potter and the Philosopher's Stone.* First, there is a cupboard under the stairs in that house and it's much like where Harry lived during his stay with the Dursleys. Second, a trap door, hidden under a rug, opens into a basement in a similar way to how the path to the Philosopher's Stone begins in the first book of the series. There was also a small detail in the window frame of Joanne's old room. Written on it, in black marker, is says, "Joanne Rowling slept here circa 1982." In 2020 it was revealed that the person who bought the house in 2011 was J.K. Rowling herself.

Of course, the merchandising, theme parks, tours and the different ways to leverage the series helped make it what it is today. But they did not have the impact on the phenomenon that the fandom had.

* * *

The "fandom" term is used to talk about the group of followers of a hobby, an activity, a genre, or even a fashion trend. Those who are part of a fandom don't have a casual interest, but one that is constant and is reflected in different activities that they carry out both as individuals, and as a group.

The first fandom of the modern era can be assigned to Sherlock Holmes; its followers organized public demonstrations of mourning in 1893 when Sir Arthur Conan Doyle decided to kill the character, and by the end of 1890, the first pieces of fanfiction had appeared, stories created by fans based on the characters and characteristics of an original author, but with a different plot. Fans sent their Sherlock tales to Conan Doyle himself. During the 20th century, the different communities of fans began to grow, especially in the second half of the 20th century, those that focused on the science fiction and fantasy genres. The fandom began to detach itself a bit from the analysis of the product they were consuming and began to make their own creations—fanarts, fanfics and fanvids, as well as their own conventions where fans from different parts attended to celebrate and carry out thematic activities.

Although the Harry Potter fandom grew thanks to the internet, it was not the first. The followers of *The X-Files* are those who have this merit of having created the first entirely online community. But the Harry Potter fandom has undoubtedly been not only the one that has gotten the most out of it, but also the one that has shaped the online fandom culture as we know it today. The key to this was that Harry Potter began to grow while the internet became massive. The key year could be 1999. When *Prisoner of Azkaban* was released, Harry Potter was not only beginning to appear in mass media, but also the internet reached 25% of the population of England and a third of the households in North America. It's no coincidence that in the middle of that year the first fan websites, The Unofficial Harry Potter Fan Club and Harry Potter's Realm of Wizardry, were created. The latter, created by Gypsy Silverleaf, was intended not only to be a mere informative site about the series, with information and synopses of each book, but also to add editorials of what would become the backbone of the fandom—fanfiction. Such is the case that Gypsy is possibly the author of the first online fan fiction of the Wizarding World, *Harry Potter and the Man of Unknown*, a story in which Harry Potter, Dumbledore, and Snape, were featured, alongside characters that other fans had created. The text was first uploaded to FanFiction.net on September 4, 1999, marking an iconic day for the fandom. Over the next few months, the websites that would become the most popular over the years would be created.

Emerson Spartz, from Indiana, was 12 when he convinced his parents to let him become a homeschooled student. That same year, he created the MuggleNet website which is updated with the latest Harry Potter news: phenomenon, rumors, and theories. It also featured a forum where fans could discuss this new content. Spartz never imagined how popular the website would be. In 2006, he would become the co-author of the book *What Will Happen in Harry Potter 7* which speculates about the final work of the series. That not only took him on a tour throughout the country to promote it, but also the book remained on *The New York Times Bestseller List* for 6 months with over 350,000 copies sold. By 2007, the MuggleNet website generated revenues of more than $100,000 per month and Spartz considered it a job, with over 120 volunteers and 6 paid employees. "As I became less motivated by my passion for the books, I got obsessed with the entrepreneurial side of it." (Marantz, 2015)

As time went on, Spartz left Harry Potter and, in 2009, created Spartz Media, now called Dose, a company that works with viral content from the internet on more than 30 websites that receive hundreds of millions of visits daily.

A few months after the creation of MuggleNet, what would become the second most visited Harry Potter site also came to light a day after *Goblet of Fire* was released. The Leaky Cauldron, created by Kevin C. Murphy, and turned over to B.K. DeLong soon thereafter, came to life. In 2001, Melissa Anelli joined as editor, writing web news, and shortly after became General Editor and took control of the website. The Leaky Cauldron was the first fansite to publish exclusive news. While the other websites only posted news from other mass media, Anelli directly contacted the people involved in the franchise to get the information from them, which made the website stand out from the others. The Leaky Cauldron was the first fansite to also cover the film premiere of *Chamber of Secrets* and visit the film set of *Prisoner of Azkaban.* Although it now seems like a normal situation, it was something revolutionary in those days where firsthand contact was reserved for the big media.

J.K. Rowling herself in 2004, on her own website, created the "Fan Site Award" section, where she gave a symbolic award to different Harry Potter websites. Among others, MuggleNet received it that same year, and in May 2005, The Leaky Cauldron received it as well. On that same day was also announced what was possibly the highest point of both websites: the author invited Spartz and Anelli, the two leaders, for an interview at her home in Edinburgh on the evening of the book launch of *Half-Blood Prince.* Both fans read the text throughout the night to be prepared for the moment of the meeting. There, both asked questions that fans wanted to hear. At one point in the interview, Emerson called fans who expected Harry to end up in a relationship with Hermione "delusional", prompting laughter and tacit approval from Anelli and Rowling herself. This generated hundreds and thousands of messages of anger later by fans who still believed in the couple, and they had felt that they had been disrespected. This was not only from Anelli and Spartz who were their "ambassadors," but for part of the author herself too.

Despite MuggleNet being the most popular Harry Potter site, the author seemed to lean in favor of The Leaky Cauldron. In August 2005, Anelli's site launched *PotterCast*, the Harry Potter podcast. Hosted by Melissa, the internet radio show featured film actors, directors, Scholastic editors and, in December 2007. J.K. Rowling herself was interviewed on two milestone episodes in a row, and *PotterCast* became the podcast #1 on iTunes worldwide. Rowling always maintained an excellent relationship with Anelli, and when she published her book in 2008 about Pottermania and its fandom called, *Harry, A*

History[28], J.K. Rowling assisted in writing the foreword. The relationship came to an end when Anelli heavily criticized the author for her views on transgender people, and The Leaky Cauldron and Mugglenet (no longer owned by Spartz) published public letters against Rowling's opinions.

Although it may not seem like it, the relationship between official entities and fansites was not always on good terms. The first clash was in 2000. Warner Bros. had taken the franchise rights over, and apparently did not yet know how to get along with the fans. Lindsay Warde was 12 years old, lived in Ohio, and loved Harry Potter. She had decided to make a website about books and call it BestHogwarts.com. However, by choosing that name, she would never have imagined that Warner Bros. lawyers would send her threatening letters, saying that Lindsay was infringing on a trademark, breaking the law, and that she had also angered Rowling herself. Not only that, but Warner Bros. also took ownership of the domain of her website since it legally belonged to them. But Lindsay's case was not an isolated incident. It happened with fans from all over the world. Claire Field was 15 years old and living in Ipswich, England, when she received a similar letter about her website HarryPotterGuide.co.uk. But despite legal threats, Claire hired lawyers to defend her website. But Claire's case was unique in a sense: the dozens of fans who received these threats could not defend themselves, and they ended up losing their website. For this reason, 16-year-old Heather Sewell, who ran a fan site called The Daily Prophet, and Alastair Alexander, a man over thirty from London, created a website that planned to boycott the franchise. They knew that Warner Bros. had invested $150 million and questioned what if the profits did not arrive?

[28] A pun on *Hogwarts, a History*, Hermione Granger's favorite book.

"Teaching Warner Bros. a Lesson" was Heather and Alastair's project name. Both did not think it would have success.

In February 2001, an article on the matter appeared in the *USA Today* newspaper, which concluded with a plea for the case's closure in favor of the children. This made the press pay more attention to the case and it appeared in media around the world: *ABC News*, *Época* in Mexico, the *BBC* in the United Kingdom, among others. Of course, the articles were in favor of the fans and against the giant, which had created bad press for Warner Bros. and it affected its profit.

Heather and Alastair received calls from different businesses asking them to stop their campaign because people were no longer buying Harry Potter products they had in stock. Of course, Heather and Alastair continued with their project for the next several months, during which they were in negotiations with Warner Bros. while speaking with the press so as not to let the case be forgotten.

Diane Nelson, Vice President of Warner Bros. at the time, was the woman in charge of the Potter War on the giant's side. She publicly denied that the company threatened minors, but in April she personally contacted Heather, informing her that she would be sued for libel against the company, and that these comments had caused losses of thousands of dollars. Heather contacted the reporter who had written the original article for *USA Today* and told him about Nelson's call in the case, and it quickly came to light. Faced with so much negative gaze from the public, Warner Bros. had no choice but to publicly agree and dismiss the cases against fansites, especially the one against Claire Field.

One would think that from this case Warner Bros. would have learned that the best way to deal with the fandom was to join in and help it grow, because if the fandom did expand (along with their websites, for example), it would just mean good news for Harry Potter as a global brand. But this took a few years for Warner Bros to understand.

The next conflict that occurred was not with the fansites themselves (in that case Warner did seem to have learned their lesson), but with the authors of fanfiction. The FanFiction.net website, where the first known text based on Harry Potter had been uploaded, was starting to receive fictions with a lot of sexual content for adults, so the company decided to ban all Harry Potter fan fiction on its own platform. At the end of 2001, RestrictedSection.org was born, a platform specialized in fan fictions in this category, but it did not last long. In January 2002, the authors' lawyers decided to shut it down, claiming that children could find the texts that were explicitly sexual and relate them to the franchise, which was not convenient for anyone. The communication made it clear that it was the adult content that was intolerable but that they supported fanfiction aimed at children. Over the years this was confirmed, because in 2009, Rowling allowed G. Norman Lippert to continue her unofficial spin-off of James Potter. Lippert started his James Potter novels right after the release of the seventh book and posted a preview of the first on a very professional website, which caused rumors and theories that claimed that it was an eighth book in the series. The publishers of Harry Potter, as well as Warner Bros., had to come out to deny it, and Rowling's representatives requested a preview of the story to analyze it. By reading it, they authorized its publication if it was free of charge, and they extended these conditions to any Harry Potter fan fiction that was to be shared. It must not have commercial purposes, and it must not have sexual or racist content.

Some fanfiction authors knew how to give it a twist to avoid these restrictions, such as the case of Cassandra Clare, who published three stories about Draco Malfoy in her *The Draco Trilogy*. The trilogy, which contains almost 3,000 pages, had quite a positive reception among readers of the genre, which motivated Clare to rewrite the stories, making changes but keeping some of the original passages. Thus, Clare published *City of Bones*, the first book of *The Mortal Instruments* series, which has had moderate success and has even been adapted for the big screen.

The most iconic case of the legal battles towards the Harry Potter fandom starred Steve Vander Ark. In July 2000, just after the release of *Harry Potter and the Goblet of Fire*, Steve launched The Harry Potter Lexicon, a website about the series with a different approach. As a librarian, Steve was obsessed with organizing information and the project was born: an encyclopedia of all objects, characters, places, events and more in the world created by J.K. Rowling.

The website grew rapidly due to the quality of its content and was featured in different media in the United States and on the official sites of publishers, as it was an inexhaustible source of information for fans of the series. The Lexicon followed a fundamental rule to catalogue the canon of Harry Potter. Thus, while everything that appeared in the books was considered canon and was included in the online encyclopedia, everything from the films was discarded, since they were creations of the technical team and had no relation to Rowling's vision. The seriousness with which Steve Vander Ark and his group of collaborators treated the Harry Potter canon granted him a lot of respect in the environment. Steve not only catalogued the information that was available through Rowling's books and interviews, but he also cross-referenced data and expanded it. For example, he created maps of Hogwarts based on different passages in the books, and timelines and calendars for each of the books, discovering exact dates of some events even before the author herself confirmed them. Thus, when Warner Bros. wanted to add a Wizarding World timeline to the extra sections of the *Harry Potter and the Chamber of Secrets* DVD, they used the same timeline Steve Vander Ark had created for his website. Even Cheryl Klein, who was in charge of the continuity in the editorial process of the latest Harry Potter books, thanked Steve via e-mail, as she acknowledged that her team had used the web to confirm data.

In September 2006, Steve was invited to the set of *Order of The Phoenix*. He was able to meet David Heyman who confessed that Warner Bros. used his Harry Potter Lexicon daily to check data and not make any mistakes. In July 2007, Steve also visited the Electronic Arts studios, who were in charge of the video games in the series, and noticed that the office walls were full of prints from his site.

The greatest recognition for The Harry Potter Lexicon came in 2004 when Rowling awarded it with one of her Fan Site Awards. Steve was the second recipient for the award. The words that Rowling dedicated to him speak for themselves: "This is such a great site that I have been known to sneak into an internet café while out writing and check a fact rather than go into a bookshop and buy a copy of Harry Potter (which is embarrassing). A website for the dangerously obsessive; my natural home" (Rowling, 2004a). But unfortunately, the good relationship between the author and the Michigan librarian eventually came to an end.

Everything started in July 2007, just days after the seventh book was published, when director of RDR Books, Roger Rapoport, from Michigan, saw a story in local media about Steve Vander Ark as a Harry Potter expert. Rapoport contacted Vander Ark, offering him the possibility of publishing an encyclopedia based on his website. Although Vander Ark was convinced that publishing such material was illegal, he changed his mind when speaking with Rapoport, who convinced him that the guide fell under what is called "fair use" in US law. Thereby they moved forward with the project. However, Vander Ark requested a clause in his contract in which RDR Books undertook to indemnify him and bear any legal expenses in the event of a lawsuit by J.K. Rowling or any representative of their brands or licenses.

Rapoport was a businessman above all, and he wanted to take advantage of this book. So, he defined October as the deadline for publication, and forced Vander Ark to deliver the manuscript in three weeks. He wanted to take advantage of the current Harry Potter fever in the bookstores, and at the same time have the first Wizarding World encyclopedia out there since he knew that MuggleNet was working on something similar (which was later abandoned at the request of Rowling's lawyers). Rapoport wasted no time and began offering the rights to the book in other countries, such as the United Kingdom, Canada, France and even China, and even tried to sell it directly to bookstores in the United States to pave the way. The publisher wanted to keep everything shrouded in mystery. When he offered the rights in Brazil for the translation, he asked that the Harry Potter publisher in that country not be informed about the book. However, his ads looking for more and more countries to sell the translation rights was his downfall. In September, Neil Blair, lawyer to Christopher Little, saw one of these ads and took action immediately. They contacted the publisher, ordering that they do not publish the book in its current state, and that they should provide the original manuscript so that Rowling's people could review and approve it, or suggest changes. However, RDR Books refused all requests, claiming that the book was completely legal under its analysis, and even during those weeks the publisher became irate with Warner Bros. for using Steve Vander Ark's timeline created for The Lexicon website. Finally, on October 31, 2007, J.K. Rowling and her representatives filed a lawsuit against RDR Books. In January 2008, the full lawsuit consisting of 1,100 pages was filed and RDR Books had three weeks to respond. The request was based on the following points. First, The Lexicon compiled and repackaged Rowling's writing, without adding critique or comments of its own. About 80% of the text was copied from what Rowling had written. Not even certain descriptions had been changed. Second, The Lexicon would conflict with Rowling's plans to publish an encyclopedia, which she had made public. Third, the plaintiff alleged that the book contained summaries and spoilers for all seven novels, which would spoil the experience for children reading it, and it would also decrease the sale of companion books (*Quidditch Through the Ages* and *Fantastic Animals and Where to Find Them*), since these were summarized within the encyclopedia. Finally, Rowling claimed that a ruling in favor of RDR Books would hurt the future relationship between fan communities and artists as the latter would lose control over their creations. With the publication of the lawsuit, the author's closest fan sites, such as The Leaky Cauldron, came out in support of her, distancing themselves from The Harry Potter Lexicon and trying to get the rest of the fans to take the writer's side.

RDR Books responded to the lawsuit in a timely manner, in early February, arguing that Rowling wanted to claim a monopoly on reference guides over a particular text, in this case of her own, having full control over non-fiction texts that could be published about the world of Harry Potter. Communication between the two parties continued in the public sphere but also in the private one. During a private meeting, RDR Books agreed to change the title of the book from *The Harry Potter Lexicon* to *The Lexicon: An Unauthorized Guide to Harry Potter Fiction and Related Materials.* The agreement met also required the removal of a quote by J.K. Rowling which had praised the Harry Potter Lexicon website. The quote in question was meant to help promote the book and was originally featured on its cover. From April 14th thru April 16th, 2008, the trial took place in New York City, presided over by Judge Robert P. Patterson Jr.

J.K. Rowling testified on the first and third day while Steve Vander Ark testified only on the second day and could not be present the other two. The author traveled exclusively to the United States for the trial, demonstrating the importance that the matter had been for her even though it limited her to the novel she was working on[29].

During her testimony, Rowling insisted on the reasons that she believed to be fair and that she had already communicated in the lawsuit, further adding that she had taken the time to note how most of the entries in the encyclopedia copied different parts from her books, considering that "17 years of my work are being exploited here," referring to The Lexicon (Warner Bros. Entertainment, Inc. and J. K. Rowling v. RDR Books, 2008a). She also added that the book was "lazy" and that "there were many [errors]" (ibid). Although as Anthony Falzone, a lawyer for RDR Books, objected: "Copyright law does not, your Honor, permit an author to suppress a book simply because she doesn't like it" (ibid).

Steve Vander Ark did not seem happy with the situation; he burst into tears and implied that he did not want this resolution,

---

[29] Years later we would find out that she was referring to *The Casual Vacancy*.

and that he was forced by the publisher to continue with the procedure. Judge Patterson seemed to feel the same way. He went so far as to recommend that the parties should reach a common agreement, since the case seemed to be motivated more by the lawyers rather than by the clients themselves. "I repeatedly tried to say to Mr. Vander Ark, do your book, but please change it so it does not take as much of my work," (ibid) said Rowling in her role as a witness. Rapoport assured the team that this possibility never presented itself to them and that Rowling and her team only wanted to block the publication of the book without providing any opportunity to correct it or modify it.

After the three days of trial, in September, Judge Patterson made his verdict in favor of J.K. Rowling and Warner Bros., assuring that The Lexicon appropriated too much work from the writer, so a permanent ban on the book was necessary to avoid future similar works that would largely copy other original authors. However, he made it clear that this was the only problem with The Lexicon, as the guidebooks were totally valid. He also rejected Rowling's argument that a possible Harry Potter encyclopedia interfered with the author's plans, claiming that "the market for reference guides to the Harry Potter works is not exclusively hers to exploit or license" (Warner Bros. Entertainment, Inc. and J. K. Rowling v. RDR Books, 2008b). This verdict was favorable to both parties. Rowling managed to win the case and ban the publication, while RDR Books got publicity for the book, and the possibility of publishing it by making the necessary modifications. If the material did not copy as much from Rowling and included more comments and material from the author, it would be totally legal. And that is how *The Lexicon* was finally published in January 2009, almost a year and a half after the date it was intended to be released.

Steve Vander Ark privately acknowledges that his relationship with Rowling and her agents has since improved, and that the text that was finally released met with the approval of Christopher Little's team, with whom he worked closely with to meet all the requirements.

* * *

The growth of the fandom at the same time as the internet was important for teenagers around the world to adopt Harry Potter as more than just a book series. It encouraged millions of readers worldwide to explore the online discussion forums and websites and meet other fans from different countries with whom they could interact with, relate to, and feel identified with. A strong sense of belonging grew, forging friendships and creating families of those who met due to the passion that the Wizarding World brought forth.

However, the internet was small, and the fandom also moved to the "real world." HP Education Fanon, Inc., a non-profit organization focused on the dissemination of academic programs on Rowling's creation, held the first fan convention in 2003 at Disney World. Named Nimbus 2003, it was the first occasion where fans gathered to discuss, learn, and have fun. There were even talks from scholars who specialized in Harry Potter. The event had approximately 600 attendees, a number that would grow at subsequent Harry Potter conventions.

In the future, there would be at least one convention per year, and up to five, as in the case of Phoenix Rising 2007, Sonorus 2007, Enlightening 2007, Sectus 2007 and Prophecy 2007 (the first three in the United States and the last two in London and Toronto respectively). At that time, fans were no longer looking for academics or serious exhibitors. Reactions to the talks by older researchers were generally boredom and disappointment. The topics that were presented as revolutionary had been already discussed by fans on online forums. Perhaps the most well-known convention for the Harry Potter fandom is LeakyCon, organized by The Leaky Cauldron site, which had its first event in 2009 in Boston, Massachusetts, and so far, it has had more than ten different events, spread across the United States, England and Ireland. On average, at its last event, LeakyCon received 5,000 attendees.

Harry Potter fans don't only go to talks when they leave the internet. One of the phenomena that the fandom created was Wizard Rock, a musical genre of thematic songs about the series. Most of them are sung in the first person by a character in the story, and almost always in a humorous tone. In 2000, an American punk and pop band called Switchblade Kittens wrote the first Wizard Rock song, *Ode to Harry*, from Ginny Weasley's point of view. But the first authentic band of the genre was Harry and the Potters, formed by the DeGeorge brothers almost as a joke in 2002. During its first months it gained followers on its MySpace profile and played in different bookstores in the United States, and in 2003 Harry and the Potters decided to release its first self-titled album which coincided with the release of *Order of The Phoenix*. The brothers had the idea of doing a show in some events that the stores organized for the release of *Harry Potter and the Order of the Phoenix*, and what they achieved was more than they expected. They were booked for five different shows in a period of 24 hours.

In 2004, they released their album *Voldemort Can't Stop the Rock!*, which was very well received overall, and allowed them to go on tour not only in the United States, but the following year in England and Netherlands. During this tour, Warner Bros. contacted them to inform them that they were violating copyright laws with that project, although it all ended in a formal arrangement between the parties in which Warner Bros. authorized them to sell their music online and tour, but the sale of merchandising had to be done only in their concerts and not through websites. Harry and the Potters inspired other people to create their bands within the same genre, such as Draco and the Malfoys, The Whomping Willows and The Remus Lupin. Like Harry and the Potters, the other bands take the stage disguised as the characters who give the group its name. Although they played in bookstores and fan conventions (such as LeakyCon), their growth was such that in 2007 Wrockstock[30], the first Wizard Rock festival, was organized in the city of Ozark, Missouri. It was planned as an annual event, and its last event was in 2013, with an average of 500 people and 15 bands in each of them.

The DeGeorge brothers not only changed the fandom with music, but through social activism as well. In 2005, together with Andrew Slack, they founded The Harry Potter Alliance, a non-profit organization that "fights the Dark Arts in the real world by using parallels from Harry Potter". Over the 10 years that the organization has been active, it has fought against social inequalities and abuses in work environments, with campaigns against Wal-Mart and Warner Bros, requesting that the chocolate for the Chocolate Frogs sold in the theme parks should come from factories where working conditions are respected. Due to pressure from The Harry Potter Alliance, in 2015, Warner Bros. committed to meeting this requirement for its products.

In addition, The Harry Potter Alliance has social action campaigns such as Accio Books, in which book donations are received in communities that need them most. This campaign,

---

[30] A pun for the Woodstock Rock Festival.

which is repeated every year, has already donated almost 100,000 books to public libraries or schools where children with the lowest resources go. In 2010, after the earthquake that struck Haiti, the organization created a rapid campaign to send aid to the country. About 100 items were auctioned, including signed books and a letter that Rowling herself donated to the initiative, and raised $123,000, which was used to send five planes to Haiti filled with medical supplies (each of the planes was named after a Harry Potter character).

Rowling often collaborates with the organization, donating signed books for the auctions she runs, and the author has also publicly congratulated them. In 2008 she gave them the last Fan Site Award: “Long overdue, I give you the HP Alliance (as mentioned in Time Magazine!) I am honoured and humbled that Harry's name has been given to such an extraordinary campaign, which really does exemplify the values for which Dumbledore's Army fought in the books. To Andrew and all the others who work on this most inspirational website: the world needs more people like you.” (Rowling, 2007m)

Just as the fandom expanded in the field of music, so it did in the field of sports. In 2005, at the University of Middlebury in Vermont, Muggle Quidditch, an adaptation of the sport invented by J.K. Rowling, but played “in the real world,” combining soccer, handball and rugby, was created.

The players run across a grass field and must score points by throwing the *quaffle* through the goals that stand in for the three hoops, the original Quidditch goals. If a player is hit by a *bludger*, they are out of the game until they touch one of their goals again. The golden snitch is another ball, attached to the snitch runner's waist, a neutral player who will try to prevent the Seekers from catching it. Unlike the ‘original Quidditch,’ catching the snitch in Muggle Quidditch is worth only thirty points.

The sport was quickly adopted by different universities in the United States, and in 2007, the first Quidditch World Cup was played in Vermont (despite being a World Cup, only universities in the US participated). Since then and so far, Muggle Quidditch has spread throughout the world, with amateur leagues in France, Italy, Germany, Australia, Canada, Belgium, Argentina, Spain, and Mexico.

Currently, it is estimated that there are more than five hundred Muggle Quidditch teams in the world which belong to an association affiliated with the International Quidditch Association (IQA), a registered non-profit organization that tries to group and organize the new sport worldwide. The IQA also promotes sport as a tool to increase athletic participation and encourage LGBT activities, as it is mandatory that all teams have at least two players of two different genders (regardless of sex). The IQA is also in charge of the IQA World Cup, the World Cup that is held every two years and was hosted by Oxford (England, 2012), Burnaby (Canada, 2014) and Frankfurt (Germany, 2016), and which saw the United States as champion of the first two competitions and Australia in the last.

* * *

Harry Potter as a brand for Warner Bros. was the springboard that allowed the company to grow and be the business it is today. It has given the opportunity to expand and reach markets that, before Harry Potter, had been unthinkable for a series based on books. Even with the limitations imposed by Rowling herself, Harry Potter products (and projects) have been of all sorts of varieties, but more importantly, successful.

However, the growth of Harry Potter was not based on Warner Bros. alone.

Without thinking of an economic reward, the fans appropriated Pottermania as such and have taken it beyond limits with all kinds of creations: from fanfics and fanarts to their own musical genre and a new sport. If Harry Potter is a global and generational phenomenon as we know it today, it's not only by monetary investment of a company like Warner Bros., but also by the passion of fans who saw themselves reflected in the ideals of history and found a sense of belonging to other fans as well. That is why the phenomenon will continue to grow in two different sides. On the one hand, related products, attractions, and new media where people can continue to expand the story of the boy wizard; and on the other hand, the fandom that will continue feeding back not only the story of J.K. Rowling, but of the series itself with more creativity and passion. The most important question is whether one can survive without new stories or new material. It will be difficult, because it is unlikely that the enthusiasm for the series will be relived as in those years when the wait for a new book was enjoyed as much as the launch itself. New generations have the difficult task and responsibility to take the legacy and continue revolutionizing the world with it. It's difficult, but not impossible as long as Rowling's magic lives in a movie, in a play, or in a *Wizarding World* book.

CHAPTER NINE

19 Years Later

"Is it true that Harry and Draco
will have to get together and fight evil?"
"Don't believe everything you read on the net!"
J.K. Rowling to a fan (JK Rowling chat, 2000c)

Poetically, as if it had been planned for almost two decades, nineteen years after the publication of *Harry Potter and the Philosopher's Stone* in the UK, the Wizarding World of J.K. Rowling returned, not with one, but two stories that expanded the past and the future of the Harry Potter universe. While one of them featured Harry as the protagonist, along with his children and his now-adult friends, the other goes back seventy years and shows the war of the *Wizarding World* at the time, though it does with characters we already know.

As already developed in previous chapters, by 2001, after the publication of the *Goblet of Fire*, JK Rowling published two Hogwarts textbooks for charity, one of them being *Fantastic Beasts and Where to Find Them*, written by the fictional author, Newt Scamander. That was the book that Lionel Wigram, executive producer of the Harry Potter films, chose in 2011 as a possible continuation of the series. Feeling nostalgic over the series end, he wanted to expand the Wizarding World, though he knew that Rowling had promised not to publish any more books, so he was forced to investigate what had already been written.

Originally, Wigram devised the adaptation of *Fantastic Beasts and Where to Find Them* as a fictional documentary presented by Newt Scamander, where viewers would see the different creatures in their natural habitat. This adaptation would be comprehensible if it had a similar format as in the book, which is a kind of encyclopedia of creatures from the Wizarding World. Wigram and Heyman brought the idea to Warner Bros., and it seemed viable. It was an opportunity to keep alive the flame of Harry Potter, that had brought to the studio many opportunities and benefits. The next step was to convince Rowling.

Heyman and Wigram brought the proposal closer to the author. "That was suggested to Jo who liked the idea but said that she had been thinking of a feature film with Newt Scamander at its centre" recalls Heyman, who needed Kevin Tsujihara, the CEO of Warner Bros. Entertainment, to finish convincing her. Tsujihara was the main person responsible in doing it: "When I say he made 'Fantastic Beasts' happen, it isn't P.R.-speak but the literal truth," says Rowling (Barnes, 2014).

Tsujihara traveled to the United Kingdom in 2012 for a personal dinner with the author and tell her the proposal. Apart from the meal, only one subsequent phone call was needed to persuade Rowling. Nonetheless, the author was not entirely delighted with the idea of the documentary, and she proposed something else. She took out an old sketch of a story that she had written and then developed it further. Although the people of Warner Bros. couldn't be more delighted with the idea, the negotiation was not that straightforward. It took more than a year, including several trips to the UK for meetings, to convince Rowling to go forward with *Fantastic Beasts*. They had to discuss the creative control of this new series, which had no fixed material on which it would be based. While Rowling would provide the background, what limits and freedoms would Warner Bros. have at the time to carry it out? The author was always very careful of what was done with her wizarding world, and very overprotective, especially in the control of the cinematic studio, so the arrangement was not easy.

Rowling demanded total creative control, but the studio wasn't convinced that she could handle the job, since the author had no experience in creating films. They finally agreed that she would write the script by herself. The deal was closed, and the author also got the concession that Warner Bros. was not allowed to hire anyone else to make significant changes to the script. Moreover, should the series continue, Rowling would have the privilege to approve or reject any scripts to be written for the following films. As we now know, Rowling wrote the first three films of the series herself, although the third one was in collaboration with Steve Kloves.

The official announcement was on September 12, 2013. Warner Bros. communicated a new partnership with J.K. Rowling and the Harry Potter franchise; and it claimed it would be a series of films, without specifying the number. The press released quoted Rowling saying, "It's not a sequel or a prequel to the Potter adventures" (Tartaglione, 2013). What was not yet announced was the producer or director.

David Heyman finished production of the acclaimed feature film *Gravity* (2013), starring Sandra Bullock and directed by Alfonso Cuarón. On October 1st, twenty days after the official announcement by Warner Bros, at the premiere of *Gravity* in New York, MTV News reporter, Josh Horowitz, interviewed Heyman about *Fantastic Beasts and Where to Find Them*. The producer confirmed (unofficially, but sufficient for fans) that he would work on the film.

With Heyday Films behind the film, Rowling writing it, and Warner Bros. as the distributor, there was only the director missing, and it would take a few months to find him. The author was frantically working on the script, and by November she had several drafts completed. Writing a screenplay was, if not easier, faster for her compared to writing a novel. In an interview with Emma Watson for *Wonderland* magazine in February 2015, Rowling said that the first version of the script took her only twelve days to write. As David Heyman recalls, there were differences between this new series and Harry Potter when it came to working: "We had a very clear sense of where the story was going [with Harry Potter] and in great detail. With Fantastic Beasts, that was not the case" and he adds that "We also didn't have the security of knowing that millions of readers would be interested in watching the films we were making. But we do have Jo and her boundless imagination [...]. On *Beasts*, as the screenwriter and a producer, she is more present and involved."

But while the story continued forward, a director was still being sought. In May, Alfonso Cuarón was considered. He had left a very good impression with *Harry Potter and the Prisoner of Azkaban*, had done a very good job on *Gravity* and had an extraordinary relationship with David Heyman, but the director was quick to decline, claiming that after so many years working on films with a high degree of special effects, now his interest was in simpler productions.

In the same month, Warner Bros. confirmed the film's release date: November 18, 2016, two and a half years into the future. As rumors from other directors continued, in August, *Variety* magazine exclusively confirmed ahead of the official announcement that David Yates, who had directed the last four Harry Potter films, was in command of *Fantastic Beasts and Where to Find Them*. The negotiation was almost non-existent. David Yates was vacationing in the south of France when he received a call from Heyman, commenting on a new script to read. Yates was only 100% interested when he was told that it had been written by Rowling. When reading the material, there were no longer doubts.

It was only in October that Warner Bros. announced the director's role, confirming what had also come out unofficially that they received three films, to be released in 2016, 2018 and 2020. The return of David Yates also included other names from Harry Potter's previous films, as Steve Kloves, who would serve as an advisor and consultant on the script, answer questions and give advice to the inexperienced Rowling; Stuart Craig, again in Production Design; and Tim Burke, Special Effects Supervisor, among others.

With the production team already formed, it was time to find the cast members. There were many candidates who were considered to play the main character, and, considering that the Harry Potter universe was an already-known brand, it was possible that most of them would accept the role. But once Eddie Redmayne was mentioned in the talks between the two David (Yates and Heyman), they were convinced that the actor was the chosen one. But of all the candidates, he was one of the most difficult to get to. Redmayne had just won an Academy Award for his portrayal of Stephen Hawking in *The Theory of Everything* (2014) and was about to start filming *The Danish Girl*

(2015). However, around Christmas 2014, Redmayne agreed to meet David Yates in a small pub in London's Soho, and Yates started telling him little things about a script that J.K. Rowling was writing. Redmayne knew the Harry Potter story, knew Yates had directed it, and had even fantasized about being a Weasley once. Nonetheless, at that time, before him, the story of Newt Scamander was being unfolded.

The encounters in which Yates continued to divulge details of the plot were held during the following months in London, where Redmayne was filming *The Danish Girl* (2015). By April, it had already been leaked in the media that Redmayne was the main candidate, although the name of Nicholas Hoult from *X-Men: First Class (*2011) and *Mad Max (*2015) was also rumored to be in the running. Finally, in June it was confirmed that Eddie Redmayne would play the magizoologist, Newt Scamander. What had been leaked was that three main roles were missing, since the story, which would take place in New York, will have four Americans as protagonists: two men and two women (later it would be known that this was false, since one of them was the British Scamander).

With the contract already signed, Redmayne began to work. He got his hands on the entire Rowling script, which he studied scrupulously. He reread all the books of the original series and watched the movies. He admits that he copied movements from Daniel Radcliffe and Emma Watson, especially wand movements. Redmayne spent a lot of time with experts who worked with animals daily to learn about their relationships with the creatures and all their techniques—from the way they move to the way they speak. Even the original script describes Scamander as the magical version of David Attenborough, the British naturalist known for being the television host of BBC documentaries about life on Earth.

Even with Redmayne, other actors were still missing. David Yates was too interested in the chemistry that would exist between the other actors with the already chosen one, more than the names themselves. For this reason, during a weekend in New York, Redmayne repeated the same scene in a hotel room with groups of three other actors in front of Yates. They wanted to see what the best possible combination was, and which of all of them managed to get along the best as a group. This is how Katherine Waterston (Porpentina Goldstein), Alison Sudol (Queenie Goldstein) and Dan Fogler (Jacob Kowalski) obtained their roles. However, they competed against other great actors. The role of Tina Goldstein could also have been obtained by Elizabeth Debicki or Lili Simmons; for Queenie the names of Kate Upton, Dakota Fanning and Saoirse Ronan were mentioned, and for Jacob Kowalski, Steve Zissis and Zack Pearlman. Dan Fogler achieved one of the film's most acclaimed performances and received positive feedback from both critics and fans who even started an online petition for a Jacob Kowalski spin-off. Fogler carries the character in his blood. He was born and raised in Brooklyn, and his great-grandfather was also a baker. On July 2015, Fogler was at the San Diego Comic-Con, promoting the ABC series *Secrets and Lies*, but he was also selling the *Moon Lake* comic, written and edited by himself. As he walked through the crowd, Fogler received a call from David Heyman confirming that he had gotten the role. Comic-Con would no longer be the same for the actor.

Unlike the other Harry Potter films, most of the story in *Fantastic Beasts* takes place in a city, and in fact, in a real city in the muggle world. Stuart Craig, who had been production manager for the entire Harry Potter series, returned to his role in this new film and had the enormous task of designing the film sets. The idea of filming in New York was initially considered, but there were two problems. The first one was obvious: getting the permits and filming in real city streets would have been chaotic; the second, that there was not much left standing of the architecture of the 1920s. That is why it was decided to build several streets of New York from 1926 at Leavesden Studios; this set became the largest to be used in J.K. Rowling's *Wizarding World*. In addition, visual effects were applied to extend the set, creating a digital version of the entire city that was used as a background and in aerial shots. “New York is probably the biggest creature we have had to design,” says Christian Manz, Special Effects Supervisor (Nathan, 2016). Manz had worked on some of the Harry Potter films (*The Prisoner of Azkaban, The Goblet of Fire* and *The Deathly Hallows - Part 1*), while Tim Burke had held the same position in all the films in the series (except the first). Both returned to deal with special effects in *Fantastic Beasts* (and continue to do so in the new films of this series). Despite having built a great set, Stuart Craig and his team saw that Liverpool had an architecture very similar to the New York of the time that was needed, and they decided to film certain scenes in the English city. The resemblance is caused by the connection between the two cities: the port of Liverpool was a departure from Great Britain and was the starting point (and arrival) on the routes that connected with New York. They were short scenes in large interiors, so it was not worth building the places that would not be used again; even transferring actors, technicians and crew members were cheaper. They used the Cunard Building in Liverpool for the Christmas-decorated shop scene, where the protagonists search for the Demiguise, and the interior of Saint George Hall for Shaw's gala dinner.

The Woolworth Building is located at 233 Broadway Street in New York. Built over three years, it opened its doors in 1913 with a height a little higher than 240 meters and was the tallest building in the world until 1930. This may explain why J.K. Rowling chose it to be the headquarters of MACUSA, the Magical Congress of the United States of America, or perhaps because of its architectural style which resembled that of the Gothic European cathedrals, the same style of Hogwarts. Stuart Craig took advantage of this to draw another connection between the magical societies of the different continents. While a lot of attention was paid to the MACUSA headquarters, another of the places in New York that is important to the plot is the Central Park Zoo. The minor issue with it is that in 1926 the park was not as we know it today, nor was it close to the way in which it is represented in the film.

For the Death Cell, where Percival Graves (played by Irish Colin Farrell) leads Tina Goldstein and Newt Scamander to be executed, Stuart Craig relied on an art installation. Yates did not want the typical torture chamber, dark corridors, or medieval dungeons. He imagined something more peaceful and clinical. They worked on the idea of this room with a chair floating on a potion – resembling a Pensieve– where the victims deposited their happy memories and watched them to feel a state of inner peace, until the executioners turned the potion into a black liquid where the victims sank to face their fate. Craig was inspired by the installation from the artist Richard Wilson called *20:50*, and which is now permanent at the Saatchi Gallery in London. It is a room flooded with oil at rest which gives the impression of an infinite floor that in turn reflects everything like a swimming pool totally black.

Percival Graves is one of the most mysterious characters in the film. During the promotion, through posters and clips, he was shown holding the symbol of the Deathly Hallows. Throughout the film he grows closer to the character of Credence, played by Ezra Miller. Miller, who had worked with Emma Watson on *The Perks of Being a Wallflower* (2012), confesses that he is an authentic fan of the series and admits that the Harry Potter books helped him in his teens. “This is like the achievement of my craziest, private dreams,” he says (Nathan, 2016).

Credence is the son of Mary Lou, who on the big screen is played by Samantha Morton from *Minority Report* (2002. Mary Lou runs the New Salem Philanthropic Society, a “no-maj” organization seeking to unmask and destroy wizardkind who hide in society. Although the name of the society appears in the script, it is only named this way once in the film, and not correctly. When Langdon Shaw introduces the society to his father, he names it as the Society to Preserve the New Salem (and it’s difficult to know if it was an improvisation by part of the actor to demonstrate his superiority or if it really was a mistake). The original script also described the society's insignia as a broken wand and a dove, but Miraphora Mina and Eduardo Lima, the prop and banner designers of both the original films and this new series, wanted to show a more aggressive attitude, and for that they decided to change it to a pair of hands breaking a wand over flames, symbolizing the Salem witch burnings to which the name refers.

One of the places where another important scene happens is in The Blind Pig[31], the illegal den where Scamander and his friends go in search of information. Although it is used by wizards and creatures to hide from the no-majes, it is a clear metaphor for the prohibition of alcohol that was implemented

[31] This was the name by which illegal low-class bars were known.

in America during the 1920s, and the similar speakeasies (hidden, dark, under the law) that were in all the country. The owner of the place is the goblin Gnarlak, and was played by the actor Ron Perlman, who always considered himself a fan of the films. He began to watch them with his children but then he followed the tradition alone and thinks that J.K. Rowling "is one of the great examples of literary brilliance to emerge in the last twenty-five to thirty years" (ibid).

Shooting was something totally different for the actor. He first filmed his scenes on set with marks on his face, while a computer took and recorded his facial expressions. Then another actor who was 1.2 meters (Gnarlak's height) remade the scene on set, while Perlman spoke his lines behind the camera to keep synchronization. Finally, the scene was filmed again, but without people, just the studio. Everything was then digitally mixed to give birth to the Gnarlak as we see in the final version.

However, there were some improvisations. For The Blind Pig bartender, who is a house elf, they could not find anyone who looked the way the concept artists designed. Until Pablo Grillo, animation supervisor, walking around the set saw Paul, one of the electricians, and realized that he was the face they were looking for. He told Yates about it, and they decided to give it a try. They digitally scanned the electrician's face, and Paul now tells his children that he is the one serving the drinks to Queenie and Jacob, albeit retouched to look like an elf.

Not only were new creatures introduced in the film (that did not appear on the original *Fantastic Beasts* book published in 2001), but also new terms. Until this film, fans thought that Muggle was a universal term used to refer to non-magical people. However, in this film we learn that in North America they use the term "no-maj" to talk about the non-magical folks.

This change introduced by Rowling makes sense, since in 1920s, Muggle was a slang term for marijuana cigarettes in the United States of America.

The soundtrack of the film was done by James Newton Howard: *Pretty Woman* (1990), *The Sixth Sense* (1999), and most recently the first two films of Nolan's trilogy of *Batman: The Dark Knight*, and also *The Hunger Games* series. However, the scene in The Blind Pig contains a composition that was not his own. Written by J.K. Rowling and musically composed by Mario Grigorov, the homonymous song to the bar is the author's debut as a composer, and although the lyrics and the music were there, the voice was missing.

Emily Joy Green was born in Devon, England, but moved to Perth, Australia, when she was a child. She studied dance in her teens, and in 2015 she released her first single, "My Kinda Swag," as Emmi, and it was very well received by critics. Her second single, "Sleep on It", was recommended by Taylor Swift on her Instagram account. It was August 2015 when, while vacationing in Perth, she received an email from Peter Cobbin, a sound engineer at the famous Abbey Road recording studios. The e-mail included the lyrics of a song, and Cobbin asked her to record it but not to show it to anyone. Emmi almost refused, justifying that she was on vacation, but Peter recommended that she not miss the opportunity. That same night, using a 50£ microphone, she recorded the song in her room. Although the project was secret, the song gave clues. The lyrics had references to "hippogriffs," "phoenixes" and "billywig." Emmi quickly searched the internet and soon remembered who they belonged to. "I read all the books, saw all the movies! I grew up with J.K. Rowling, like most kids in my generation." Considering that she never recorded it again, Emmi was almost certain that this was the final version. "To be able to sing the words penned by a legendary writer like J.K. Rowling is an inexplicable honour."

The fantastic beasts are what give the film its title, and their behavior (the escape from Newt's suitcase) is what builds the plot. Producer David Heyman assures that there were more magical creatures in this film alone than in all the Harry Potter films combined. In contrast to the previous films, this time the personality of each animal was very important, and the different interactions with their surroundings, both environmental and with humans. It was no longer just a matter of just designing each of the beasts but understanding their nature. The challenge was interdisciplinary: director, producer, designers, concept artists, puppeteers, animators, and special effects groups came together to bring all the animals to life, with J.K. Rowling approving every detail. The creatures were divided into two groups: "the hero beasts", those which had escaped in New York, and "the not-so-important beasts", which are the ones that we only see in Newt's suitcase. The process, much more detailed for those from the first group, consisted of designing them on paper, then making a sculpture, which was finally scanned and digitized, allowing it to be animated. In this last stage, there were ideas and concepts which had to be discarded because they did not work as well as was initially imagined.

To Yates it was very important that the different beasts look authentic and real; they should not be noticeable in a natural environment. Although they come from a fantastic world, the animals are not extravagant, and could easily be part of the fauna of the planet Earth that we know (in appearance, of course). Most of them, in the version that spectators came to appreciate, are entirely digital. But unlike *Harry Potter and the Chamber of Secrets*, where Daniel Radcliffe filmed scenes with

Dobby using a tennis ball as a guide, in *Fantastic Beasts and Where to Find Them,* Eddie Redmayne was luckier. In the first tests, an actor took the place of the creatures in the filming, which allowed for more natural movement, and reactions that Redmayne could work with. But the design team quickly became more excited, and life-size replicas of the animals were built, even with movement, as in the case of the erumpent, which needed four operators at a time to move all its joints. The one who benefited from this was Redmayne, who had something as similar as possible to the creature itself in front of him, and that allowed him to react accordingly. In this way, the actor developed movements, signals and even the different sounds and tones of voices to address each of the beasts in different circumstances. The animals that Newt Scamander rescue find a new habitat in his suitcase. Eddie Redmayne believed that the suitcase was Newt's whole world. Inside his suitcase is where Newt makes progress with his book, *Fantastic Beasts and Where to Find Them.*

Anna Pinnock, the studio decorator, bought dozens of suitcases from the epoch, and together with Yates, they discarded them until they were left with two or three that would be a good fit. From those, they created a suitcase entirely from scratch, using different parts from the previous suitcases, and then produced hundreds of copies of the suitcase to be used at different times during the shoot and by different teams. With the suitcase already made, other challenges began. The first was to decide how Newt (and later Jacob) were to enter it. Different ideas were considered: from visitors being "eaten" by the suitcase, as if it was just another creature, to images projected in the air in the best *Star Trek* style. All these ideas that were discarded. For several months, Manz and his team struggled without being able to solve the issue until they relied on

Rowling's script. The author had put Newt simply going down, and they used that concept: going down by ladder. The filming was even oversimplified, since it did not need special effects. The bottomless suitcase was located precisely on a hole in the ground, and the actor could descend normally.

The second challenge, a little more complex, was the design of the inside of the suitcase. It took the entire period of pre-production to complete, and it was the toughest job when it came to special effects. Originally it had been thought that, when entering the suitcase, one entered a kind of entire universe where different environments coexisted. A real forest, which after many hectares, at its limit, became a desert, which in turn, bordered with a meadow, and so on infinitely. But Rowling was blunt in saying that creating such a place would require a wizard more powerful than even Voldemort[32]. The result is Newt's shed, which expands into different environments created by Atmospheric Charms. The place where these environments meet with each other is not delicate or tidy, but a bit diffused, to give the idea that Scamander was not so concerned with being a good wizard, but with taking care of the creatures he managed to rescue.

But if we talk about the beings that Newt Scamander rescues, the most important is the obscurus, the manifestation of Dark Magic that occurs when a child with magical gifts represses them due to physical or psychological abuse. Harry Potter fans did not take long, once the film was released, to associate it with the story of Ariana, Dumbledore's younger sister. Fans even asked J.K. Rowling about it on Twitter, but she simply liked the tweets, without responding. The idea of obscurus may have existed in the author's mind for years (in fact, when she

---

[32] Notice that Rowling, according to the book *Inside the Magic of Fantastic Beasts*, used Lord Voldemort as an example and not Albus Dumbledore.

published *Fantastic Beasts and Where to Find Them* in 2001, the fictional publisher of the magical universe was called Obscurus Books). While the final form of the obscurus is the closest thing to a nebulous fluid, in the early conceptual arts it was different, a kind of cube that contained the fluid within its limits, which tried to escape, and there facial features could be seen of the person who inhabited it. Max Kostenko, one of the conceptual designers, recalls the difficulty of working on it: "The Obscurus is the most complex character: Just imagine that you need to draw an invisible villain" (Power, 2016).

Beyond the revelation of this new magical entity and its possible relationship with the world of Harry Potter, one of the biggest surprises was the appearance of the character Gellert Grindelwald, known for his rivalry with Albus Dumbledore. The final twist in which he makes his appearance is even more surprising by the actor who brings him to life, Johnny Depp.

The participation of Depp, known for his roles in *Edward Scissorhands* (1990), *Charlie and the Chocolate* Factory (2005) and *Pirates of the Caribbean* (2003), among others, was kept secret throughout filming and different promotional events. He did not participate in the Avant premiere, press conferences, or in any kind of interviews, not even in those published after the premiere. The fandom in general did not welcome the actor being part of the Harry Potter world due to allegations of verbal and physical abuse from his ex-wife, Amber Heard. Heard filed for a legal divorce in May 2016, presenting the evidence of her complaints, and an agreement was reached in August; the divorce was finalized only in January 2017. Fans were not complaining about Depp's original inclusion in the cast—as the filming had been from August 2015 to January 2016, months before the incidents were made public—but that the studio had not bothered to find a replacement. The scenes in which Depp participates are short, and even in one of them his face is not even seen, which made some fans say that the change wouldn't have been difficult to do with CGI. The story of Depp's involvement in the franchise would continue into the following years with J.K. Rowling and David Yates defending his casting, but Warner Bros. was not so happy with Depp.

The first photographs appeared almost a year before the film's premiere, in November 2015, in *Entertainment Weekly* magazine, under the title "Harry Potter Prequel." The first minute-long trailer was released on December 15th, and it began with the main track from the Harry Potter series, "Hedwig's Theme." In fact, this is the only allusion to the original series, since at no point in the trailers or posters, or any other original material, is the character referred to. The way the studio decided to associate the new series to the Harry Potter series was through the tagline "From J.K. Rowling's Wizarding World."

The film had its Avant premiere in London and New York in November, and both events were attended by Rowling. A month earlier, in October, Warner Bros. had held an event for a small group of fans, although broadcasted live on the internet, where Rowling surprised fans by saying that the series of these new films would not be three films, but five, and that we would see the relationship of Albus Dumbledore and Gellert Grindelwald. The second film, which would take place mainly in Paris, would show both characters.

The film was released on November 18, 2016, and a day later, its script was published as a book. Although it has the format of a screenplay, and the author is J.K. Rowling, the published text is not the text written for the film but it is a transcription of the dialogue that is a part of the final version of the feature film. It does not include deleted scenes and the dialogue from the characters are as performed by the actors, including improvisations and differences with the original text. This caused criticism from the more purist fans who hoped to be able to access Rowling's original creation but they, instead, found themselves with a packaging of the film in text format.

The film grossed $814 million, surpassing only that of *Harry Potter and the Prisoner of Azkaban* from the original series, but still achieved good revenue for a film that was not promoted or related to the Harry Potter name during the previous months. The reviews were very good, especially for the author, who made her debut in the matter of writing screenplays. One of the points in favor, at least for the fans, compared to the other Harry Potter films, was that in this one there was a surprise at the end. Not knowing what would happen was something new for the followers, who were used to knowing in advance what story they would find on the big screen.

Although highly anticipated by the fandom, the second film of the series didn't do so well. The main cast returned (except Colin Farrell), including Johnny Depp, who this time had a more prominent role since Gellert Grindelwald was going to be one of the main characters of the picture. As it happened with the first film, the news of the casting was not well received by the public due to domestic violence allegations against him. In December 2017, J.K. Rowling published a text on her website explaining that her and the rest of the producers were completely happy with having Depp playing the antagonist, which again was not completely well received by the fans. Depp acknowledged this months later, closer to the film release, saying, "I'll be honest with you, I felt bad for J.K. having to field all these various feelings from people out there. I felt bad that she had to take that." (Hibberd, 2018). The other major addition to the casting was Jude Law, who portrayed a young Albus

Dumbledore. According to different journalists, many actors were considered for the role, such as Benedict Cumberbatch and Christian Bale, and even Jared Harris, son of Richard Harris, who played the powerful wizard in the first two Harry Potter films.

The filming took part in the United Kingdom, again in the Leavesdean Studios, where production had to recreate a replica of Paris from 1920s, where the film is set. They shot from July 2017 to December 2017, and in that time the title of the film was released. *Fantastic Beasts: The Crimes of Grindelwald* was announced on November 2017, one year exactly before the release date of the movie.

In the next months, teasers and trailers were shared with the public that generated excitement but also some doubts over story and plot elements. The first doubt was of the origin of the character named Nagini. The snake "friend" of Lord Voldemort was a woman once, with a curse that makes her transform into a snake. A lot of fans protested over this, saying that these were not Rowling's original plans for the character. However, one of the titles that was trademarked back in 2006 for the seventh book was "Harry Potter and the Curse of Nagini". That title in some way could prove that the idea of Nagini being affected by a curse could have been in Rowling's mind since then.

It is interesting to note that, in the original screenplay, Hogwarts was no part of the film. "In the original, the very first draft of the screenplay, Hogwarts didn't actually exist. It was very much grounded in Paris and in London and then, of course, over a period of about six months, eight months, there's a lot of back and forth, a lot of discussion, and it felt right to explore that side of Jo's world. And Jo was reticent at first to go there, she said, 'I don't think we need to go there' and we felt it would be intriguing to sort of..." (Dayez, 2018). This is one of the many quotes that proved that, although Rowling wrote the screenplay, she was heavily influenced by the whole crew who suggested scenes, passages, lines of dialogue and many changes for the story. The second doubt comes from this very specific scene. Despite the fans being happy with seeing the castle on the big screen again, some noticed that an important canon rule was broken. In the trailer (and later this was confirmed when the film was released), a group of people *apparated* onto the grounds of Hogwarts. But what bothered the canon purists more was the fact that Minerva McGonagall, who was (thought to) be born in 1935, was featured as a Hogwarts Professor in 1927, contradicting the established timeline. A lot of fans tried to find an explanation for this, tweaking the known facts based on the information from the books and even articles published in Pottermore (written by Rowling herself), but no one could find a way to make it work with all the data available. Some people are expecting this to be answered or solved in the following films, maybe explaining the use of a magical time-turner (as it happened in *Harry Potter and the Cursed Child*). Others just consider it a minor mistake that does not alter the plot that much.

There was another kind of mistake during the filming that was solved on time, with the help of CGI. Albus Dumbledore, at that point of time, did not own the Elder Wand, so the prop department had to design a new wand for him. This wand is what Jude Law uses and has in some promotional footage and photos, but it isn't what it is depicted in the final trailers. When asked about the change, Pierre Bohanna (head of the prop department) explained that the original wand was at first built with a lot of details in mind, and was even loved by J.K. Rowling, but she noticed it looked too similar to the Elder Wand. To avoid confusion for the viewers (who might think that

Dumbledore had the Elder Wand), they decided to change the design of the wand in post-production using CGI. Due to the change, The Noble Collection, the company that builds and sells props for fans and collectors, did not have the wand ready for the film release.

Fantastic Beasts: The Crimes of Grindelwald had its world Avant premiere in Paris on November 8, 2018, and another premiere in London on November 13th. The whole cast attended both events, alongside directors, producers and of course J.K. Rowling. The film was released worldwide on November 16th, and the screenplay was published in book format as with the first film.

The film grossed only $160 million in the United States, totalling $655 million worldwide and became the lowest grossing Wizarding World film to date. Some people blame this on the early critical response: those reviewers who had the chance to see the film before its release criticized its excessive plotting, a complex narrative and too many plot twists. The cast, especially Jude Law, was praised, but it was not enough for a film which was expecting much more from the public.

One of the main criticisms of the film, the overloaded plot, can be explained through a quote said by VFX supervisor, Christian Manz. In an interview in 2019, he admitted that the VFX team decided to change the main ability of one of the beasts introduced in the film. “In the script, it said a Zouwu can travel, I think, 1000 miles in a day. Originally, Tim and I were thinking ‘wow, that’s really fast’, but then Tim realised that’s only about 35mph, which isn’t that fast. Tim worked again with Andy at Framestore and they came up with him being able to warp space and time” (Beasley, 2019). This is the confirmation that, although J.K. Rowling wrote the script and signed it and it is published under her own name, the final version that is used on the film was changed by a lot of people, including the team who created the visual effects.

The third film, despite the efforts from Warner Bros., seems to have a complicated fate. Originally planned to be released in November of 2020, it was postponed for the first time to November 2021, almost one year later. The reason? Warner Bros. understood the critique of the second film and wanted to have more time to work on the script and address notes. One way to do this was to assign Steve Kloves (who was working as a consultant) to the role of co-writer. Instead of the screenplay being created by Rowling alone, now the two writers had to work together, which would trigger a better balance, since Kloves has had plenty of experience working on films (while Rowling does not).

Principal photography for this new film, which was going to be set in Rio de Janeiro, Brazil, and Berlin, Germany, was planned for March 16, 2020. However, the COVID-19 pandemic forced Warner Bros. to cancel shooting, and they could only restart in September of 2020.

Two months later after the production restarted in London, we would know two big pieces of news related for the film. The first one would come directly from Johnny Depp, who announced he would not return to play Gellert Grindelwald, after being asked by the production company to step down from his role. The request from Warner Bros. came a few days after Depp lost a defamation lawsuit which had found that allegations of domestic violence committed by him against Amber Heard were substantially true. Campaigns to boycott the film started online, with petitions to bring the actor back. On the same day, Warner Bros. announced that the film had to be postponed again to a new date: July 15th, 2022, because an actor had to be replaced. Later, the studio announced Mads Mikkelsen as the replacement to play Gellert Grindelwald in the third film (and, if nothing bad happens, through the fifth film). It is interesting to note that despite Depp had filmed only for one day, he had a "play-or-pay" contract which makes Warner Bros. pay him fully even if he was not part of the film (a term in the contract that possibly was required by Depp himself to be added in case something like this happened).

Curiously enough, in August 2021, less than a year away from the film release, not much is known about it. No leaks have happened, besides some aerial shots from the set (which are not confirmed to be from the film), and Warner Bros. hasn't released a synopsis, trailer, promotional photo or even the title (for the previous films, the title was released one year exactly before the release, which made a lot of fans think that July 15th 2021 was going to be the date, but nothing was announced). Some trusty online sources have said that they saw a test screening of the film in Los Angeles, but the spoilers shared cannot be confirmed until the film is released.

The future of the series is uncertain, with some rumors saying that Warner Bros. is thinking about finishing the series as an HBO Max TV show (considering that some people are trying to boycott the rest of the films because of J.K. Rowling's views on transgender people, and others because of how the studio handled Depp's firing). Only time will tell when and how we will see the ending of this new set of films.

But with all its obstacles, the Fantastic Beasts film series had something that the Harry Potter films series never did. The advertising campaign for the first *Fantastic Beasts* film featured new text by Rowling, something the author had never done before to promote any film. Perhaps because she had developed the story down to the last detail, she decided to be more active in the promotion, and to generate more interest. She published her own texts on the Wizarding World on Pottermore but focused on the United States. Under the title "History of Magic in North America," Rowling published four parts which expand on the Wizarding World of Harry Potter to the country where the film takes place. Not only did she tell the story of the Ilvermorny School of Witchcraft and Wizardry (the American Hogwarts), but she went further back in history, and talked about the natives of the country, more precisely the Navahos, a Native American tribe. Rowling mentions in her texts that what the Navahos call skin-walkers, a kind of people who after committing a crime can transform into animals, do not exist and are simply a legend created to demonize wizards. It's common for Rowling to cite these legends and stories from the real world in her writings, but this time it was not well received by the different native communities of the United States who accused her of appropriating their legends, and even worse, to deny them. Despite being contacted on social networks by different academics and scholars on the subject, who demanded a public apology, Rowling never spoke about it.

The texts were published on Pottermore, which had begun development in 2008 and was under construction for more than two years. Different creators of fansites worked as consultants because of their experience with fandom in the online world.

Initially, Pottermore was created by the demand that existed to buy the Harry Potter books in digital format. The platform would be the exclusive place where the Harry Potter texts could be purchased as eBooks, which would not be available even on Amazon, the most popular site for buying digital books. Pottermore was announced in 2011, when it was promoted as Rowling's mysterious new project. However, it quickly became clear that it was not a new book. With a video where the author told what and how it would be, it was explained that it was a new online experience to relive the known story, but this time adding a new variable: the reader. The idea of the website was to go through the story of Harry Potter, chapter by chapter, while the reader (the user) was also experiencing it as its own story. Thus, when a person registered in Pottermore, after playing some chapters, one could be sorted into one of the four houses of Hogwarts (after answering a questionnaire designed entirely by J.K. Rowling), buy his or her own wand in Diagon Alley, and even brew potions. The most interesting point was that one could access new writing by the author, never published material on a particular topic in the series. Thus, Rowling published biographies of characters like Minerva McGonagall and Remus Lupin, and the history behind objects and places, like Azkaban. At launch, the author was claimed to have written more than 18,000 words of content for the website.

After the announcement made in June 2011, it took just two months, until August, for the first users to receive their invitation email to start testing the site. Although the original idea was that the closed trial version would last only until October, when the site would be launched to the public, it was extended until April 2012, when the Pottermore Shop also opened. At first, only the *Harry Potter and the Philosopher's Stone* experience was available, and the following books were added over time. *Harry Potter and the Deathly Hallows* was only released in June 2015. In 2014, to give a nod to the FIFA World Cup, which was taking place in Brazil, Rowling decided that the Quidditch World Cup was taking place at the same time, during the months of May and July. To celebrate that, she wrote articles as if they were by Ginny Weasley (now the senior Quidditch correspondent for the Daily Prophet) and Rita Skeeter (still working for the Wizarding newspaper) reporting the matches from Argentine Patagonia, where the tournament took place. For the final match, Rowling (as Ginny Weasley) reported that the whole Potter family visited the country and saw how Viktor Krum finally got his well-deserved World Cup Trophy.

During the first half of 2015, however, Pottermore had announced that the site would have a total change. The platform, which was born for commercial purposes, suffered from the problem of user retention. Those who had already explored it completely, hardly returned, except for the rare exception of the announcement of a new Rowling material uploaded there. This change came not too long after the rupture of the partnership between Pottermore and Sony. The Japanese company had been a partner in the project from the beginning, even launching a digital book reader for the occasion, and producing exclusive games from the world of Harry Potter for the PlayStation console. However, with this twist on the Pottermore idea, the partnership was already at an end.

The new Pottermore, which was launched in September 2015, had removed the interactive parts, but in January 2016 added a simple system of users who, after a questionnaire, were assigned to a Hogwarts house and received a wand, but nothing more. Subsequent questionnaires were added over time: one to find out which house in Ilvermorny each user belonged to and another to find out each user's Patronus. The new website, which promised more Rowling material, was heavily criticized by fans. On the one hand, the experience on which so much emphasis had been placed had disappeared, since the new version simply looked like a generic (although official) fansite, and secondly, the quality of the new articles (written by the staff and not Rowling) was sometimes not the best, since the canon created by the author was not considered.

Pottermore then became the official site of the brand of The Wizarding World of J.K. Rowling, publishing exclusive news, trailers, interviews with people involved in the movies and books, while still occasionally publishing new material from the writer. In the store fans could buy eBooks and digital audiobooks (although the former is no longer exclusive, as they can already be purchased through iTunes, even an improved digital version that includes animated illustrations). The online store also allowed the user to purchase exclusive posters and illustrations, parts of its own art collection launched on the website. However, the most interesting thing for sale at Pottermore was the *Pottermore Presents* collection, three books published only in digital format that contain the texts that had already been shared on the website. Although the news was welcomed because it implied the possibility of adding to one's collection (although only electronically) the latest information that Rowling had revealed about the Wizarding World, other fans took the opportunity to ask (and criticize) the reason in selling material that could already be read for free on the platform. The official response was that it was the only way to add this text to devices and read them offline. A lot of fans didn't notice that these ebooks also contained new material by J.K. Rowling in the form of new articles or repurposed articles with expanded details.

In 2019, Pottermore mutated again, and this time, completely. The website was rebranded into Wizarding World Digital, an online portal labeled as the "new online home of Harry Potter and Fantastic Beasts". The new website, that kept original content from Pottermore (such as the original writings by J.K. Rowling but also content created by collaborators), also allowed user registrations and provided new tests to be sorted into a Hogwarts House or discovering one's Patronus. Through registering into the new platform, one becomes a Silver Member of the new Harry Potter Fan Club. To become a Gold Member, one has to pay an annual fee to access some exclusive perks such as an exclusive customized journal, discounts for merchandise, event tickets, and priority access to some collectibles.

In 2017, and independently from Pottermore, Portkey Games, a new video game label from Warner Bros. Interactive Entertainment, that develops videogames for phones, consoles, and computers based on the Wizarding World of J. K. Rowling, was founded. Only four games have been released so far bearing the Harry Potter name: *Wizards Unite*, *Hogwarts Mystery*, *Puzzles & Spells*, and *Magic Awakened*. *Hogwarts Legacy*, an action role-playing video game set in the late 1800s in the Wizarding World is currently in development and will allow players to create a student in Hogwarts and explore an open world consisting not only of the school castle and grounds but also locales near the school such as Hogsmeade. While set to originally be released in 2021, the launch of the videogame was postponed until 2022. It will be the first videogame from the company that will be released on consoles such as PlayStation 5 and Xbox One, among others.

Possibly to have more freedom (and to not repeat below-mentioned criticisms of *Harry Potter and the Cursed Child*), from the beginning Portkey Games announced that, although the content of its games would be governed by the rules and regulations of the known Wizarding World, it would not be canon. This allowed developers not to require the author's approval for every detail or action to be taken to be, while staying within known limits.

* * *

Although the film series of *Fantastic Beasts and Where to Find Them* and the Pottermore platform were well received, neither one nor the other was the extension of the original story that was desired by the fandom. Despite including new writings from Rowling, Pottermore is a digital platform, and the material is not even narrative, but closer to encyclopedia entries. Fans always wanted a story set in the past of the Wizarding World. Most would have opted for a Marauders prequel, which would tell the adventures of James Potter, Sirius Black, and company in their years at Hogwarts, and even further back, the Founders, a plot starring the founders of Hogwarts School of Witchcraft and Wizardry. But what fans ultimately received was a story with Newt Scamander as the protagonist, although it slowly veers towards the duel between Albus Dumbledore and Gellert Grindelwald.

What fans always wanted, an extension of Harry Potter's own story, started being developed around the same time as *Fantastic Beasts*. The news appeared on December 19, 2013 in the *Daily Mail online*, reported by Baz Bamigboye, renowned entertainment journalist in Great Britain, who had the exclusive. According to the article, Harry Potter would reach the West End, London's theatre district, the largest nucleus of theatrical works globally after Broadway. The production, authorized by Rowling who was also involved, would see light in 2015 and would be under the command of Sonia Friedman and Colin Callender. For Bamigboye it was not easy to get the news. "Each week, for months, I would make literally hundreds of calls just to get splinters of information and then piece it together. In the early days, I received no official assistance or guidance from those close to the production," recalls the journalist.

Friedman and Callender had experience in large theatrical productions. Among so many plays, in 2013, Callender had been a part of *Lucky Guy* (with Tom Hanks), the highest-grossing non-musical play in Broadway history. For his part, Friedman worked in the world of theatre since the late 1980s, and in 2002 she founded her company, Sonia Friedman Productions, which through its productions won awards such as the Tony and the Olivier awards, prizes for works in the United States and England, respectively.

They knew that to have Rowling they had to partner up and present her with an impressive idea that would completely convince her. It was not the first time that the author had received proposals to take Harry Potter and company to the theatre. She had even declined Michael Jackson, who wanted to do a musical about Harry.

The first meeting was in Edinburgh, at the home of the writer, where the producers met her personally. They did not talk about money or merchandising, but about the idea they wanted to devise. Thus, Friedman and Callender hit the nail on the head. "Sonia and Colin's vision was the only one that really made sense to me, and which had the sensitivity, intensity and intimacy I thought appropriate for bringing Harry's story to the stage," explains Rowling (Sonia Friedman Productions Limited, 2013).

The day after Bamigboye published the news, the official press release was distributed, and the rumor was confirmed. Fans learned that they would see Harry's early years, living with his aunt and uncle while he still didn't know about his magical abilities. This plot, which correctly classified the work as a prequel, changed in its final version. There were no further details on the press release, just a thank you to Warner Bros. for their support of the venture, and the news that directors and writers were already being sought. Rumors about these positions began in May of the following year when the names John Tiffany and Jack Thorne appeared.

The original idea of Harry Potter in his years before Hogwarts had brought certain comments on the part of some groups of fans who assured production that it would be boring to see a history of the Wizarding World in a muggle world. Now, the idea of showing James and Lily Potter in the years before they became parents was floated.

Tiffany and Thorne had previously worked together on *Let the Right One In*, the stage adaptation of the Swedish novel about vampires. Tiffany had stood out in the past for his work on *Once*, inspired by the film of the same name, for which he won a Tony Award for Best Musical Director. In addition to the rumors concerning the production team, there were also rumors of which theatres were interested in hosting the performance. But for a long time, everything was kept secret.

The reveal only came on June 26th, 2015, more than a year later, on the 18th anniversary of the publication of *Harry Potter and the Philosopher's Stone* in the UK. Through her Twitter account, J.K. Rowling revealed the title of what would be the continuation of her famous series: *Harry Potter and the Cursed Child*. The play would premiere in London the following year, and it would be directed and written by those most strongly rumored: Tiffany and Thorne. The base story had come from their collaborative work, but Thorne wrote the script. Also, Rowling clarified that this eighth story was not a prequel. Along with the information on Twitter, producer Sonia Friedman published the official statement revealing that the premiere date would be in the next summer at the Palace Theatre in London, and ticket sales would begin almost eight months prior, in autumn.

In September, a month before ticket sales began, it was announced that the play would be divided into two parts because of the complexity of the story. The intention with this decision was for fans to see both performances on consecutive days or on the same day (early afternoon and early evening). This situation had also been discovered by the journalist Bamigboye days before: "The breakthrough for me was discovering that it was to be in two parts. That opened my eyes to the scale of the piece." The news prompted comments stating that the decision was only monetary, as fans now had to pay for two tickets to see the full story. But the comments were only just that, since on October 28th, when the tickets went on sale, all the showtimes from June 7th to September 18th sold out in just one hour. The sale, exclusively for those who had pre-registered in the system, not only generated disappointment but also anger, since just minutes after the seats were sold-out, tickets were found on resale sites for more than $2,000. Official sources claim that more than 70,000 people tried to buy their tickets on that pre-sale.

Pottermore was no longer just posting stories on *Fantastic Beasts*, but news about *The Cursed Child* was also posted. In September the official synopsis of the play was released, which was totally different from the first press release which mentioned Harry's story before he knew he was a wizard. Fans would see Harry Potter as an adult, an employee of the Ministry of Magic with difficulties being a father, especially with his son, Albus, who suffered from carrying the weight of being the son of Harry Potter. In the second half of December, two years after the first announcement, Baz Bamigboye was re-publishing information before the official sources. This time, he revealed the name of the actors who would portray Harry Potter, Ron Weasley and Hermione Granger.

Jamie Parker and Paul Thornley would play Harry and Ron respectively, two experienced and award-winning actors in the West End. The news that broke the internet was that Hermione Granger would be played by Swaziland-born actress, Noma Dumezweni. Noma is the daughter of South African parents and lived her childhood in Uganda and Kenya until she was eight years old, when she arrived in England with her mother and sister as refugees. With vast experience on London theatre, in 2006, she won an Olivier Award for Best Supporting Actress for her role in *A Raisin in the Sun.*

What caused a heated discussion was that Noma Dumezweni is dark-skinned, something that was unthinkable for the character of Hermione Granger. While certain fans claimed that it was a good choice which added diversity to the story, something important in times of racism, others said that it contradicted the established canon, since that was not Hermione Granger's skin color. These fans claimed that they were not against diversity and that their argument was not racist. They simply wanted this new story in the Harry Potter series to remain consistent with the previous canon. The discussion reached the mainstream media and Rowling had to go out and say on Twitter that none of her books mentioned that Hermione Granger had a white complexion, so that it is not canon, and the choice of Noma Dumezweni did not contradict anything. Matthew Lewis, the actor who portrayed Neville Longbottom in the films, joined in adding that his character is blonde in the books. While it is true what Rowling affirms, that Hermione is never described as having white skin, there are traits that could associate her with having that tonality in her complexion. In Rowling's own drawings, which have been made public, it is evident that Hermione Granger has fair complexion, and her illustrations have always been considered canon because they come directly from her.

The rehearsals for the play began on February 22nd and lasted five months, until the first performance, which took place on June 7th. This was part of what the production called "previews," a common practice where plays are performed in front of an audience but not in their final version. These performances allow the team to analyze reactions and to have time to make necessary changes until the release date. For example, in these previews, real owls were used for certain acts, but in the first show one of them escaped from the stage, which led to the use of prop animals from that moment on.

The premiere date, which included a red carpet where everyone involved was present, including J.K. Rowling, was July 30th, almost two months later. However, for practical purposes, the premiere was in June, when fans from all over the world traveled to the English capital to observe the first performance of the eighth part in Harry Potter's history.

While journalists were urged to publish any kind of review, they stayed away from spoilers and filled their reviews with praise, giving the play 5 out of 5 stars. But fans behaved differently, and they flooded the internet with details of the plot, new characters and more. Months earlier, J.K. Rowling launched the *Keep The Secrets* campaign to ask that those lucky enough to see the play not to tell the details so that everyone could enjoy it when they had a chance to see it. Although many sites published the plot in detail, it was always with respect and warnings, ensuring that those who did not want to know what was happening did not read it by mistake. This would have been natural for those fans from the rest of the world who were unable to travel to London to see the play. In fact, when announcing that *Harry Potter and the Cursed Child* would be a play, the fandom criticized it a lot, as it had been a very different experience so far. Books and movies could be enjoyed anywhere in the world while the play involved traveling to one of the most expensive cities on the planet. Perhaps due to the pressure that was exerted (or perhaps it was already decided from the beginning), in February 2016, months before the premiere, it was announced that the script of the play would be published as was later done with *Fantastic Beasts*. The release date would be July 31st, one day after the official premiere. This caused most fans to prefer to avoid spoilers and read the play themselves.

It was published by Scholastic in the United States, but in the United Kingdom by Little Brown and Company, the publisher that published Rowling's other novels post Harry Potter. It was promoted under the slogan "Nineteen Years Later ... The Eighth Story", as *Harry Potter and the Cursed Child* begins with the last scene of *Harry Potter and the Deathly Hallows*, on Platform 9$^{3/4}$.

Although it was neither a novel nor written by the author, bookstores around the world did treat it as such, organizing events at midnight for the launch of the book, trying to replicate the launch parties for the Harry Potter series. Certain fans were even confused and noted that the book was not a novel, but a theatre script. But despite the subtle differences, it was a bestseller. In the UK it sold 680,000 copies in its first three days, making it the fastest-selling book since the last Harry Potter; by the end of the year, it had reached 1.5 million copies sold. Scholastic had a first print run of 4.5 million copies, and sold 2 million in the first 48 hours, unthinkable for a theatre script.

The play has received positive reviews, and even was rated with the highest possible ratings. From the sets, the costumes, the special effects and even the performances, everything has been highlighted. So much so, that it obtained eleven nominations for the Olivier Awards. Not only was the number of nominations a record for a theatrical production, but also the awards it won, nine statuettes: Best Actor, Best Actress, Best Director, and Best New Play, among others.

Although the experience of enjoying the play live is truly magical, the script alone did not cause the same effect. Those who only read the story and did not see the play, for the most part, were disappointed and even surprised. The main complaints were the contradictions with the canon established during the original seven books, and the poor plot that seems more like a fanfiction than an original creation of J.K. Rowling.

Jack Thorne changed how time-turners work, and more so, the flow of time in the Wizarding World. While the Harry Potter books always were improving in quality and plot, with this eighth part a creative conflict was expected, but the story seemed to fall into childish knots and worn-out clichés such as the villain's daughter who returns to avenge her father.

Even though J.K. Rowling claims that the story of *Harry Potter and the Cursed Child* should be considered canon, certain fans don't agree and ignore what happens in it. Complaints fall heavily on Jack Thorne, but the author may be just one more victim. He wrote the script for a play to be acted and performed on stage, not for millions to read in the comfort of their home as if it were just another novel. But even with the criticism from the fans, the play continues to be successful. With each new batch of sales, tickets are sold out in just hours for performances in the coming years.

Harry Potter and the Cursed Child made its Broadway debut in April 2018 at the Lyric Theatre in New York, and in 2019 it arrived in Melbourne, Australia. Sonia Friedman, who received an Order of the British Empire appointment for her work with the English Theatre after the premiere of *The Cursed Child*, assures that she wants to take it to more than ten countries, but it's not easy to do with a production of such magnitude which imposes many conditions to get to a new city. The play also opened in San Francisco, California, and Hamburg, Germany (the first production in a language different than English). It was also planned to open in Toronto, Canada, and Tokyo, Japan, but those openings had to be delayed due to the COVID-19 pandemic, and their proper dates are still to be confirmed.

Although their names do not appear as big as Rowling's on the cover of the book, John Tiffany and Jack Thorne are largely responsible for this work. Tiffany recalls seeing Rowling in the Traverse Theatre Café in Edinburgh in 1995, when the author was in the habit of writing in public places. Thorne considers himself as a fan of the series, having read all the books and seen all the movies. They both met Rowling at her home in Edinburgh, just as Friedman and Callender had done before, and that same day the three of them outlined the basic path the story would follow. Thorne and Tiffany then returned to London and continued to develop the story and add the necessary details to turn it into a production. Thorne reread the books over and over again, taking notes and gathering details to serve his plot.

One of the most frequently asked questions is who came up with the main story. Was it Rowling? Did they write all together? Was it Thorne and Tiffany, and Rowling just approved and declined certain decisions? "I did most of the physical writing, but everyone fed back into it," says Thorne (Shenton, 2017). As an example, Thorne asks himself about Ron's lines: "Did I write them or did Paul Thornley?" (ibid), alluding to the actor who collaborated in the dialogue, and then adds "We did so many workshops, so there are a lot of people whose voices played a huge role in how the show turned out" (ibid). But despite having assured interviewers several times that the work was done by them, Thorne feels responsible: “Nobody else had ever written anything that Harry Potter has ever said before apart from J.K. - so that was terrifying” (Morris, 2017). Although it was never confirmed, some theorize that the idea of Delphini (the most controversial twist of this new story) came directly from Rowling. The author is an admirer of Jessica Mitford, the writer and activist whom she named her first daughter after. Interestingly, one of Jessica's sisters, Unity Mitford, joined the Nazi movement and became obsessed with Adolf Hitler, who noticed Unity's passion for her project and included her in his privet circle, appearing in public with him. To this day, several historians and researchers believe that Unity had a secret daughter with Hitler, and certain fans of the series cannot help but see a clear parallel between that and the relationship of Bellatrix Lestrange and Lord Voldemort, ensuring that it served as inspiration for the writer and the new daughter these characters had. On the other hand, some fans cannot believe Rowling came up with the plot of Voldemort having a daughter, and they cite an answer from the author during 2004 World Book Day Chat, organized by the BBC. A kid named Harry asked her “Has Voldermort any children?”, at which she replied: “No. Voldemort as a father... now that's not a nice thought.” (J.K. Rowling chat, 2004e)

Another theory claims that Scene Four of Act Four, where Harry Potter has a conversation with Dumbledore through the headmaster painting, is the product of Rowling's pen. The reasons? They say that this scene has much of the author's style, and even more, the conversation gives one of the phrases from the book that even most of those who do not accept the work as canon liked. A source who participated in the work itself confirmed this theory but preferred to remain anonymous in the face of such a claim.

Whether or not Rowling devised most of *The Cursed Child* story, the truth is that if she keeps her word, it will be the last part of Harry Potter's life.

At the play's official premiere at London's Palace Theatre, the press asked if fans could still expect more from the now grown wizard with glasses, to which Rowling replied, "[Harry] goes on a very big journey during these two plays and then, yeah, I think we're done. This is the next generation, you know. So, I'm thrilled to see it realized so beautifully but, no, Harry is done now" (Lazarus, 2016).

It's not the first time that Rowling has said something similar, but it does seem to be the end. Harry Potter has already suffered enough. We witnessed his entire adolescence, and now also his most complicated adult moment. We are left with the *Fantastic Beasts and Where to Find Them* film series, which promises to show the duel between the young Albus Dumbledore and Gellert Grindelwald, anticipated for the first time since *Harry Potter and the Philosopher's Stone*, and all the written material that J.K. Rowling has decided to give away at Pottermore. Let's enjoy that 19 years after the publication of the first book, Rowling is still as involved as in her best moments and continues to expand the Wizarding World that we love so much.

Epilogue

It's cold in Scotland, especially on winter mornings. Through the window of The Elephant House, where J.K. Rowling wrote parts of the Harry Potter story more than twenty years ago, you can see the cemetery where the author used to walk through to get inspiration for names for her characters. A little farther away, a school can be seen and its towers bears some resemblance to Hogwarts. The walls of the café's bathrooms became a canvas where fans from all over the world could leave messages in multi-colored ink, a mark of having passed through one of the meccas of the Wizarding World. A few streets away is Victoria Street, a curving street lined with small, huddled shops that immediately resemble Diagon Alley, where young witches and wizards do their shopping before going to Hogwarts. It's clear that the development of the Harry Potter story took place here, and some will even say that it was easy, and that anyone, under the stimuli that Edinburgh offers, could have written a similar story. But the reality is that, as years go by, and although other series strive to be as popular, none have even come close to being the new Harry Potter.

J.K. Rowling did not invent magic schools, children who make friends by fighting monsters, or magic wands. She also doesn't own the trademarks for flying brooms, unicorns, phoenixes or centaurs. The idea of the old wizard with the long white beard who works as a mentor, guide, and source of knowledge, is not necessarily original. But she does know how to tell a good story, with the construction of the mystery, its unexpected twists, and its endings that don't disappoint. All of that is the foundation that makes these books so loved.

Rowling's imagination is highlighted by many as central to Harry Potter, and while her ingenuity is undeniable, her talent lies in the foundation of the fable and in the construction of the characters. Her books could be considered mystery novels instead of fantasy, and even the writer herself has said on different occasions that the central theme is not magic, but death. The spells, the creatures, and the artifacts are excuses that can be replaced, because the true charm of the story lies in its characters and in itself—in the turns taken by the plot, in the facts concealed but not entirely so, in how a plot is woven, which at the end is perfectly revealed, and in the secrets that, hundreds of pages ago, were briefly mentioned. They are later revealed and, those with good memory, remember the details which were missed the most.

Readers, journalists, and other professionals appreciate how Rowling, through her seven books, has planned the Harry Potter series without leaving any loose ends. Most of the criticism comes from colleagues, other authors who consider that the writing lacks quality, believe that Rowling's success has only been a stroke of luck. They claim that the idea lacks originality, that the story is vague and predictable, adding the usual criticism to everything that is successful claiming that if it is consumed by the majority, who know little about literature, it may not actually be high-quality.

The truth is that yes, Rowling was very lucky. The timing and pace at which the different parts of the series were released could not have been better. Harry Potter took hold at the end of the 20th century, at which time the internet was also becoming massive. She took advantage, almost by chance, of the avalanche of online globalization and forged a parallel world driven by the fans themselves who invested with their own creations: theories, discussions, fanfics and fanarts.

The publication of news became a profession and what began as websites carried out by followers of the series became professional media outlets that booked interviews, were invited to events, and even generated income. Almost parallel to the "official" world of Harry Potter that was carried out by the publishers and studios of the films, was another world of its own that grew unprecedented, which, little by little, began to set the agenda for the "official" and also served as an example for many other fandoms that came after. But while the Harry Potter franchise knew how to side with the internet, the franchise also had to compete against it. At a time when children around the world were fascinated by computers and videogame consoles, the book triumphed. It was a book where the characters live in an ancient world, where they write with quills using parchments, travel by train, and don't even know about the existence of the internet. It was a book that managed to get the bookstores open during the early hours of Saturday because of the lines that were formed to acquire the final book.

Harry Potter was also attractive because of the Wizarding World, which is parallel with our own world and hidden in woods, in buildings, and in telephone booths. It is a school in a castle but has students with very similar experiences, such as exams, teenage angst, and even a sport to play with friends. It has a governmental body with the same flaws as those of the Muggle world which Rowling knew very well how to criticize through her characters—and a society that can't escape racism or class discrimination either. It's very easy to identify and feel within the Wizarding World, because the differences are almost nonexistent.

But the J.K. Rowling books have not only come out at exactly the right time, but at the best possible pace. Her novels were published as her readers were growing up, becoming one of the best marketing campaigns ever. While the early books in the series were aimed at children, the later books grew in complexity, violence, and darkness at the same rate as the readers grew up. Those who started the series in their childhood may have been in their late teens, like the protagonists, by the time the seventh book was published. A book that, as the English journalist and writer Tibor Fischer said, generated so much excitement that not even a "lost novel by Shakespeare with a cover by Michelangelo could generate this much excitement" (Fischer, 2007). The series of the Owl Post turned millions of children around the world into readers, opened the doors to other books (even of different genres), and transformed a large part of them into potential and established writers. Recent studies show that the number of teenagers who dream of becoming published authors has grown considerably in recent years, and teenagers claim to have been influenced by Rowling's work. As proof, a girl in her twenties scribbles on a notepad two tables away, here at The Elephant House, mimicking what Rowling did nearly two decades ago, and dreams of the same stroke of luck.

The Harry Potter phenomenon has left a mark on an entire generation and promises to do the same with many children and teenagers who go on discovering the Wizarding World every day. These new generations are still in awe whenever they read or watch Harry Potter. It is highly unlikely that any other work of fiction for young readers can have the same effect and response in a worldwide audience. After 20 years, the story of Harry Potter is timeless and its phenomenon, limitless.

Edinburgh, January 2018

Acknowledgements (2018)

My entry into the Wizarding World occurred in 1999, when the first three books had recently been published. Years later, when I first got the internet, I began to interact in several online communities and collect different editions of the books. Since 2011, I have run The Rowling Library, a news portal about all the works of J.K. Rowling, including her new novels for adults. We also publish a monthly digital magazine with articles and interviews which can be downloaded and read around the world. With The Rowling Library we were fortunate to publish, even before official announcements, exclusive news that generated great impact such as the confirmation of the release of Harry Potter and the Cursed Child in book form. This type of news led us to be cited by major media such as Newsweek, Entertainment Weekly and The Independent, among others.

As time went by, I became interested in everything that revolved around the novels rather than the story itself: fans, businesses, and the evolution of a book published by a small publishing house becoming the literary phenomenon that we all know. I felt that there was an interesting story to tell, guarded by the protagonists who did not want, with good reason, to reveal secrets of one of the greatest businesses of the late twentieth century.

It took a lot longer than I thought, and I have learned a lot along the way. Not just about the task of writing a book, but about Harry Potter itself. I have spent weeks investigating, looking for that missing piece of information. I contacted the person who might have known the information I needed and urged them to please reveal it to me. This book could not have become a reality without the help of many people who have contributed to it over the past year.

First, I must thank Cristina Alemany, who from the beginning trusted me in this project and ended up guiding and editing it; to Erika Wrede, whose attention to detail enhanced it substantially; and to the entire editorial team who have done a lot to make this book a reality.

My goal was always to make a book that tells the truth, and for that I had to go directly to the protagonists who were part of the process. I must thank all of them for their patience, for taking the time to answer my questions and concerns, and for contributing their valuable testimony. To Nigel Newton, Barry Cunningham, Fleur Howle, Lindsey Fraser, Rosamund de la Hey, Thomas Taylor, Cliff Wright, Hira Digpal, Daphne Durham, Katy Reilly, David Heyman, Nisha Parti, Emmi, Andrew Williamson, Dermot Power, Ben Hibon, Tiago da Silva, Baz Bamigboye and many others who preferred to remain anonymous due to contractual issues. To Bryony Evens, for the reasons stated above and for the foreword that she agreed to write.

This book is also part of a process that began many years ago for me. To Germán Gallo, an irreplaceable friend, who helped me create my first Harry Potter website back in 2001, which is where I think it all began. To Martín Losardo, from whom I learned a lot, with whom we founded RedFlu.com more than fifteen years ago. Martín always wanted us to write a book like this; I know that he would be very happy to know that it finally happened. To Ariel Bosi, friend, initiator, and guide in this mess of buying repeated books. To Fepe and Pupi, to whom few things matter less than Harry Potter, but they helped anyway. To Ibid and Laurent Garcia, specialists in canon and the history of the Harry Potter phenomenon like few others.

To my mom, who always encouraged me to read, and when I asked her for the first Harry Potter book, she was able to get it for me, and (many) years later she helped me build my first bookcase. If she were here today, she would buy all the copies of this book. To my dad, who dared to cross platform 9 3/4 in London. And to my brother Leandro, who always told me that I had to do this.

Finally, to Belén Salituri, my life partner who is still not tired of being with me every day despite my Harry Potter obsession to know every tiny detail about this phenomenon, but also agrees to live with hundreds of books by J.K. Rowling which occupy more space than they should. And if that was not enough, she also helped me in all possible aspects of this work, which is why I also consider her to be the author a bit, too. This book is also yours.

Acknowledgements (2021)

Since this book was published in Spanish back in 2018, I felt that the natural next step was to publish it in English (and update it, of course). I felt that the fandom from all over the world would love to know the facts and details that are shared in this work. But it was not easy, and it was possible after all these years thanks to many people who helped in one way or another.

First, I want to thank to LBL for his help on the translation, and to A.E. Williams, who edited and corrected this book, improving it in a way that exceeded any expectations. To Ibid, again, because thanks to his attention to details and knowledge, the book is much better. To Laurent García and Sean McLennan, who are crazy enough to want to be part of this new crazy project called *TRL Books*.

And to Belén, again, because after adding hundreds of new Harry Potter books to our house, she is still here with me.

References

Alexander, T. (2017, October 18). Jason Isaacs didn't want to play Lucius Malfoy in Harry Potter and was 'mightily pissed off' by his audition. *Digital Spy*. http://www.digitalspy.com/movies/harry-potter/news/a840896/jason-isaacs-lucius-malfoy-harry-potter-audition/

Armitage, S. (2021, July 24). The Poet Laureate Has Gone to His Shed. *BBC Radio 4*.

Ballard, N. (2001, November 12). Interview, *BBCi Bristol*.

Barnes, B. (2014, March 29). Warner's C.E.O. Is Bullish on the Big Screen. *The New York Times*. http://www.nytimes.com/2014/03/30/business/media/warners-ceo-is-bullish-on-the-big-screen.html

BBC News. (2003, June 22). Potter 'is fastest-selling book ever'". *BBC News*. http://news.bbc.co.uk/2/hi/entertainment/3005862.stm

— (2005*a*, July 18). Read the FULL JK Rowling interview. *CBBC News*.

http://news.bbc.co.uk/cbbcnews/hi/newsid_4690000/newsid_4690800/4690885.stm

— (2005*b*, July 18). Potter book smashes sales records. *BBC News.* http://news.bbc.co.uk/2/hi/entertainment/4692093.stm

— (2006, February 22). Potter star buys Rowling document. *BBC News.* http://news.bbc.co.uk/2/hi/entertainment/4739474.stm

— (2008, June 11). Potter 'prequel' sold at auction. *BBC News.* http://news.bbc.co.uk/2/hi/7446337.stm

— (2016, April 10). Harry Potter: GCHQ “intervened over Half-Blood Prince leak”. *BBC News.* http://www.bbc.com/news/entertainment-arts-36010426

Beasley, T. (2019, January 26). Exclusive Interview – Fantastic Beasts VFX supervisor Christian Manz on The Crimes of Grindelwald, his love for Nifflers and awards season success. *Flickering Myth.* https://www.flickeringmyth.com/2019/01/exclusive-interview-fantastic-beasts-vfx-supervisor-christian-manz-on-the-crimes-of-grindelwald-his-love-for-nifflers-and-awards-season-success/2/

Bloomberg (2005, May 30). Nigel Newton. *Bloomberg* http://www.bloomberg.com/news/articles/2005-05-29/nigel-newton

Bloomsbury (2003). Meet Emma Matthewson, the Editor of the Harry Potter books. *Bloomsbury.com.* http://web.archive.org/web/20040823141635/http://www.bloomsburymagazine.com:80/harrypotter/wizard/section/creation_editor2.asp

Blue Peter (2007, July 20). Harry Potter: A Blue Peter Special. *CBBC.*

Carvajal, D. (1999, April 1). Children's Book Casts a Spell Over Adults; Young Wizard Is Best Seller And a Copyright Challenge. *The New York Times.* http://www.nytimes.com/1999/04/01/books/children-s-book-casts-spell-over-adults-young-wizard-best-seller-copyright.html

Collette-White, M. & MacMillan, R. (2007, July 19). Rowling anger as New York Times reviews last Potter. *Reuters.* http://www.reuters.com/article/idINIndia-28562520070719

Creating the World of Harry Potter Part 7: Story. *Harry Potter Wizard's Collection.* Warner Bros. Pictures, 2012.

Cuccinello, H. (2017, June 19). How J. K. Rowling Earned $95 Million In A Year. *Forbes* http://www.forbes.com/sites/hayleycuccinello/2017/06/19/how-j-k-rowling-earned-95-million-in-a-year/#12d88b2ed429

Dayez, H. (2018, November 16). L'interview de David Heyman et David Yates, à propos des "Crimes de Grindelwald". *RTBF Culture.* https://www.rtbf.be/culture/cinema/detail_l-interview-de-david-heyman-et-david-yates-a-propos-des-crimes-de-grindelwald?id=10074902

Dunn, E. (1997, August 2). From the Dole to Hollywood. *Electronic Telegraph.* http://www.accio-quote.org/articles/1997/0897-telegraph-dunn.html

Errington, P. (2015) *J. K. Rowling: A Bibliography 1997-2013.* Bloomsbury.

EW Staff (2001, July 27). Meet J. K. Rowling's accomplices. *Entertainment* http://ew.com/article/2007/07/27/meet-jk-rowlings-accomplices/

Farber, C. (1999, October 17). Harry Potter's Toughest Foe. *Sunday Herald.* http://www.accio-quote.org/articles/1999/1099-sundayherald-farber.html

Feldman, R. (1999). The Truth about Harry. *School Library Journal, 45* (9), 136-139.

Fisher, L. & Nettleton, P. (1999, July 9). Potty Over Potter. *The Mirror.*

Fischer, T. (2007, July 21). Harry Potter review: Is all well in the end? *The Telegraph.* http://www.telegraph.co.uk/news/uknews/1558079/Harry-Potter-review-Is-all-well-in-the-end.html

Fraser, L. (2002, November 9). Harry and me. *The Scotsman.* http://www.scotsman.com/lifestyle/culture/books/harry-and-me-1-628320

Fraser, L. & Rowling, J. K. (2001). *Conversations with J. K. Rowling.* Scholastic.

Fry, S. & Rowling, J. K. (2005, December 10). Living with Harry Potter. *BBC Radio 4.*

Greig, G. (2006, January 10). There would be so much to tell her.... *Tatler Magazine, 301* (2), 128-134.

Gritten, D. (2005, Ocobter 28). I was so fearful of breaking the spell. *The Telegraph.* http://www.telegraph.co.uk/culture/film/3647492/I-was-so-fearful-of-breaking-the-spell.html

Grossman, L. & Sachs, A. (2007, June 28). Harry Potter and the Sinister Spoilers. *Time Magazine* http://content.time.com/time/specials/packages/article/0,28804,1637886_1637891_1637864,00.html

Harry Potter and Me (2002, November 13). *A&E Biography.*

Hibberd, J. (2017, November 28). Fantastic Beasts director defends keeping Johnny Depp. *Entertainment Weekly.* http://ew.com/movies/2017/11/28/fantastic-beasts-director-defends-johnny-depp/

— (2018, October 11). Johnny Depp breaks silence on Fantastic Beasts sequel role. *Entertainment Weekly.* https://ew.com/movies/2018/10/11/johnny-depp-grindelwald-interview/

J. K. Rowling chat *a* (1999, March 19). *Barnes & Nobles Interview.* http://www.accio-quote.org/articles/1999/0399-barnesandnoble.html

— *b* (2000, May 4). *AOL Live.* http://www.accio-quote.org/articles/2000/0500-aol-umkc.html

— *c* (2000, October 20). *Barnes & Noble & Yahoo!* http://www.accio-quote.org/articles/2000/1000-livechat-barnesnoble.html

— *d* (2001, March 12). *Comic Relief.* http://archive.li/lssEb#selection-295.0-297.92

— *e* (2004, March 4). *JK Rowling's World Book Day Chat* http://www.accio-quote.org/articles/2004/0304-wbd.htm

Jensen, J. (2000, August 4). J.K. Rowling talks about writing *Harry Potter and the Goblet of Fire. Entertainment* http://ew.com/books/2000/08/04/jk-rowling-harry-potter-and-goblet-fire/

Johnstone, A. (1997, June 24). Happy ending, and that's for beginners. *The Herald* (Glasgow), p. 15.

— (1999*a*, January 26). We are wild about Harry. *The Herald.* http://www.accio-quote.org/articles/1999/0199-herald-johnstone.html

— (1999*b*, August 27). Oh, to hide behind a cloak of secrecy. *The Herald* (Glasgow) http://www.heraldscotland.com/news/12270006.Oh__to_hide_behind_a_cloak_of_secrecy/

— (2000, July). The hype surrounding the fourth Harry Potter book belies the fact that Joanne Rowling had some of her blackest moments writing it –and that the pressure was self-imposed; a kind of magic. *The Herald* (Glasgow) http://www.heraldscotland.com/news/12193670.The_hype_surrounding_the_fourth_Harry_Potter_book_belies_the_fact_that_Joanne_Rowling_had_some_of_her_blackest_moments_writing_it___and_that_the_pressure_was_self_imposed_a_kind_of_magic/

Khan, S. (2003, June 22). At the stroke of midnight, J. K. walked in. *The Guardian*. http://www.theguardian.com/uk/2003/jun/22/harrypotter.books2

King, S. (2009, August 1). *Harry Potter and the Order of the Phoenix*: Stephen King Review. *Entertainment Weekly*. http://ew.com/books/2009/08/01/harry-potter-and-order-phoenix-4/

Kruhly, M. (2011, July 15). Harry Potter, Inc: How the Boy Wizard Created a $21 Billion Business. *The Atlantic*. http://www.theatlantic.com/business/archive/2011/07/harry-potter-inc-how-the-boy-wizard-created-a-21-billion-business/241948/

Laurence, C. (2002, December 29). J. K. Rowling read unfinished book to dying girl. *The Telegraph*. http://www.telegraph.co.uk/news/worldnews/northamerica/usa/1417303/J.-K.-Rowling-read-unfinished-book-to-dying-girl.html

Lazarus, S. (2016, July 31). JK Rowling confirms Harry Potter's story is complete: "we're done". *RadioTimes.com*. http://www.radiotimes.com/news/2016-07-31/jk-rowling-confirms-harry-potters-story-is-complete-were-done/

Leonard, D. & Palmeri C. (2017, April 19). Disney's Intergalactic Theme Park Quest to Beat Harry Potter. *Bloomberg*. http://www.bloomberg.com/news/features/2017-

04-19/disney-s-intergalactic-theme-park-quest-to-beat-harry-potter

Levine, A. (1999, October 13). Why I Paid So Much for a Children's Book. *The New York Times.* http://www.nytimes.com/library/financial/101399manage-levine.html

Linder, B. (2001, February 6). Screenwriter Kloves Talks Harry Potter. *IGN.* http://www.ign.com/articles/2001/02/06/screenwriter-kloves-talks-harry-potter

Los Angeles Daily News. (2004, June 4). Harry Potter: The past and the future. *Chicago Tribune.* http://articles.chicagotribune.com/2004-06-04/entertainment/0406040340_1_harry-potter-katie-leung-steve-kloves

Lydon, C. (1999, October 12). J. K. Rowling Interview. *The Connection (WBUR Radio).*

Marantz, A. (2015, January 5). The Virologist. *The New Yorker.* http://www.newyorker.com/magazine/2015/01/05/virologist

Martin, D. (2009, June 17). 'Harry Potter' countdown: Steve Kloves on a 'haunting moment' in 'Half-Blood Prince'. *LA Times.* http://herocomplex.latimes.com/uncategorized/countdown-to-harry-potter-and-the-half-blood-prince-steve-kloves-talks-up-the-final-moments-between

McCabe, B. (2011). *Harry Potter Page to Screen: The Complete Filmmaking.* Harper Collins.

Mclaughlin, D. (2000, July 8). Harry Potter 'madness' stuns author Rowling. *Reuters News.* http://www.accio-quote.org/articles/2000/0700-reuters-mclaughlin.html

Memmott, C. (2007*a*, July 25). J. K. Rowling's fond look back at Harry Potter. *USA Today* http://usatoday30.usatoday.com/life/books/news/2007-07-25-jk-rowling_N.htm

— (2007*b*, July 25). Spoiler alert! Rowling discusses Harry's fate here. *USA Today.* http://usatoday30.usatoday.com/life/books/news/2007-07-25-harry-potter-spoilers_N.htm

Morris, L. (2017, April 6). Jack Thorne: "Writing Harry Potter and the Cursed Child was terrifying but JK Rowling got me through". *Daily Post.* http://www.dailypost.co.uk/whats-on/jack-thorne-writing-harry-potter-12851141

Mzimba, L. (2001, July 8). JK Rowling talks about Book Four. *cBBC Newsround.*

Nathan, I. (2016). *Inside the Magic: The making of Fantastic Beasts and Where to Find Them.* Harper Collins.

O'Donnell, R. (1999, June 21). *The Rosie O'Donnell Show.*

Paxman, J. (2003, June 19). OOTP Interview. *BBC Newsnight.*

People Magazine. (1999, December 31). J. K. ROWLING: The 25 Most Intriguing People Of '99. *People, 52* (25).

Perring, R. (2013, April 26). The Duke and Duchess of Cambridge and Prince Harry enjoy a wizard time on Harry Potter studio tour. *Watford Observer.* http://www.watfordobserver.co.uk/news/10383234.the-duke-and-duchess-of-cambridge-and-prince-harry-enjoy-a-wizard-time-on-harry-potter-studio-tour/

Pottercast. (2007*a*, December 17). PotterCast Interviews J. K. Rowling, part one. *Episode 130.*

— (2007*b*, December 23). Rowling Along. *Episode 131.*

Power, D. (2016). *The Art of the Film: Fantastic Beasts and Where to Find Them.* Harper Collins.

Puig, C. (2004, May 27). New 'Potter' movie sneaks in spoilers for upcoming books. *USA Today.* http://usatoday30.usatoday.com/life/movies/news/2004-05-27-potter-movie-book_x.htm.

Raincoast Books. (2001, March). Interview.

Reuters. (2007, December 13). J. K. Rowling and Bonnie Wright at "Beetle the Bard" Auction.

Rowling, J. K. (2004*a*, June 28). *Section: Fan Sites – The Harry Potter Lexicon.* JKRowling.com http://web.archive.org/web/20071103060904/http://www.jkrowling.com:80/textonly/en/fansite_view.cfm?id=14

— (2004*b*, June 28). Section: Rumours – Book Six is called 'The Pillar of Storgé'. *JKRowling.com.* http://web.archive.org/web/20051125035227/http://www.jkrowling.com:80/textonly/rumours_view.cfm?id=21

— (2005*c*, April 6). Do you like 'Half-Blood Prince'? *JKRowling.com.* http://web.archive.org/web/20051124055807/http://www.jkrowling.com:80/textonly/faq_view.cfm?id=93

— (2005*d*, September 7). E-Bay Users Once Again. *JKRowling.com.* http://archive.li/bv2Oe

— (2005*e*, December 25). Welcome! *JKRowling.com.* http://web.archive.org/web/20060101025644/http://www.jkrowling.com:80/textonly/en/

— (2006*f*, February 28). February 28th. *JKRowling.com.* http://web.archive.org/web/20060301065927/http://www.jkrowling.com:80/textonly/en/

— (2006*g*, March 16). At the end of 'Goblet of Fire', in which order should Harry's parents have come out of the wand? *JKRowling.com.* http://web.archive.org/web/20060417232842/http://www.jkrowling.com:80/textonly/en/faq_view.cfm?id=19

— (2006*h*, March). Opening Chapters of Philosopher's Stone. *JKRowling.com.* http://web.archive.org/web/20060316221021/http://www.jkrowling.com/textonly/en/extrastuff_view.cfm?id=1

— (2007*i*, February 6). February 6, 2007. *JKRowling.com.* http://web.archive.org/web/20070315005334/http://www.jkrowling.com:80/textonly/en/

— (2007*j*, May 14). May 14, 2007. *JKRowling.com.* http://web.archive.org/web/20070516043237/http://www.jkrowling.com:80/textonly/en

— (2007*k*, July 20). Acknowledgements. *JKRowling.com.* http://legacy.hp-lexicon.org/about/sources/jkr.com/jkr-com-door.html#ninth

— (2007*l*, November 1). Auction of The Tales of Beedle the Bard. *JKRowling.com.* http://web.archive.org/web/20071115233345/http://www.jkrowling.com:80/textonly/en/news_view.cfm?id=100

— (2007*m*, December 21). Section: Fan Sites – The Harry Potter Alliance. *JKRowling.com.* http://web.archive.org/web/20090313195557/http://www.jkrowling.com:80/textonly/en/fansite_view.cfm?id=20

Scholastic *a*. Meet the Editor: Arthur Levine, Harry Potter V. *Scholastic.com.* http://teacher.scholastic.com/scholasticnews/indepth/harry_potter_v/editor.htm

— *b*. Scholastic and Harry Potter and the Order of the Phoenix Break All Publishing Records With 5 Million Copies Sold in 1st 24 Hours. *Scholastic.com.* http://mediaroom.scholastic.com/press-release/scholastic-and-harry-potter-and-order-phoenix-break-all-publishing-records-5-million-c

— *c*. "An Evening With Harry, Carrie & Garp" J. K. Rowling, Stephen King and John Irving. *Scholastic.com.* http://www.scholastic.com/harrycarriegarp/Press_Release.pdf.

— *d*. Scholastic Releases Both Front and Back Covers of Highly Anticipated "Harry Potter and the Deathly Hallows". *Scholastic.com.* http://web.archive.org/web/20070707013929/http://www.scholastic.com/aboutscholastic/news/press_03282007_BA.htm

— *e*. Scholastic and Harry Potter and the Deathly Hallows Make Publishing History with 8.3 Million Copies Sold in First 24 Hours. *Scholastic.com.* http://mediaroom.scholastic.com/press-release/scholastic-and-harry-potter-and-deathly-hallows-make-publishing-history-83-million-cop

— *f*. Scholastic Reports Q4 and Fiscal 2017 Results and Fiscal 2018 Outlook. *Scholastic.com.* http://mediaroom.scholastic.com/press-release/scholastic-reports-q4-and-fiscal-2017-results-and-fiscal-2018-outlook

Shenton, M. (2017, March 2). Jack Thorne: "I don't know if I wrote the script for Harry Potter and the Cursed Child or the cast did". *The Stage.* http://www.thestage.co.uk/features/interviews/2017/jack-thorne-dont-know-wrote-script-harry-potter-cursed-child-cast/

Singh, A. (2008, May 28). JK Rowling pens a Harry Potter prequel. *The Telegraph.* http://www.telegraph.co.uk/news/uknews/2044760/JK-Rowling-pens-a-Harry-Potter-prequel.html

Smith, S. (2003). *J. K. Rowling: A Biography.* Michael O'Mara Books.

Sonia Friedman Productions Limited. (2013, December 13). Statement from J. K. Rowling. http://www.soniafriedman.com/news-press/statement-from-jk-rowling

Sotheby's. (2013, July 10). Lot 368, Rowling, J. K. Harry Potter And The Prisoner Of Azkaban. Bloomsbury, 1999. *English Literature, History, Children's Books & Illustrations.*

— (2014, June 4). Lot 140, Rowling, J. K. Harry Potter and the Chamber Of Secrets. London: Bloomsbury, 1998. *The Library of an English Bibliophile, Part IV, Sotheby's.*

Stahl, L. (2002, October 3). The Magic Behind Harry Potter. *CBSNews.*

Tartaglione, N. (2013, September 12). Warner Bros, J. K. Rowling Team For New 'Harry Potter'-Inspired Film Series. *Deadline Hollywood* http://deadline.com/2013/09/warner-bros-j-k-rowling-team-for-new-harry-potter-inspired-film-series-585122/

The Guardian. (2001, September 4). "Potter movie no challenge for Spielberg". *The Guardian* http://www.theguardian.com/film/2001/sep/04/news.steven spielberg.

Treneman, A. (1997, November 21). Joanne Rowling's Secret is Out. *The Independent* http://www.independent.co.uk/life-style/joanne-rowlings-secret-is-out-1295267.html

— (2003, June 20). I'm not writing for the money. *The Times* (London). http://www.accio-quote.org/articles/2003/0620-times-treneman.htm

Universal Studios. (2007, May 31). Harry Potter 'Theme Park within a Theme Park' Scheduled to Debut in 2009, Press Release. *Thestudiotour.com.* http://www.thestudiotour.com/usf/ioa_harrypotter.php

Vieira, M. (2007*a*, July 29). Harry Potter: The Final Chapter. *Dateline NBC*.

— (2007*b*, July 27). JK Rowling One-On-One: Part Two. *Today Show NBC*.

Vineyard, J. (2007, June 25). Kreacher Comfort: MTV Solves A "Harry Potter" Mystery. *MTV Movies Blog*. http://archive.is/Diz2

WalesOnline. (2004, June 2). Rowling reveals debt to Welsh friend who was inspiration for Ron Weasley. *WalesOnline*. http://www.walesonline.co.uk/news/wales-news/rowling-reveals-debt-welsh-friend-2432102

Warner Bros. Entertainment, Inc. and J. K. Rowling v. RDR Books, 575 F.Supp.2d 513 (2008a).

— (2008b) 575 F.Supp.2d 513, Opinion and Order.

Weir, M. (1999, March 13). Of magic and single motherhood. *Salon*. http://www.salon.com/1999/03/13/featureb_18/

Williams, S. (2010, November 15). Wizard job: the end of the line for Harry Potter. *The Telegraph*. http://www.telegraph.co.uk/culture/harry-potter/8123297/Wizard-job-the-end-of-the-line-for-Harry-Potter.html

Womack, P. (2011, July 5). Harry Potter and the Deathly Hallows, Part 2, review. *The Daily Telegraph*. http://www.telegraph.co.uk/culture/harry-potter/8619487/Harry-Potter-and-the-Deathly-Hallows-Part-2-review.html

About the Author

Patricio Tarantino (1990) is a J.K. Rowling and Harry Potter collector, who created his first Harry Potter website back in 2001. Since then, he has been actively participating in the Harry Potter fandom with different projects. From 2001 to 2008 he directed *Redflu.com*, one of the most popular Harry Potter websites in Spanish. In 2010 he founded *The Rowling Library*, a fan website focused not only on Harry Potter but also on other J.K. Rowling's works. With *The Rowling Library* he oversees several projects, such as a monthly magazine and the creation of *The Rowling Index*, a digital archive of everything J.K. Rowling has written through the years.

He lives with his girlfriend Belén in Buenos Aires, Argentina.

www.ingramcontent.com/pod-product-compliance
Ingram Content Group UK Ltd.
Pitfield, Milton Keynes, MK11 3LW, UK
UKHW011407290525
6142UKWH00029B/275

9 798889 921660